WOODLANDS
ENGLAND A
1994

A guide to over 600 woodlands and forests where visitors are welcome for enjoyment and education.

The Forestry Trust for Conservation and Education

The Old Estate Office, Englefield Road, Theale,
READING, Berks RG7 5DZ

Telephone 0734-323523

Registered Charity 327856

CONTENTS

Cover illustration by Hazel McGlashan
Text printed and bound by   Severn Print, Gloucester

ISBN 0-9521001-1-8
ISSN 1352-6324

WELCOME

Although this is the second edition of the "Green Book" it is the first to cover every county in England and Wales. Following the success of the 1993 version, which concentrated mainly on four counties, we issued open invitations to woodland owners throughout both countries to join the scheme, and received a response well in excess of our expectations. A glance at the maps will show that most people are now within easy motoring distance of a number of woodlands which can be visited.

It is pleasing to be able to report that a very significant proportion of the woods listed have not previously been open to the public; or, if they have, the fact has not been widely publicised. Privately owned woodlands are prominent although often no entrance fee is charged.

It is already clear that owners of the woodlands and their visitors are achieving a close rapport with one another. Owners are able to show that continuous management of a woodland is a necessity not only to grow timber, on which we all depend so much, on a sustainable basis; but also to conserve the plants and wildlife in them, as well as the scenery. If the timber is grown properly, there is income for improved conservation measures.

Timber production is therefore an essential goal for the majority of forest managers who cannot rely on external subsidy to maintain their trees. Neglect brings in its wake many problems. Very often an untended forest reaches a point when drastic measures are essential, involving perhaps unacceptably heavy felling with an adverse effect on landscape as well as local wildlife. The Forestry Trust seeks to show how sustainable forestry is also multi-purpose, capable of giving the greatest possible amount of recreational opportunities so necessary in a crowded island. While some forms of recreation may clash at times with others, a woodland can absorb far more people and activities than, say, hill land.

I have a seat inscribed with the claim "One is nearer God's heart in a garden than anywhere else on earth". Perhaps so, but the inter-relation of man and nature in a forest seems to me to be more basic and a constant source of wonder. The exciting challenge to foresters is that we can produce man's biggest renewable resource - timber - at the same time as enhancing the environment.

Over 70% of Britain was once covered with trees, seven times the forest area we have now. There is a renewed will to build up our forest cover not only for conservation and recreational purposes, but in order to reduce the scale on which we buy timber from other countries and deplete and sometimes plunder their resources. The Trust's role is to help visitors to enjoy and understand the positive and many-sided benefits of this vital industry. I hope readers enjoy many hours of peace, joy and wonder among the trees.

BN Howell
Chairman
Forestry Trust for Conservation and Education

WOODLANDS: THEN AND NOW

All of us will remember as children, the excitement of exploring in the woods. For thousands of years the magic of the forest has been at work. People like to visit woodlands for that magic, for the peace and quiet, to touch the past and to absorb the special atmosphere. The smell of the pines, the rustle of the beech leaves underfoot - each woodland has its own blend of magic, its own fingerprint. Visiting woodlands is like dipping into a library. Like a library, the woodland reflects the characters of those who adopt it, own it, shape it, visit it or care for it. Each woodland and each tree, young or old, will have a story of its own.

Some stories go back a long way. Think what it must have been like five thousand years ago. The wood provided homes, shelter, food; a source of building materials, of fuel, of charcoal to sketch with, of plant stuffs to eat, to make dyes or medicines. The wood was a hunting ground, a sports field and a meeting place for social gatherings. The wildlife and the trees gave inspiration for music, songs and drama. Some trees had a special meaning. Rowans warded off evil spirits. The wood was full of mystery. Its secrets learnt from families and from ancestors. Now advance to the year 1079. William the Conqueror creates his New Forest. People become distanced from woodlands. If you interfered with any aspect of the running of the Royal hunting forest you could expect severe punishment. Records show around 15% of Domesday England was wooded.

Centuries later the amount of woodland cover reached an all time low of 4% in 1919. Concentrating people in towns created more barriers between people and woodlands. However, great strides have been made since then to clothe our land with trees once again. Planting woods around our towns will help to re-unite people and trees. It takes a long time for a tree to grow. It takes very much longer for a woodland to develop. A woodland is more than trees. It is a system; a community of trees, other plants, animals and spaces of all kinds. Amongst the most rewarding of woodlands to visit are those with variety of species and ages, colours, forms, spaces and water. Woods like these attract wildlife and people.

Deer, woodpeckers and badgers abound in most woods. One way to be sure of seeing them is to be taken by a guide. A good field guide will help you to look in the right places. There are many smaller woodland creatures rather easier to watch. Look under logs, under leaves and along stream-sides, but with care. In the best woods for visitors you will be unaware that any great effort has been made on your behalf. You will arrive and be put at ease by your surroundings. You will easily find a place to leave the car, be made welcome and be led along a path that just seems to be natural. You may find reassuring waymarks or a simple map which shows where you can go. You stop to enjoy a picnic taken with friends. There are few signs and these are welcoming. There is no litter nor other signs of previous visitors. You complete your walk or return to the car with memories to store away. On the way back, members of the group each tell of special things found or enjoyed. You add it to your library of places to visit and places to show your friends.

The foresters in these woods put themselves in the shoes of those who will visit. The visit is natural and planning, designing and managing not obvious. The paths are routed where they give good views and a pleasing experience, where maintenance is kept to a minimum. The car parks and picnic sites are designed to fit in naturally with their surroundings. Productive woods are unique amongst other forms of land use in their capacity to accept many forms of recreational activity without prejudicing their main objective of growing timber. We hope each year many more owners will open their woods for your enjoyment. Your comments will help us and them to make your next visit even more rewarding.

IN SUPPORT OF WOODLANDS TO VISIT IN ENGLAND AND WALES

Together with the Forestry Trust - the Countryside Commission, the Countryside Council for Wales and the Forestry Authority are cooperating in this venture to publish a guide to woodlands and forests where visitors will be assured a welcome. Over three years the funding partners are supporting the venture with the expectation that the project becomes self financing. We wish the Forestry Trust every success in this project which should encourage and increase the enjoyment for woodland visitors and also recruit more woodland owners and managers to extend a welcome.

This guide focuses on private woodlands but also lists some Forestry Commission and other woods where visitors are welcome. There are of course many other woods owned by public and other bodies in which you will be welcome, only some of which are listed here. These include:

● national woodlands managed by Forest Enterprise where visitors on foot generally have the freedom to roam throughout the forest.

● local authority owned woods whether in urban or country parks.

●woods owned by National Parks and in some National Nature Reserves; and

● woods managed by the National Trust, Woodland Trust and other voluntary bodies.

For further details of such woods in your area contact the relevant local office. Meanwhile we hope that visiting the woods in this guide will add to your enjoyment.

5

The Countryside Commission

The Countryside Commission works to conserve and enhance the beauty of the English countryside and to help people enjoy it.

The Countryside Council for Wales

The Countryside Council for Wales is the statutory adviser to government on sustaining natural beauty, wildlife and the opportunity for outdoor enjoyment in rural Wales and its inshore waters and is the national wildlife conservation authority.

The Forestry Authority

The Forestry Authority, part of the Forestry Commission, promotes good forestry and the expansion of woodland and forest, so increasing the social and environmental benefits of forestry in Great Britain. The Forestry Authority does this through research, setting standards, providing advice, grant-aid and training.

A CODE FOR VISITS TO PRIVATE WOODLANDS

Do remember when you visit a wood you are a guest and:-

1. Respect trees, plants and wildlife

2. Guard against all risk of causing fire

3. Leave no litter and do not pollute water

4. Leave things as you find them and take nothing away

5. Keep to paths and trails where indicated using gates and stiles

6. Leave all gates as you find them, shut or open

7. Dogs and other animals are not allowed unless otherwise stated. Please keep dogs under close control, where allowed.

8. Move quietly, respecting the habitats of wildlife

9. Observe all signs and, for safety, keep clear of forestry operations, falling timber and dead trees

10. Follow any instructions given by the Forester or Woodland Owner (Please obey special instructions at each individual wood)

11. Park your car so as not to cause obstruction

If you follow the code you will hear more, see more, understand more and enjoy more!

HOW TO USE THIS BOOK

The key to using this book is to first establish:

1. How far are you prepared to travel? Start by looking at the map of England and Wales and then focus down to the relevant regional and, where appropriate, county map.

2. Are you looking for informal recreation on the spur of the moment or a visit from which you may learn something about the working countryside? Do you mind if there are likely to be lots of other people there or do you wish to visit somewhere not usually open to the public? The guide divides access into four categories which are described in more detail below but for quick reference on the map these are divided into two broad categories of readily available (categories F and R combined) and more limited access (categories L and A combined). Where access is readily available it is denoted by a square outline - ☐ - round the size symbol.

3. Are you looking for a quick or detailed visit to a small wood or a long walk in a large forest? It is important to check the size carefully first to avoid disappointment. On the map the woods and forests are shown by size symbols; which are approximately reproduced here - ■ for less than 10 hectares, ■ between 10 and 100 hectares, ■ between 100 and 1000 hectares and ■ for forests over 1000 hectares. A hectare is 100 metres square. Even copses smaller than this can be a source of considerable enjoyment and learning but are unlikely to fit the bill for a bracing country walk. At the other extreme it is not possible to gain more than a superficial insight to forests such as Kielder, at 60000 hectares, on a day visit.

4. Is the purpose of your visit educational? Those woods that provide opportunities to study both timber production and wildlife conservation (Study Woods) are shown in the key below each map with a *.

Once you have decided the area, size and level of access you are looking for you can find out further details from the individual woodland entry by looking under the relevant county in the gazetteer. Entries are listed firstly under England or Wales, alphabetically by county and finally alphabetically by the name of the wood. The key to individual entries is described below:

The name of the wood is shown in **large bold print**. Woods that provide educational opportunities to study both timber production and wildlife conservation are preceded with a *. The name of the owner, and/or where the responsibility for management has been given to another organisation, the manager, is shown in (brackets) . The size of the wood is shown in hectares - ha. *Please note this carefully before you commit yourself to a long journey*. The name is followed by a letter in bold print denoting the level of access:

F denotes full and free access for walkers and dogs though some areas or even whole woods may have to be temporarily closed off for safety or conservation reasons. Access off paths and rides should not be assumed unless stated. Organized group visits of more than 10 people to privately owned woodland should, out of courtesy, be cleared with the owner whether or not this is stated as a specific requirement. Access for horses should not be assumed unless bridleways or horses are specifically mentioned.

R denotes regular or routine access but with some restrictions. These may be of time (seasons, days of the week or times of day), of space (rights of way, permissive paths, self guided trails or zoned areas), of payment (for car parking or an admission charge) or a combination of these or other specific conditions.

L denotes limited access - where a wood is open only for a very short season, where there is only one right of way running through the wood or where only set days are specified. Limited access does not in itself preclude visits at other times by appointment. See individual woods for details.

A denotes by appointment only. Access to some woods may need to be carefully controlled. Almost without exception those who have restricted access to their woods to visits by appointment have expressed a willingness to conduct visits for schools and special interest groups.

Dogs. Unless otherwise stated it should be assumed that dogs are not allowed in private woods or those managed by wildlife trusts. As a general rule Forest Enterprise and local authority woods do allow dogs but if in doubt check with the owner, forester or agent. Dogs may not appear to cause much disturbance but in some woods and in specific

seasons their presence may be harmful to wildlife.

Horses. Allowed only where bridleways are specifically mentioned. Riders must keep to bridleways unless specifically permitted to use other tracks. To do otherwise is an abuse of the owner's hospitality and a disservice to visitors on foot.

A further letter or letters in bold print - C, D or E - denotes the award in the last ten years of one or more of the three main woodland management prizes. Uppercase denotes overall winners and lowercase denotes placed or commended woods. Woods which have won these awards are strongly recommended for visits . These major awards are:

The Duke of Cornwall's Award for Forestry and Conservation (C) - the premier award of the Royal Forestry Society of England, Wales and Northern Ireland presented annually to encourage the owners of commercial woodlands to manage them in a way which is sympathetic to the landscape and likely to conserve and enhance the wildlife interest in them, in both the short and long term, whilst still consistent with the primary purpose of timber production.

The Dulverton Flagon (D) - the principal award of the Timber Growers Association (TGA) presented annually for demonstrating the principles of the TGA's Forestry and Woodland Code by combining good environmental practice with timber production.

The Centres of Excellence Award (E) - the principal award of the Forestry

Authority for trees, woods and forests that demonstrate the highest management standards in at least one of the following categories: improving the quality of the landscape, creating benefits for wildlife, providing access for people or growing timber in environmentally-sound ways.

The Ordnance Survey Landranger 1:50000 Map Sheet Number and National Grid Map Reference are given in most instances to get you to the meeting point or close to the wood with the aid of a map. Please note that some woods cannot be reached by car and the meeting point may be some distance from the wood itself. Whilst every effort has been made to verify the Grid References given, they should be used in conjunction with any directions. The Forestry Trust regrets it cannot guarantee that the six figure reference will put you within 100 metres of the described point.
☎ (Telephone Number) or ✉ (address) are given for most woods. This is the contact for further information, of particular relevance for visits by appointment.

Most entries give the directions, facilities, any charges, opening times and special instructions followed by a brief description of the wood itself. These entries are in the words of the respective owners or their agents. The Forestry Trust is extremely grateful to all the entrants for contributing to this book but cannot verify the accuracy of any claims made for individual entries.

Abbreviations. We have tried to restrict the overuse of abbreviations but the following land use designations have been abbreviated - Area of Outstanding Natural Beauty (AONB), Environmentally Sensitive Area (ESA), Site of Special Scientific Interest (SSSI).

For a summary of forestry education opportunities refer to page 254 for those woods that provide educational visits on a regular basis, on specific days or by appointment. There are notes for educational visitors, for teachers and about educational publications available from the Forestry Trust. These will help you interpret what you see and, in the case of schools, to link it with programmes of study.

After this there is a section on management, for visitors who wish to gain an insight into how and why woods are managed - for timber, for wildlife conservation, for landscape or other objectives. Whilst it may not exactly reflect the management of the wood being visited it provides a first step in the principles involved.

Towards the end there is a questionnaire section on which to provide feedback, for advance orders for the 1995 book, and, for woodland owners whose woods are not currently listed, an opportunity to reserve an entry for 1995.

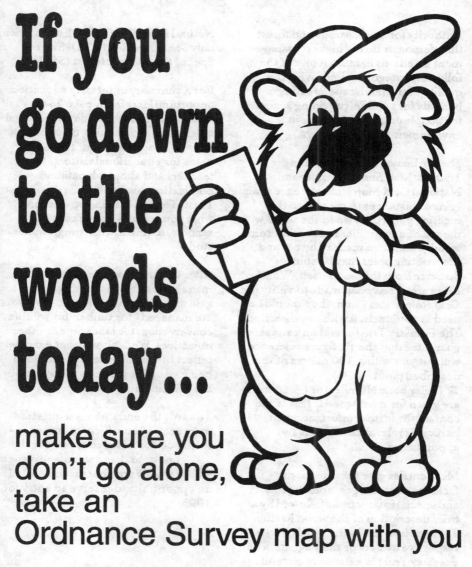

EASTERN

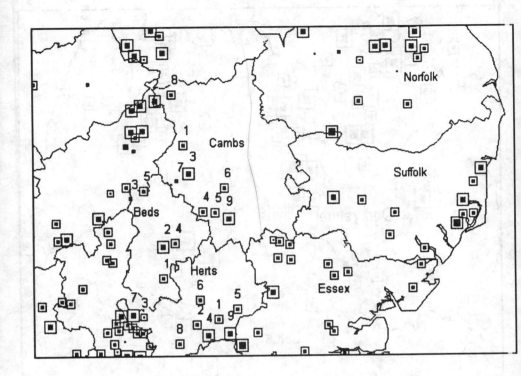

See separate maps for
Essex p 92
Norfolk p142
Suffolk p179

Bedfordshire (p20)
1 Bramingham Wood
2 *Maulden Wood
3 *Park Wood
4 Rowney Warren
5 West Wood

Cambridgeshire (p39)
1 Aversley Wood
2 Bedford Purlieus
3 Brampton Wood
4 Gamlingay Wood

5 Hayley Wood
6 Overhall Grove
7 *Perry Woods
8 Southey Wood
9 Wimpole

Hertfordshire (p121)
1 *Broxbourne & Bencroft Woods
2 *Bullens Green Wood
3 Hardings
4 Northaw Great Wood
5 Post Wood
6 Sherrardspark Woods
7 *Tring Park Estate
8 *Wall Hall Estate Woods
9 Wormley Wood

EAST MIDLANDS

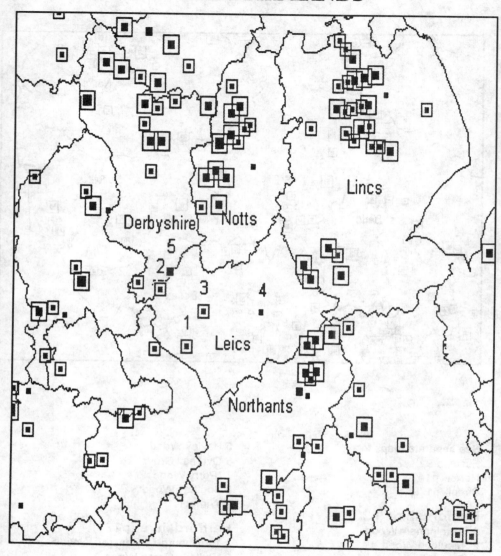

See separate maps for
Derbyshire p57
Lincolnshire p135
Northamptonshire p148
Nottinghamshire p158

Leicestershire (p133)
1 Burbage Wood & Sheepy Wood
2 Land at Willesley
3 Martinshaw Wood
4 *Red Lodge Wood
5 *Staunton Harold Estate Woodlands

NORTH EAST

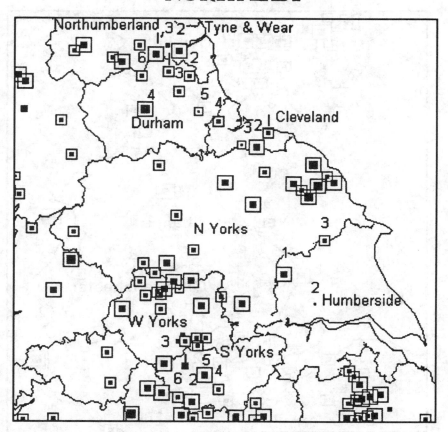

See separate maps for
Northumberland p152
Yorkshire North p208
Yorkshire West p216

Cleveland (p44)
1 Errington Wood
2 Guisborough Forest
3 Newton Wood
4 Thorpe Wood

Durham (p89)
1 Carrickshill Wood
2 Cocken Wood Picnic Site
3 Durham Riverbanks

4 *Hamsterley Forest
5 Hardwick Hall Fen Carr
6 Pontburn Wood

Tyne & Wear (p198)
1 *Chopwell Woodland Park
2 Gibside
3 Spen Banks

Yorkshire South (p214)
1 *Cawthorne Park
2 Ecclesall Woods
3 Langsett Reservoir
4 Roe Wood
5 Wharncliffe Woods
6 Wyming Brook

NORTH WEST

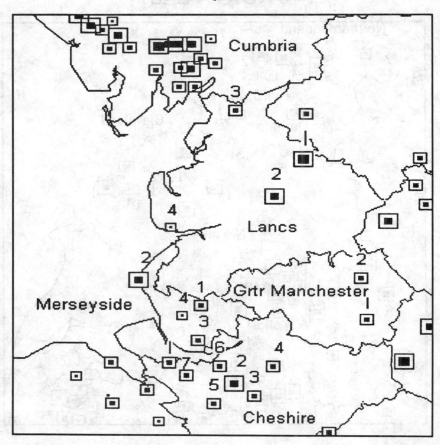

See separate map for Cumbria p48

Cheshire (p42)
1 Church Wood & Clayhill Wood
2 *Delamere Forest Park
3 *Little Budworth Country Park Woods
4 *Marbury Country Park Woods
5 Primrose Hill Wood
6 Snidley Moor & Woodhouse Hill Wood
7 Stanney Wood

Greater Manchester (p108)
1 Hulmes Wood

2 Tandle Hill Country Park

Lancashire (p132)
1 Gisburn Forest
2 Longridge Fell
3 Lords Lot
4 Witchwood

Merseyside (p140)
1 Acornfield Plantation
2 Formby
3 Halewood Triangle Country Park
4 Littlewood Community Wood

SOUTH EAST

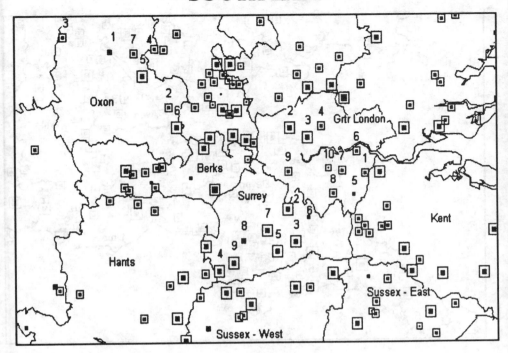

See separate maps for
Berkshire p21
Buckinghamshire p28
Hampshire p109
Kent p126
Sussex East p186
Sussex West p192

Greater London (p104)
1 Chalk Wood
2 *Fryent Country Park
3 Highgate Wood
4 Hampstead Heath
5 Hockenden Wood
6 Lesnes Abbey Wood
7 Petts Wood
8 Rookery Estate Woods
9 Sheen Common
10 Sydenham Hill Wood

Oxfordshire (p63)
1 *Blenheim Estates
2 Cowleaze Wood
3 Foxholes
4 Piddington Wood
5 Shabbington Wood
6 Warburg Reserve
7 Whitecross Green Wood

Surrey (p183)
1 *Alice Holt Forest
2 Ashtead Common
3 Box Hill
4 Hindhead
5 Leith Hill
6 *Nower Wood
7 Ranmore
8 *Winterfold Forest
9 Witley Common

SOUTH WEST

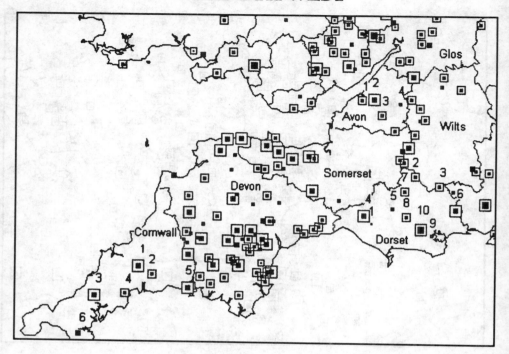

See separate maps for
Devon p61
Gloucestershire p99
Somerset p169
Wiltshire p202

Avon (p18)
1 Avon Gorge
2 Leigh Woods
3 Lords Wood
4 *Rocks East Woodlands

Cornwall (p46)
1 *Cardinham Woods
2 *Horse Wood
3 Idless Woods
4 Kings Wood
5 Mount Edgcumbe Country Park
6 *Trelowarren

Dorset (p85)
1 *Belstone Warren & Chaffins Copse
2 Duncliffe Wood
3 Garston Wood
4 *Hooke Park
5 Melcombe Park
6 *Moors Valley Forest
7 Piddleswood
8 Ruins Plantation
9 *Slepe Wood
10 *Wareham Forest

16

WEST MIDLANDS

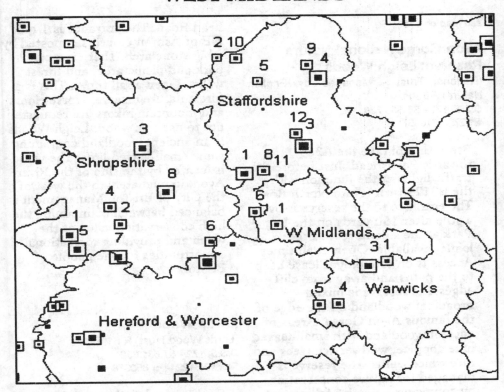

See seperate map for Hereford &
Worcester p114

Shropshire (p166)
1 Bury Ditches
2 *Edge Wood
3 Haughmond Hill
4 Helmeth Wood
5 Hopton Forest
6 Longdon & Withybed
7 Mortimer Forest
8 Wenlock Edge

Staffordshire (p175)
1 Big Wood
2 Black Firs
3 *Cannock Forest
4 Dimmings Dale
5 Hem Heath Wood
6 Himley Plantation
7 *Jacksons Bank
8 The Lower Avenue
9 Moseymoor Wood
10 Parrot's Drumble
11 Somerford
12 Stafford Plantation, Shugborough Park

Warwickshire (p199)
1 *Claywood
2 Hartshill Hayes & St Lawrence's Wood
3 Hay Wood
4 Oversley Wood
5 Thornhill

West Midlands (p201)
1 Saltwells Wood

17

AVON

see map on p16

Avon Gorge National Nature Reserve: Leigh Woods

(National Trust - Managed by English Nature) F 63ha
O.S.S. 172 - ST 555 730
☎0272-731645

From Bristol take the A369 towards Portishead. Just before the traffic lights at the junction with the B3129 turn R into North Road. The entrance to the reserve is over a stile after 150 yards on the L. Park at the side of road. Free leaflet available. Open at all times. Access is on foot only. Please keep to the paths and away from cliff edges.The reserve is mixed broadleaf woodland on the edge of the famous Avon Gorge. Areas of ancient woodland with small-leaved lime coppice, wild service trees and rare whitebeams. The reserve is managed for nature conservation by coppicing, selective felling and the clearance of scrub from areas of grassland. The wide range of plants found on the reserve supports a variety of insects and other animals. Rarities found here include the white-letter hairstreak butterfly, the dormouse and the elusive hawfinch. The woods are particularly attractive in autumn and are well known for their fungi.

Leigh Woods: Abbotts Leigh

(Managed by Forest Enterprise) F 122 ha
O.S. S. 172 - ST 559 738
☎0594-833057

Take the A369 Bristol to Portis-head Road. The entrance is 1 mile NE of Ashton Court, signposted by a big stone arch. There is a car park and picnic area, and forest walks. Open at all times. This is a forest nature reserve. Horse riders and mountain bikers are requested not to use this wood. Leigh Woods is an ancient woodland containing some small-leaved lime. The wood is located by the side of the River Avon, immediately to the west of the City of Bristol. Management is balanced between maintaining the high conservation value of the wood and providing recreational opportunities for the people of Bristol.

Lords Wood

(Lords Wood Trust) R 61.5ha
O.S.S. 172 - ST 631 632
☎0749-812244 or 850378

The junction of Birchwood Lane and A37 at Whitley Batts is exceedingly dangerous. The lane is narrow with no passing places. There are no facilities. There are footpaths through the wood, but you are free to wander off them unless there is shooting in progress. For further details ring James Lang Brown on the above number(s).
Lords Wood is mixed woodland of ancient origin - i.e. as far as records show most of the site has been wooded since time immemorial. Largely felled in 1960, and replanted with softwoods. Seedling ash, wild cherry, oak and birch have thrived among the conifers. The vegetation and shrub layer are

rich in species and the wide rides and pond support a great variety of butterflies, moths and damsel flies. Note particularly white admirals and orange tips. Wild daffodils, bluebells and wild cherry blossom in spring.

larch in the 1960s. Good natural regeneration. The site has a range of plants including garlic and comfrey. Birds include buzzard. Roe and muntjac resident; fallow deer regular visitors. Badger setts in forest.

★ Rocks East Woodlands

(Mr & Mrs A G Phillips) A 38 ha
O.S. S. 172 - ST 775 706
☎0373-858674

From M4 Jn 18 - Marshfield A420, take unclassified Colerne road. Three miles on R at top of valley. Car parking is provided for 50 cars and 2 coaches. There are 4 WCs on site. There are two lecture rooms, kitchen facilities by arrangement, caravan and camping site and picnic area. Guided walks, lectures and training courses are also offered by prior arrangement. All visits are by appointment only, please contact Mrs M E Timms, Secretary, Brokerswood House,.Brokerswood, Westbury, Wilts BA13 4EH. A minimum of 7 days notice is required for all group visits. Prices on application. Donations made to the Forestry Trust on Forestry Trust open days. Situated in AONB in St Catherine's valley. Mainly created by linking a collection of small woods and planting in the 1950s/1960s on steep slopes previously used for agriculture. Could be called farm woods 30 years on. Area of high landscape and scenic value. Victorian woodland garden, grotto and pond. Ideal site for ash, planted mainly with beech and

BEDFORDSHIRE

see map on p11

Bramingham Wood
(Woodland Trust) F 18.21ha
O.S.S. 166 - TL 068 259
☎0476-74297

From the centre of Luton take the A6 towards Bedford. Near the outskirts of the town turn L into Icknield Way. Take the R fork after about 1/2 mile, then the first R (Northwell Drive), then turn R at the roundabout into Lygetun Drive. There is space for a few cars at the end of this drive. National Tree Week events may take place in this wood during late Nov-Dec. Please phone the Woodland Trust for details in the Autumn. Bramingham Wood is one of the Trust's community woodlands. There is a rich variety of flora from spring right through summer with flowers such as snowdrop, bluebell, red campion and enchanter's nightshade. Most typical woodland birds can be seen during the year, including tawny owl, treecreeper and sparrowhawk. A wide variety of animals live in and around the wood but many, like the voles and shrews, are difficult to see. Several species of fungi are found in Bramingham Wood which are not found elsewhere in the country.

★ Maulden Wood
(Managed by Forest Enterprise) F 183ha
O.S.S. 153 - TL 073 395
☎0296-625825

Lay-by off A6, at the top of hill between Clophill and Haynes West End. There is car parking in the lay-by. The wood is an SSSI and has forest trails.

★ Park Wood
(Heygate & Sons) A 65ha
O.S.S. 153 -SP 933 595
☎0234-720932

The wood is situated between Harrold and Hinwick, 10 miles NW of Bedford. Visits for at least 6 people can be arranged any time, by appointment with Peter Hall, Forester, on the above telephone number. No dogs. There is natural regeneration of ash at various stages up to 10 years old, plus general conservation work and rehabilitation of semi-derelict woodlands.

Rowney Warren
(Managed by Forest Enterprise) F 71ha
O.S.S 153 - TL 124 404
☎0296-625825

From A600 follow sign for RAF Chicksands, in approx 2 miles, NW of Shefford. Car Park. Forest walks.

West Wood
(Forest Enterprise) F 84ha
O.S.S. 153 - SP 986 623
☎0780-83394

BERKSHIRE

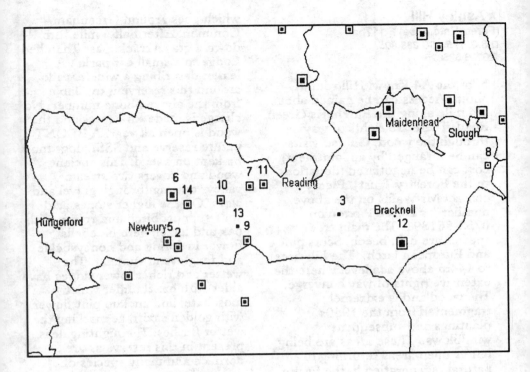

1. *Ashley Hill
2. Baynes Reserve
3. *Bearwood
4. Bisham Woods
5. Bowdown Woods
6. *Fencewood
7. Moor Copse

8. Poyle Poplars Community Woodland
9. *Round Oak Piece
10. *Rushall Woods
11. Sulham Wood
12. *Swinley and Bagshot Forest
13. *Ufton Park
14. Westrop Wood

★ Ashley Hill

(Forest Enterprise) F 117ha
O.S.S. 175 - SU 833 805
☎0296 625825

N of the A4 Knowl Hill round-about. Access can be gained about 1/4 mile along the Burchetts Green Road. There are rights of way through the wood. Guided visits can be arranged by appointment; cost can be negotiated (donations to the Forestry Trust). Please contact Mr Wallis on the above number, or Derek Paxton on 0753-861891. The main tree species are oak, beech, Scots pine and European larch. The hill rises to 144m above sea level where the extensive rights of way converge. The woodland is extremely fragmented from the 1950s plantings and subsequent windblows. These areas are being left as open areas returning to natural regeneration in the future, There is an ex-Forestry Commission house at the centre of the wood: woodland users are asked to give the occupants privacy and consideration whilst in the vicinity. The wood is especially pleasant on a frosty morning or a summers evening.

Baynes Reserve

(Berks, Bucks and Oxon Naturalists Trust) F 16ha
O.S.S. 174 - SU 511 649
☎0296-433222

Take unclassified road S past Thatcham station and as the road rises fork R (Burys Bank Road) which goes around Greenham Common. After half a mile turn R down a gravel track, pass Thatched Lodge to a small car park. . A leaflet describing a widlife walk around this reserve is available from the above phone number. No charge is made for access and the wood is open all year. A BBONT nature reserve and SSSI: dogs must be kept on a lead. This ancient woodland covers two stream valleys cutting through gravel and clays. On the higher slopes acid soils support birch and rowan with oak and hazel; here bluebells flower in spring and honeysuckle and foxglove in summer. The wetter and richer lower slopes have alder with hazel under which moschatel and cuckoo pint flower with golden saxifrage marking the wetter flushes. The nightingale is present in this reserve as are dormice and many species of dragonflies.

★ Bearwood

(Royal Merchant Navy School Foundation) A 25ha
O.S.S. 175 - SU 777 692
☎0734 787645

A329 Reading - Wokingham road, at Winnersh lights take B3030 for Arborfield Cross, L at mini roundabout, College is first R. Parking, WC. By appointment only; a small charge may be required. Until the early 1800s the estate was an outlier of Windsor Forest. During this time Bearwood House was built and turned into a gentlemans estate. Exotics were planted, the lake dammed and the area landscaped. Among the exotics were rhododendron ponticum which have in places taken over and swamped out the native species. In addition to the Wellingtonia Avenue, there are a number of unusual trees - Japanese cedar, swamp cypress, Himalayan spruce and others. Fauna includes usual animals - roe deer, muntjac, viper and grass snake. Bearwood lake has a wide variety of birds, depending on the season.

Bisham Woods
(Woodland Trust) F 153ha
O.S.S. 175 - SU 856 850
☎0476 742297

From Maidenhead take the A308 towards Bisham. Follow this road to the roundabout where it joins the A404. Turn L at the round-about then immediately L again and park in the council car park. Apart from the car park there are no facilities on the site. There is no charge made to walk in the wood and it is open at all times of the year. National Tree Week events may take place in this wood during late Nov-Dec. Please phone the Woodland Trust for details in the Autumn. Ancient maps at Bisham Abbey indicate that most of this 153 hectare woodland is at least 500 years old. It is understood to be the inspiration for the Wild Wood in Kenneth Grahame's "Wind in the Willows". There are excellent examples of Chiltern beech; high forest on the chalk

slopes and oak, birch and sweet chestnut elsewhere. Bisham Woods have some unusual plant species including bird's nest orchid, thin-spiked wood sedge and yellow archangel. Large areas of bluebell can be seen in the spring. The great spotted woodpecker, green woodpecker and nuthatch inhabit the wood, along with muntjac deer.

Bowdown Woods
(Berks, Bucks and Oxon Naturalists Trust)
F 38 ha
O.S.S. 174 - SU 504 657
☎0296 433222

From the A34 S of Newbury, turn L at a roundabout towards Greenham village. After about 11/2 miles along Burys Bank Road turn L down the track signposted "Newbury Trout Lakes", the car park is on the R a little way down the track. A leaflet describing a wildlife walk around this reserve is available from the above phone number. No charge is made for access and the wood is open all year. A BBONT nature reserve and SSSI: dogs must be kept on a lead. Bowdown has extremely varied topography and vegetation. Gullies filled with alder coppice blend into ash and maple on the clay while old oaks and rowans are scattered throughout relict ancient heathland reminiscent of wood pasture. White admiral, purple hairstreak and silver washed fritilary are amongst the butterflies present. Spring flowers include Solomons seal, moschatel, yellow archangel and wood anemone.

★ Fencewood
(Gerald Palmer Trust) R 152ha
O.S.S. 174 - SU 513 723
☎0635 200878

From Newbury, take the B4009 to Hermitage. Turn R on Marlston Road, under the railway bridge. The wood will be found on the R. There is parking for a limited number of cars. There is full access for walkers and dogs and between 1 May and 30 Sept there is also full access for horse and pony riders. Outside this period riders must stay on the bridleway. Group and guided visits must be arranged by contacting Mr LO Birch on the above number. Please give 3 weeks notice for all such visits. Donations to the Forestry Trust. Fence Wood has been woodland for very many years. Over half the wood has been restocked since 1950 with a variety of species, retaining belts of old broadleaved trees. Grimsbury Castle is an iron age hill fort. The folly in the centre of the fort is a private house. The wood has been open to the public for many years but visitors are asked to obey the rules set out on the notice boards at the principle entry points.

Moor Copse
(Berks, Bucks and Oxon Naturalists Trust)
F 26.8ha
O.S.S. 175 - SU 635 742
☎0296 433222

Leave Pangbourne southwards on the A340. Just past Tidmarsh, as you rise to cross the M4, turn L into a layby with a car park. A leaflet describing a wildlife walk around this reserve is available and there is an Open Day on Sun 24 Apr 1994: contact the woodlands officer on the above number for further details. No charge is made for access and the wood is open all year. A BBONT nature reserve and SSSI: dogs must be kept on a lead. An ancient woodland lying in the flood plain of the river Pang, Moor Copse is a diverse mixture of wet ash and alder standing on peat and gravel. Coppicing has taken place over the last seven years and the regrowth has provided habitats for various plants, insects and breeding birds. Primroses, bluebells and early purple orchids can be seen in the spring. White admiral butterflies (on the wing in Jul and Aug) lay their eggs on honeysuckle which can been seen hanging from many trees.

Poyle Poplars Community Woodland
(Thames Water Utilities Ltd) F 6ha
O.S.S. 176 - TQ 023 757

1 mile W of M25, junction 14, on Horton Road. There is a park for 16 cars. Pub at eastern end on Colne Valley Way. This is a 20 year old hybrid poplar plantation being converted by phased felling to native species deciduous woodland. Nearly 10,000 trees have been planted by local schools, volunteers and contractors from 1990 to 1993. 26 species of native trees and shrubs have been planted to create different woodland

characters. The path through the wood is part of the Colne Valley Way.

nightjar population

★ Round Oak Piece

(R H R Benyon) F 60.7ha
O.S.S. 175 - SU 627 651
☎0734-302504

W of Reading and S of the A4(T). From junction 12 of the M4 take the A4, Theale bypass, for about two miles, then take first road L through Ufton Nervet towards Mortimer, then R at T junction towards Tadley and Heath End. Parking is being provided at the Round Oak pub, about 800m on L. There will be four Forestry Trust Open Days starting at 2 o'clock on the first Sundays in May (1st), Jul (3rd), Oct (2nd), Dec (4th). These will cover the changing habitats and seasons, the different stages of forestry operations, the benefits for wildlife arising from them and the opportunity for visitors to carry out practical work and see its effect on a subsequent visit. A predominantly long established Scots pine wood, with trees of varying ages, with larch and Douglas fir interspersed. There is a pond, originally designed as a fire dam to provide an emergency water supply in case of fire at the listed Ufton Court (c.1600) which is in the middle of the wood, providing both an attractive area for visitors and for many species of dragonfly. Alder, oak and birch grow in the gulleys leading to the pond and the large clearfelled areas, where the pine is regenerating, support a

★ Rushall Woods

(W Cumber & Son (Theale) Ltd) F 40ha
O.S.S. 174 - SU 588 714
☎0734-744547

Reading M4 junction 12: A4 past Theale: A340 towards Pangbourne, take the first L to Bradfield. Go through Bradfield, just L towards Stanford Dingley, then first L for New Farm or second L for Rushall Manor Farm. There is parking for 20 cars and 2/3 coaches. There are WCs (including disabled). Disabled path, picnic area, pond, recreational woodland walks between 1 and 5 miles long. There are rights of way on foot and bridleways through the woods. There are also self guided trails - please keep to the marked trails. Guided visits and school visits can be arranged by appointment between 1 Mar and 30 Nov. Please give two weeks notice. Charges: adults and children £1. To make arrangements contact John Bishop on the above number. Donations to the Forestry Trust. Rushall Woods are mainly ancient woodland which has been brought into management over the last five years. There is a coniferous plantation which is being felled and both natural regeneration and replanting of Douglas fir and Scots pine is underway. Work in the main has been limited to underwood coppicing and ride widening. One area of hazel is being rotationally coppiced. There are new plantings in some important landscape positions. The woodlands have a good variety of species with some outstanding cherries. They are a beautifully rich area of wildlife and especially attractive in the spring. There are a number of statutory footpaths and access is encouraged but avoiding Saturdays in the winter. The farm supports the John Simonds Trust as it seeks to encourage a love and understanding of the countryside.

Sulham Wood
(Managed by Forest Enterprise) F 53ha
O.S.S. 175 - SU 647 745
☎0296-625825

Take the minor road S from the A329 Pangbourne - Reading Road, at 'T' junction turn L, car park on L at the top of the hill.

★ Swinley and Bagshot Forest
(Crown Estate Commissioners) F 1000ha
O.S.S. 175 - SU 876 662
☎0753-860222

Start from The "Look Out" heritage centre on Nine Mile Ride, Bracknell, half mile to the W of the Bracknell to Bagshot dual carriageway (A322). Ample car parking, toilets (including those for disabled persons), cafe, schoolroom, and displays of local commerce and wildlife. Maps, interpretative material and educational packs are available for self guided walks. Guided walks can be arranged by contacting the Crown Estate Office (see above). Swinley and Bagshot Forest extends to about 1000 hectares and is part of the much larger Windsor Forest. Scots and Corsican pine are the dominant species, grown mainly for commercial reasons. Spinneys of natural birch and elderly Scots pine are interspersed and add diversity to landscape and wildlife, which is rich and includes an SSSI in the vicinity of Mill Pond. This and other features of scenic and archaeological interest are served by waymarked trails. Principal amongst these are Caesar's Camp, dating to about 700BC, and Napoleonic redoubts.

★ Ufton Park
(R H R Benyon) A 30ha
O.S.S. 175 - SU 626 667
☎0734-302504

W of Reading and S of the A4(T). From junction 12 of the M4 take the A4, Theale bypass for two miles., then take second road L to Ufton Nervet, follow signs to Ufton Court. Guided visits can be arranged. Please book for ALL visits at least 3 weeks in advance. Contact Mr K R McDiarmid on the above number. Donations made to the Forestry Trust. A mixed wood forming part of the Englefield Estate. Mixed age compartments all in production. The wood was originally planted with oak and coppice, much of which has been felled and replanted for the purposes of timber production and conservation. Species include oak, sweet chestnut, ash, red oak, larch, Scots pine, Corsican pine and

Norway spruce. Flora and fauna include roe and fallow deer, foxes, badgers, wild flowers, butterflies, and birds including all three woodpeckers, nightjar, nightingale, various warblers and gamebirds.

Westrop Wood
(Mrs S J Constantinidi Will Trust) F 25ha
O.S.S. 174 - SU 517 708
☎0761-470765

From Newbury travel east on A4; turn L in Thatcham to Cold Ash, pass through village and turn R at crossroads into Bucklebury Alley signed to Westrop Green. Entrance to wood is on R after the houses, approx. 1/2 mile. The wood is open all year round - please observe notices when tree felling operations are underway. This is a most attractive mixed wood containing a wide variety of species. A group of very old Scots pine on the top of Westrop Hill is a fine feature protected by covenant. Bluebells and primroses in abundance.

BUCKINGHAMSHIRE

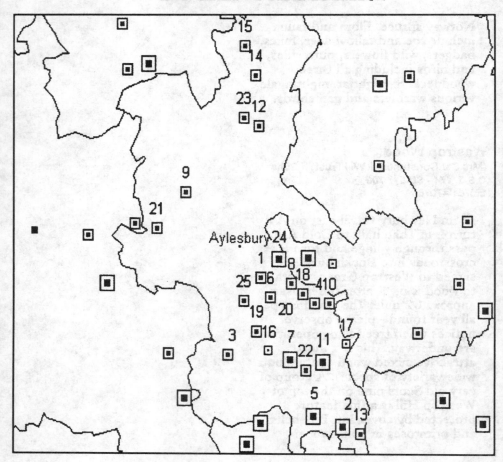

1. Bacombe Hill
2. Black Park
3. * Bottom Wood
4. Captain's Wood
5. Burnham Beeches
6. * Cockshoots
7. Common Wood
8. Dancersend
9. Finemere Wood
10.* Hockeridge & Pancake Woods
11. Hodgemoor Wood
12.* Howe Park Wood

13. Langley Park
14. Linford Wood
15. Little Linford Wood
16. Millfield Wood
17. Old Hanging Wood
18. * Pavis Wood
19. Piggots Wood
20. Priestfield Arboretum
21. Rushbeds Wood
22. Sandells and Netherlands
23. Shenley Wood
24. * Wendover Woodland Park
25. Whiteleaf Wood

Bacombe Hill

(Buckinghamshire County Council) F 25ha
O.SS. 165 - SP 864 074
☎0296 383394

From Wendover High Street, take Ellesborough Road past the Station. 1/2 mile up this hill on the L of the RH is the small parking area (3 cars) for Bacombe Hill. Other facilities include the Ridgeway National Trail, bridleway and network of premissive paths. There is full and free access all the year. Situated on the Chilterns scarp slope above Wendover, Bacombe Hill contains open chalk grassland, recent ash woodland, hazel coppice and scrub. The site is being managed for open public access, woodland production and nature conservation. Following the introduction of coppicing in 1990 the site now provides materials for traditional hedgelaying practices in the area.

Black Park Country Park

(Buckinghamshire County Council) F 210ha
O.S.S.176 - TQ 005 833
☎0753 511060

Signed (white and brown tourist type) off A412 trunk road Slough - Uxbridge. Facilities include Visitor Centre, refreshments, WCs, partially sighted and disabled. Car park adjacent to 5 1/2hectare lake and picnic area.There is full and free access all year on foot - vehicles excluded from dusk - 0800 hours. Attractive setting almost completely woodland consisting mix of conifer and broadleaved.

Hard rides provide good access even in wet weather. 22ha heathland to the north of the park surrounded by 25 hectares managed as a local nature reserve. Good variety of birdlife. Objectives of management are multi-purpose: timber production, nature and landscape conservation, and quiet countryside public recreation.

★ Bottom Wood

(Chiltern Society) F 14ha
O.S.S. 165 - SU 795 949
☎0494 461286

Bottom Wood lies in a valley to the N of A40, 3 miles SE of Stokenchurch (Jct 5 M40) and 2.1/2 miles W of West Wycombe. Park at top end of Old Dashwood Hill, Studley Green, off A40. Take bridleway to valley bottom and turn L into wood - leaflet and management map available. Open Days and visits can be arranged. Donations for guided visits. Public Bridleway, which gets very muddy, runs the length of the wood. Please keep dogs on leads. Ancient semi-natural Chiltern beechwood with wide variety of other trees, including wild cherry, ash, oak, goat willow, whitebeam, field maple, hazel and wych elm. The wood is managed as a nature reserve and used by the Chiltern Woodlands Project for demonstration purposes. It has a rich ancient woodland flora and also, on Toothill, a remnant of chalk downland recovered from a pine plantation. 175 species of butterflies and moths have been recorded. Old sawpits, boundary banks and terraced fields add historical interest.

Burnham Beeches

(Corporation of London) FE 220ha
O.S.S 175 - SU 953 850
☎0753 647358

S from junction 2 of the M40 and N from junction 6 of the M4. Along A355 to Farnham Common and turn into Beeches Road which takes you into the Beeches. There is ample parking for cars and coaches. There are WCs (including disabled). Many local pubs, 2 cafes (1 seasonal), picnic area - common. A few facilities for the disabled including parking bays and paths near features. There is fully open access to the wood with byways open to all traffic (daylight hours only). Guided visits by appointment, please contact Mark Frater on above number. A new guide book is available from the cafes or office. The Beeches are a National Nature Reserve with ancient semi-natural woodland, mainly beech and oak with heathland, wetland, ponds, coppicing and wood pasture systems - beech pollards with rare breed ponies, cattle and pigs. Twelfth century scheduled monument. Rich social history including Mendelssohn and Jenny Lind. Varied flora, rich and diverse fauna. Ford Conservation Award for the Natural Environment.

Captain's Wood

(Buckinghamshire County Council) F 10ha
O.S.S. 165 - SP 953 032
☎0296 383394

From the centre of Chesham take Bellingdon Road from the A416 towards Bellingham. This road leads into Hivings Hill. Captain's Wood is on the LH side of Hivings Hill at the steepest part of the road. There is woodside parking for 3/4 cars, bridleway and a network of footpaths but no other facilities. Access is full and free all the year. This ancient semi-natural woodland is a superb asset to the local community. It is predominantly beech high forest with some excellent groups of beech natural regeneration. A multi-purpose woodland management approach is pursued, with emphasis being placed on enhancing the nature and landscape conservation value of the site. There is a diverse range of native tree and shrub species and ground flora reflecting the different soil conditions across the site.

★ Cockshoots

(Sir Leonard Figg) F 24ha
O.S.S. 165 - SP 872 042
☎0494 488346

2.1/2 miles S of Wendover on the Amersham Road (A413). Look for signs to Cockshoots Wood. Picnic site and car park. An old beech wood of which half has been felled in the last 20 years and replanted with oak, cherry, southern beech, larch, Lawson cypress and western red cedar. The wood is well provided with footpaths leading from the car park. Bluebells and primroses are conspicuous in the spring and many species of wild flowers throughout the summer months. Muntjac and fallow deer, badgers and foxes are present.

Common Wood

(Robin Fleming) R 118ha
O.S.S. 175 - SU 911 943
☎0295 688100

Leave Beaconsfield by the B474 for Penn and Tylers Green. Pass through Penn into Tylers Green. Turn R at the crossroads in the valley bottom into Common Wood Lane. The entrance to the wood is 400m from the crossroads on the L hand side. Parking for 10 cars. Self guided trails open between April and September but there may be restrictions during forestry operations. Please contact Peter Hale on above number ,or in writing , at Payn's House, Oxhill, Warwick,CV35 0QR, for a descriptive leaflet of the wood (£1 plus postage). Donations to the Forestry Trust. The mature beech in this wood were planted in about 1850 partly on the site of Wycombe Heath. An active policy of regenerating them is taking place with a number of stands of hardwoods and one stand of naturally regenerated European larch. The objective is to grow good quality hardwoods at the same time as creating an uneven aged wood to provide a diversity of habitats.

Dancersend

(Berks, Bucks and Oxon Naturalists Trust)
F 30 ha
O S.S. 165 - SP 900 095
☎0296 433222

A4011 from Wendover to Tring. Just before A41 turn sharp right to St Leonards. After 1 1/2 miles, at a sharp left hand bend, park on right verge or pull in on left and walk up track to reserve. No charge is made for access and the reserve is open all year. A BBONT nature reserve and a Site of Special Scientific Interest (SSSI): dogs must be kept on a lead. The reserve lies on varying soils and dry valley slopes and contains a rich variety of wildlife. The beech with oak woodland was felled in the last war and colonised by scrub. In the mid 1950s the Forestry Commission replanted most of this area with beech, larch and spruce. Original woodland survivors include stinking helleborine. There is also an area of chalk grassland carrying pyramidal, fragrant and bee orchids, clustered bellflower, Chiltern gentian, green hairstreak and dark green fritillary.

Finemere Wood

(Berks, Bucks and Oxon Naturalists Trust)
F 40.3ha
O.S.S. 165 - SP 720 215
☎0296 433222

Travel northwest from Quainton (SP 74 20), turn left at a T-junction towards Edgcott. After 3/4 mile, just over the rise, a track goes right. Park on nearby verge. Walk up track to reserve. A leaflet describing a wildlife walk around the reserve is available and there is an open day on 10 April 1994. Further details from the above phone number. A BBONT nature reserve and an SSSI: dogs must be kept on a lead. The wood is a rich mosaic of habitats resulting form its chequered history. Much of the site was replanted with conifers in the 1950s; this is being thinned and managed as a productive crop but will be replaced by native broadleaved woodland. Substantial areas of ancient woodland survive: oak with hazel, maple and ash coppice, as well as blackthorn and aspen. Coppicing is being reinstated, with great benefits for flowers and insects, and the blackthorn is being managed for the nationally rare black haristreak butterfly. Woodland rides are also being managed for the benefit of butterflies and flowers.

★ Hockeridge and Pancake Woods
(Royal Forestry Society of England, Wales and Northern Ireland) FE 74ha
O.S.S. 165 - SP 978 063
☎0442 822028

Off the A416 Chesham to Berkhamsted Road at Hockeridge Cottages on the Herts/Bucks border. There is parking for 20 cars. There are also picnic tables and 52 labelled specimen trees. Explanatory leaflets and maps are available free on receipt of an s.a.e. from the RFS, 102 High Street, Tring, Herts, HP23 4AF or

telephone as above. The site is not really suitable for the disabled. There are rights of way through the woodland and self guided trails. Please keep to the marked trails Open days with guided visits on Sundays, Apr 3; Jul 3; Oct 2 and Dec 4 1994. Guided walks and group visits by appointment at other times. Please give 2 months notice. Charges for guided walks are £2 for adults and £1 for children. Donations to Forestry Trust on open days. Walkers are welcome on the permissive footpaths elsewhere in the wood. Rights of way should be adhered to. Please keep dogs on leads. A mixed multi purpose working woodland in the Chilterns providing a microcosm of lowland forestry, woodland types and management practices in the U.K. A demonstration woodland of how to harmonise conservation, recreation, landscape and education.

Hodgemoor Wood
(Managed by Forest Enterprise) F 113ha
O.S.S. 175 - SU 969 939
☎0296 625825

Off A355 between Amersham and Beaconsfield, take minor road - Bottrells Lane - leading to Chalfont St Giles. Car parking is available. This is an SSSI with forest walks.

★ Howe Park Wood
(Milton Keynes Parks Trust) F 23.1ha
O.S.S. 152 - SP 831 345

☎0908 223322

Howe Park Wood is immediately S of Westcroft Roundabout at the junction of Chaffron Way and Tattenhoe Street in the SW corner of Milton Keynes. There is a car park and picnic area on the N side of the wood, off Chaffron Way. The wood is an SSSI with high value to nature conservation. We prefer visitors to keep to the paths and to keep dogs on a lead, especially during the bird nesting season. There is an excellent path and ride network, a number of seats and two interpretation panels, but no other facilities. Howe Park Wood is an ancient semi-natural woodland, possibly a remnant of the former Royal Forest of Whaddon Chase. Records date back to the 11th century. It has been managed as coppice with standards in the past and was part of a medieval deer park. It is a wet ash/maple/dog's mercury woodland, with stands of oak/bracken/bramble woodland on drier areas. Of special interest is the natural occurrence of small stands of hornbeam, far to the north west of its accepted East Anglian range. Aspen and willows are common in the the wet areas and the abundant blackthorn supports two colonies of the rare black hairstreak butterfly. There are also purple hairstreak, white admiral and wood white butterflies recorded. There is a very rich ground flora,with bluebells, woodrush, pendulous sedge, wood anemone, dog's mercury, primroses and violets, yellow archangel and woodruff. At least 5 orchid species may be

found and the flora is typical of ancient woodland with a long history of traditional management. About 300 species of moths have been recorded, including such scarcities as buff footman, slender brindle and pinion streaked snout. The wood is managed primarily as a nature reserve.

Langley Park Country Park
(Buckinghamshire County Council) F 55ha
O.S.S. 176 - TQ 016 821
☎0753 511060

Follow brown tourist signs off main A412 Slough - Uxbridge. Toilets open seasonally but there are full facilities in adjacent Black Park Country Park. Full and free access all year - vehicles excluded from dusk - 0800 hours. Traditional parkland features of wood pasture - views to Windsor Castle. Recommended during April/May/June during Azalea/ Rhododendron flowering period. Good mature oak woodland with fine avenues of Wellingtonia.

Linford Wood
(Milton Keynes Parks Trust) F 40ha
O.S.S. 152 - SP 845 406
☎0908 223322

Linford Wood is just over 1/2 mile N of central Milton Keynes between Monks Way and Dansteed Way. There are car parks off Brecklands and Saxon Street, on the W side of the wood. The wood has a good footpath network, suitable for disabled access, with picnic areas, seats and benches. There is also a "trim trail" for fitness exercises. We would prefer it if visitors kept to the paths and kept dogs on a lead, especially in the bird nesting season. Linford Wood is a mixture of ancient wet ash/maple woodland, old secondary woodland and recent plantation. It is an important feature of the landscape of central Milton Keynes. It is also of considerable conservation importance, with a very rich flora and fauna. Most of the wood has a high mixed canopy of oak, ash and maple standards with an understorey of hawthorn, blackthorn, bramble, wild rose and crab apple plus hazel, maple and ash coppice. Historical records go back to 1283 and a fragment of a medieval woodbank and ditch remains in the SW corner of the wood. Over 200 flowering plants have been recorded and the ground flora is dominated by bluebells and dog's mercury with such rarities as herb paris, butterfly orchid, bird's nest orchid and broad leaved helleborine. It is also an important area for recreation, used quite heavily by dog walkers, joggers, bird watchers, picnickers and horseriders.

Little Linford Wood

(Berks, Bucks and Oxon Naturalists Trust)
F 42.5ha
O.S.S. 152 - SP 832 455
☎0296 433222

Not to be confused with Linford Wood (above)! B526 from Newport Pagnell. Just before Gayhurst turn left towards Haversham. After 1/2 mile turn left along track. Reserve is 1 1/2 miles on, beyond M1 and Dairy Farm. A leaflet describing a wildlife walk around the reserve is available and there is an open day on 20 Mar 1994. A BBONT nature reserve: dogs must be kept on a lead. Although an ancient woodland site, much of it was felled and replanted 100 years ago. It still remains rich in wildflowers with 130 plant species including 23 ancient woodland plants such as herb paris (flowering in May - Jun). Suitable timber trees are occassionally cropped, coppice crafts are being re-introduced, and charcoal is made on site.

Millfield Wood

(Berks, Bucks and Oxon Naturalists Trust)
F 7.3 ha
O.S.S.165 - SU 870 954
☎0296 433222

A4128 N from Wycombe. After 1/2 mile turn L into Hughenden Manor and park. Walk back down drive, go a few yards L, cross the road and follow bridleway up hill to the reserve. A leaflet describing a wildlife walk arond the reserve is available from the above phone number. A BBONT nature reserve and a Site of Special Scientific Interest (SSSI): dogs must be kept on a lead. A rare example of a semi-natural Chiltern beechwood on chalk. Severely damged in the great storms but producing good natural regeneration of trees (ash and beech) with areas of mixed trees (holly, yew, whitebeam, field maple) and some coppiced hazel. Many spring flowers, such as goldilocks buttercup, wood anemone and a good display of herb paris.

Old Hanging Wood
(Dr J W & Mrs M A McAnuff) F 7ha
O.S.S. 176 - TQ 011 976
West Barn, Hall Place, Seer Green, Beaconsfield, Bucks HP9 2YE

Follow A404 E from Little Chalfont. 1 mile from Chalfont & Latimer Station bridleway on R leads to and through the wood after 5 mins walk. Bus stops on A404 close to bridleway. Only parking 100m E of bridleway entrance. After a series of damaging fires in 1960s this small semi ancient wood is now fully stocked with an uneven-aged mixture of native hardwoods and larch. The wood is continuously worked by the present owner, with advice and occasional practical help from the Chiltern Woodlands Project. Management includes some coppicing but the main objectives are timber production and silvicultural improvement for the benefit of wildlife, amenity and landscape.

★ Pavis Wood
(Buckinghamshire County Council) F 35ha
O.S.S. 165 - SP 914 093
0296 383394

From the S side of Tring, near the Museum, take the lane S towards Hastoe village (road passes under the A41). Bear R in Hastoe. Pavis Wood is 1/4 mile along this road opposite the next LH bend. Facilities include parking for 3 cars, bridleway (Ridgeway path) and network of footpaths. There is full and free access all the year. Pavis Wood is a diverse ancient semi-natural woodland principally comprising broadleaf high forest with a scattering of conifers. A multi-purpose woodland management approach is pursued. New plantings are a consequence of the recent storms which ravaged the exposed escarpment. Emphasis is being placed on developing a system of group regeneration, recruiting natural regeneration where possible. On the lower, less accessible slopes the thin soil over chalk has resulted in a large number of moribund standing beech - fabulous wildlife habitats.

Piggots Wood
(Dr & Mrs Wheeler Robinson) R 20.3ha
O S.S. 165 - SU 853 987
Pigotts, North Dean, High Wycombe, Bucks HP14 4MF

In Lower North Dean 4 miles N of High Wycombe park at the top of Pigotts Hill. There are no entrance charges but donations welcomed to Cystic Fibrosis Research Trust via the owner. Please keep to the paths; no access for horses; groups by appointment (schools welcomed). 20 hectares of ancient semi-natural woodland, most designated as heritage woodland by English Nature because of the interesting flora. One area of Piggots Wood South replanted in 1993; two areas in Piggotts Wood North in 1993. Some coppicing and glades to encourage variety of habitats. Ancient boundary banks and sawpits. Copy of Eric Gill crucifix. Managed by Chiltern Woodlands Project.

Priestfield Arboretum

(Mr and Mrs A Carton) A 2ha
O.S.S. 175 - SU 901 992
✉The Dendrologist, PO Box 341, Chesham, Bucks HP5 2RD

Off Stoney Lane, Windsor Lane, Little Kingshi ll Nr Gt Missenden, Bucks. Little Kingshill is off the main A413. There is limited parking in Stoney Lane, but no other facilities. There is a guide book, price £2.00 incl p&p which is available from the above address. Access is free (by appointment only through the Dendrologist) but a donation towards maintenance and planting of trees would be welcome. There are Open Days which are held in Jun and Oct. The woodland consists of 175 unsual and rare trees including representatives of all conifer genera that can be grown in this area of Britain. The Taxodiaceae have a very good representation at Priestfield. Small growing broadleaf exotics are currently being added for interest and colour. Shrub management by volunteers with grass cutting by the owner twice a year.

Rushbeds Wood

(Berks, Bucks and Oxon Naturalists Trust)
F 45 ha
O.S.S. 165 - SP 668 157
☎0296 433222

A41 W from Aylesbury. At Kingswood turn L towards Brill. After 1 1/2 miles follow road L and just before T-junction turn R over bridge into car park. A leaflet describing a wildlife walk around the reserve is available from the above phone number. A BBONT nature reserve and an SSSI: dogs must be kept on a lead. This ancient woodland has over 120 species of flowering plants, 50 fungi and 60 mosses and liver-worts. Dead wood supports beetles and other invertebrates which attract numerous woodpeckers, including the greater spotted. Part of the wood is being brought back into coppice management, a large area is being left as wildwood, and an area of blackthorn is being managed for the black hairstreak butterfly. The rides have been widened for the benefit of flowers and insects.

Sandells and Netherlands

(The Earl Howe) R 26ha
O.S.S. 175 - SU 937 924
☎0295 688100

From Beaconsfield (Newtown) take Penn Road and then turn R into Ledborough Lane. Drive for 350m and turn L into Sandells Wood End. Drive for 900m and the entrance to the wood is on the R by the public footpath sign and the

Penn Parish Council notice board. There is adequate street parking. There is fully open access to the wood from April to September and there are rights of way and self guided trails. There may be some restrictions to access during felling operations. Please contact Peter Hale on the above number, or in writing, at Payn's House, Oxhill, Warwick, CV35 0QR for a descriptive leaflet of the wood (£1 plus postage). Donations to the Forestry Trust. The mature beechwoods were probably planted in about 1850. The stand has been recently thinned and some storm damage has occurred. The belt of young hardwoods are to provide a screen when final fellings and replantings take place. The objective is to grow good quality timber. An ancient boundary ditch borders part of the wood.

Shenley Wood
(Milton Keynes Parks Trust) F 23.4ha
O.S.S. 152 - SP 825 357
☎0908 223322

Shenley Wood is between Fulmer St and Tattenhoe St on the W side of Milton Keynes, with Portway to the N and Child'sWay to the S. Access is via a path from Chalkdell Drive on the NE side, or from the car park off Merlewood Drive, by the SW corner of the wood. There is a good car park and a picnic area, a network of paths and rides with several seats, but no other facilities. Shenley Wood is an important nature conservation site and visitors are asked to keep to the paths and keep dogs on a lead, especially in the bird nesting season. The wood is a fragment of ancient semi-natural woodland, historically associated with the nearby hamlets of Shenley Brook End and Shenley Church End, with records dating back to 1693 when it was twice as large. It contains a wide variety of trees and shrubs. Being primarily wet ash/oak woodland there is a predominance of ash, with lesser numbers of oak and field maple. Some of the large standard ash and oak are growing on very old previously coppiced bases, possibly 3/400 years old. In the 1950s small areas were planted with beech, Norway spruce, Lawson cypress and western hemlock but none of the latter and very few of the first three have survived. Hazel, field maple, aspen and goat willow dominate the shrub layer. With extensive brambles and hawthorn patches, and dense blackthorn thick in places. Privet, dogwood and dog rose are all frequent, Guelder rose is also quite common and there are a very few wayfaring trees and purging buckthorn. The ground flora is also rich, being dominated, under the relatively light open canopy, by rough meadow grass, with dog's mercury in the drier areas; meadowsweet, ragged robin and pendulous sedge in the wet places. This rich and diverse flora and structure supports a wide variety of woodland birds, butterflies and moths, other insects and small mammals, though few rare species are recorded. It is currently managed to conserve its wildlife value and as a park.

Buckinghamshire

★ Wendover Woodland Park
(Managed by Forest Enterprise) F 325ha
O.S.S. 165 - SP 889 107
☎0296 625825

From A4011 Wendover-Tring Road a brown tourist sign directs visitors to the woodland entrance. Car park (£1), toilets, play area, barbecues forest trails, orienteering course, forest fitness trail. Special events programme and guided walks leaflet available. Situated on the northern edge of the Chilterns escarpment the woods afford some spectacular views of the Aylesbury Vale. These productive woods are now probably the most important nesting site for one of the smallest of our birds, the firecrest. Management has been adapted to conserve this bird and its habitat. Recreation is positively encouraged with a range of trails and play furniture.

Whiteleaf Wood
(Buckinghamshire County Council) F 10ha
O.S.S. 165 - SP 824036
☎0296 383394

From the S end of Whiteleaf village, take Peters Lane up the escarpment towards Hampden. At the top of the hill (about 3/4 mile) Whiteleaf Wood car park (20 cars) is on the L. Facilities include bridleway, Ridgeway National Trail, network of permissive paths, picnic site. There is full and free access all year. Whiteleaf Wood/Hill is a distinct north-south

ridge on the edge of the Chilterns scarp. Recent gale damages has resulted in extensive planting of native species to the site. Whiteleaf Hill contains some fascinating archaelogical features; a Neolithic long barrow, two round barrows, Whiteleaf Cross (existence first noted in 1738), a cross ridge dyke system, and First World War practice trenches. The principal management objectives are to enhance the archeological interest and grassland conservation value by clearance and containment of scrub growth, and restoration of the storm damaged areas of the woodland to broadleaf high forest.

CAMBRIDGESHIRE

see map on p11

Aversley Wood
(Woodland Trust) F 61.5ha
O.S.S. 142 - TL 158 815
☎0476 74297

Take a minor road off the A1 to Sawtry village. Park off St Judith's Lane in the parish council car park. National Tree Week events may take place in this wood during late Nov-Dec. Please phone the Woodland Trust on 0476 74297 for details in the Autumn. Aversley Wood is one of the most interesting woods in Cambridgeshire. Ash and oak are the main canopy trees, along with aspen, beech and most interesting of all, the wild service tree, for which Aversley is especially important. The wood is a haven for birds. Look out for wrens and warblers; also blue, great and long-tailed tits, which have been seen and heard among the many shrubs in the wood, including hawthorn, elder, dogwood and the wayfaring tree. The rides in this wood provide habitats for many flowers including lady's smock, bugle and meadowsweet.

Bedford Purlieus
(Forest Enterprise) R 195ha
O.S.S. 141 - TF 045 004
☎0780 83394

Brampton Wood
(Wildlife Trust for Beds & Cambs) F 132ha
O.S.S. 153 - TL 185 698
☎0223 846363

The wood is on the N side of the road between Brampton and Grafham, about 1 mile W of the A1. Car park at wood entrance. Brampton is the second largest wood in Cambridgeshire. It consists primarily of ash and field maple with hazel coppice but there are extensive blackthorn thickets, stands of recently planted conifers and many other trees and shrubs. Over 300 plant species have been recorded and it is particularly well known for butterflies, including white admiral and black hairstreak. Brampton Wood is also noted for birds including the grasshopper warbler, nightingale, spotted flycatcher and woodcock.

Gamlingay Wood
(Wildlife Trust for Beds & Cambs) F 48ha
O.S.S. 153 - TL 242 535
☎0223 846363

From Gamlingay take B1040 towards Waresley. About 1/2 mile down the road, a track on the right leads to the reserve. Please drive carefully down track and park near wood. Between 1949 and 1964, most of the wood was planted with a variety of conifers and oak. The rest of the wood is as it has been for hundreds of years, a mixture of coppice ash, hazel and field maple with pedunculate oak standards, some sallow and aspen. Wild service trees also grow here, a rarity in Cambridgeshire. Flora to see includes: oxlip, dog's mercury, bluebell, yellow archangel. Gamlingay is rich in mosses, fungi and insects which live only in ancient woodland.

Hayley Wood
(The Wildlife Trust for Beds & Cambs) F
48ha
O.S.S. 153 - TL 294 534
☎0223 846363

Hayley Wood is on the B1046
between Great Gransden and
Longstowe. The track leading to
Hayley Wood is opposite a large
water tower. Park on B1046 verge,
W of track entrance. Please close
and fasten all gates after passing
through, especially those which
protect the coppice plots within the
wood. The ancient Hayley Wood
consists largely of tall oak
standards forming a canopy above
the mixed coppice and smaller
trees of field maple, ash, hazel and
hawthorn. Bluebell, oxlip and other
beautiful spring flowers thrive in
the conditions created by coppice
management. Hayley is thought to
have one of the largest oxlip
populations in Britain and is also
famous for its mosses, liverworts
and fungi.

Overhall Grove
(WildlifeTrust for Beds & Cambs) F 17ha
O.S.S. 154 - TL 337 633
☎0223 846363

From Cambridge take A1303
which leads onto A45. 6 miles
down the A45 turn R to Knapwell;
drive into the village and take track
on R which leads to church. Please
park by church. Overhall Grove
grows on the remains of the fields,

ponds and moat of a medieval
manor house, on a gentle W facing
slope. Despite the slope, the wood
is poorly drained and provides
good habitat for many of the
beautiful woodland plants that
flower in the spring. Oxlip, bluebell
and wood anemone grow here in
profusion and there are many other
botanically interesting plants,
including alexanders, and a
flourishing fungus population.

★ Perry Woods
(A H Duberly) L 80ha
O.S.S. 153 - TL 133 665
☎0480 860305

1 mile S of Grafham Water on the
B661. Roadside parking. The wood
is open only on Good Friday, April
1st 1994 otherwise by appointment. No dogs please. An excellent
example of ancient woodland.
SSSI. Traditionally managed with
wide rides and coppiced areas.

Southey Wood
(Forest Enterprise) F 71ha
O.S.S. 142 - TF 110 025
☎0780 83394

From A47/A1 junction travel east
approximately 1.5km and turn left
(follow sign for Southorpe). Take
first right about 500m, follow to
wood. Picnic site, car park, forest
walks. Open all year but some
restrictions during forest operations. This is a working multipurpose woodland. The car park area
is situated on the site of ancient

woodland and consequently has a
good show of spring flowers.
Throughout the wood are examples
of unusual trees such as maples,
hickory and Turkish hazel. A walk
at any time of year will not be
without some interest.

Wimpole
(National Trust) **F** 112ha
O.S.S. 154 - TL 338 510
☎0223 207257

10 miles SW of Cambridge. Free
access and parking. Further
information telephone the above
number.

CHESHIRE

see map on p 14

Church Wood & Clayhill Wood
(Ellesmere Port & Neston Borough Council)
F 40ha
O.S.S. 117 - SJ 368 775
☎051-357 1991

Off B5132 signposted to Rivacre Valley. Car park. Area of oak and birch woodland with nature trail/interpretation. Wildlife includes fox and weasel. Meadow areas with lots of orchids and butterflies in summer. Orienteering course, birdwatching, bluebells in woodland in spring.

★ Delamere Forest Park
(Managed by Forest Enterprise) F 785ha
O.S.S. 117 - SJ 546 703
☎0606 882167

From Chester, take the A51 to roundabout, then A54 to Kelsall and Northwich; after Kelsall bear L onto A556 to Northwich, at cross roads turn L to Delamere, turn L again in front of forest park signs, follow track to Forest Centre. All ability trail, refreshments, forest walks, car parking, Christmas tree sales centre in December. Educational facilities. Shop open 1030-1230, 1.30-4.00 Mon-Fri and 1030 to 4.30 Sat-Sun. Mountain bikers are requested to respect other visitors and give way to pedestrians. Delamere Forest is the largest block of established woodland in Cheshire. Delamere originated as a Norman hunting ground, hence the French name "Forest of the Meres". Many of the Meres were drained by Napoleonic

prisoners of war. Those Meres which remained undrained are now SSSIs because of their importance for wildlife. As the hemlock trees on the drained Meres reach maturity and are felled, the foresters have an interesting opportunity to return some Meres back to their original flooded state.

★ Little Budworth Country Park Woods
(Oulton Estates - leased to Cheshire County Council) F 33.2ha
O.S.S. 117 - SJ 587 657
☎0244 602845

Turn E off A49 immediately S off the A54/A49 intersection signed Little Budworth. Toilets, car park, picnic area, information board, disabled access and toilet. Open from 0830 hours to dusk. Please keep to paths. The area of heathland is an SSSI. Lowland heath - rare plants and invertebrates. Birchwood fungi.

★ Marbury Country Park Woods
(I.C.I.- leased to Cheshire County Council)
F 85.2ha
O.S.S. 118 - SJ 654 762
☎0244 602845

Approx 1 mile N of Northwich. Entrance off the Comberbach/Barnton "C" Road. Brown tourist signs off main routes. Car Parking, toilets, paths, Mere birdhide, picnic tables, link to canal, interpretative information. Opening times posted on site, usually 0830 hours to dusk. Dog exercise area in operation; dogs on leads in park but free exercise in woods. Please respect fishermen and horseriders. Birdwatching with extensive species list of woodland and water birds. Historic remains of manor house. Grotto/cock fighting pit. Ice house 1800's. "Elmer" - sculpture in elm. Ghost - The White Lady. Tree Garden for Everyman - collection of trees for the senses. Avenue of limes. Canal. Guided walks and activities in annual programme.

Primrose Hill Wood
(Managed by Forest Enterprise) F 99.5ha
O.S.S. 117 - SJ 537 678
☎0606 882167

From Tarporley take the A49 towards Northwich in 2 miles turn L: at Cotebrooke towards Delamere, in 3/4 mile pass farm on R, turn L at crossroads towards Kelsall. 2 car parks on R, one in 1.5 miles, second in 3 miles.

Snidley Moor and Woodhouse Hill Wood
(Woodland Trust) F 14.16ha
O.S.S. 117 - SJ 513 753
☎0476 74297

From Frodsham take the A56 Chester road, the B5393 (sign-posted to Tarvin, Alvanley and Manley). After 1 mile, turn L on to the minor road called the Ridgeway. The wood is at the end of the track running N along this road after just under 1/2 mile.

National Tree Week events may take place in this wood during late Nov-Dec. Please phone the Woodland Trust for details in the Autumn. The woodland of Snidley Moor covers a west-facing slope of the central Cheshire sandstone ridge, which rises dramatically from the former marshland below. The wood contains many birch trees with some oak and rowan. A noisy, colourful bird which you are sure to come across on your walk through the wood, is the jay. The sandstone trail or Cheshire Way footpath from Frodsham follows the western edge of Snidley Moor.

Stanney Wood
(Ellesmere Port & Neston Borough Council)
F 20h
O.S.S. 117 - SJ 398 738
☎051 3571991

On the A5117 between M53 and A41. Woodland is signposted into car park off the A5117. Car park, surfaced footpaths, information/ ranger service. Stanney Wood is an area of semi-natural ancient woodland. Birch, oak with hazel understorey. Healthy fern population. Wildlife includes foxes, squirrels, bank and field voles. Interesting and varied bird life. Circular walks and well surfaced paths suitable for prams and wheelchairs. No gradients.

CLEVELAND

see map on p13

Errington Wood

(Langbaugh on Tees Borough Council) F
80ha
O.S.S. 94 - NZ 618 203
☎0642 231212

From the A174 take the Grewgrass
Lane exit (signposted "New
Marske") follow the road to the top
of the hill where the picnic site can
be found. There is also a car park,
woodland trail and information,
and 1.1/4 miles of footpath suitable
for wheelchairs starting from the
picnic site. Errington Wood is a
mature mixed mainly conifer wood
managed for its wildlife and
amenity value. One of the oldest
conifer woodlands in the NE
(Planted 1773). Unsurpassable
views of the Tees Bay and beyond
from its highest point.

Guisborough Forest

(Forest Enterprise) F 230ha
O.S.S. 94 - NZ 600 136
☎0751 72771

Newton Wood

(National Trust) F 8.1ha
O.S.S. 93 - NZ 575 126
☎0751 460396

8 miles SE of Middlesbrough, 2
miles SE of Great Ayton. Access by
public footpath from Great Ayton
and from the National Park car
park at Newton under Roseberry.
Newton Wood is a broadleaved
woodland flanking the SW slope of
Roseberry Topping, the famous

Cleveland landmark. A semi-
natural acid oak woodland
botanically rich with good bird and
mammal life. Spectacular displays
of bluebells. Good area for walkers
especially as the Cleveland Way
crosses nearby Newton Moor.

Thorpe Wood

(Cleveland County Council) F 17ha
O.S.S. 93 - NZ 401 246
☎0740 630011

The wood is part of Castle Eden
Walkway Country Park. Access off
A177, Stockton-on-Tees to
Sedgefield Road, opposite Thorpe
Thewles village. There is a Visitor
Centre, toilets, picnic site, play
area, circular walks, and ponds.
The wood is open during daylight
hours. The Visitor Centre is open
8.30 am-4.30 pm Mon-Fri, 9
am-4.30 pm weekends (closed Sat.
Nov-March incl.) No cycling
allowed in woodland. Dogs must be
under close control. Access is not
possible by wheelchair due to steep
gradients. Thorpe Wood is a relic
of the ancient woodland which
once covered this country. It
retains the distinctive flora of
ancient semi-natural woodland with
fine spring displays of flowers such
as wood anemone. The pond within
the woodland is also home to great
crested newts. Thorpe Wood has
undergone a variety of types of
management over the centuries.
The present policy is to retain what
is left of older coppice and to
manage for sustainable timber
production with an emphasis on
wildlife conservation. Traditional

skills such as charcoal making and bodging, "green wood turning for chairs" are being revived. The woodland is used to demonstrate traditional woodland management techniques with associated "Woodcraft Weekend" events (2 per year). These may be of interest for educational visits. Please discuss with Warden - Bruce Ferguson.

CORNWALL

see map on p16

★ Cardinham Woods
(Managed by Forest Enterprise) F 264ha
O.S.S. 200- SX 099 667
☎0208 72577 or 0409 221692

From Bodmin take the A38 for 2
miles. 400 yards beyond roundabout turn L, in 600 yards go
round sharp bend, turn L into
forest. Car parks, cafe, cycle hire,
childrens' play trail, all ability trail
and forest walks. The Forestry
Commission has managed the
woods at Cardinham since 1922.
Today their fertile soils produce
fine timber with impressive old
Douglas fir. Four walks explore the
natural beauty of the forest; one of
the walks which follows the stream
is suitable for people of all abilities.

★ Horse Wood
(Duchy of Cornwall) F 27ha
O.S.S. 201 - SX 161 613
☎0579 343149

Follow the signs on the A390 to
"Duchy of Cornwall Nursery"
between West Taphouse and
Lostwithiel. Car parking, picnic
area, retail, tree nursery, information leaflet, drinks and WC
available in the nursery. This is a
commercial woodland situated in
the picturesque Fowey Valley with
views of Restormel Castle and
plantings of Douglas fir, larch,
hemlock, cedar and broadleaved
species. A small pinetum has been
created and specimen broadleaves
planted at intervals around the
trail. A pond has been dug out with

some
adjacent ornamental planting.
School parties and groups
welcome. Contact Brian Wilson on
above number.

Idless Woods
(Managed by Forest Enterprise) F 114ha
O.S.S. 204 - SW 822 477
☎0409 221692

2 miles N of Truro. Car park and
forest walk.

Kings Wood
(Woodland Trust) F 59.49ha
O.S.S. 204 - SX 007 493
☎0476 74297

Take the B3273 S from St Austell.
After 1.1/4 miles pass through the
village of London Apprentice and
just after a road to the R called
Polgooth, turn L onto a track.
Follow the track over the bridge,
around to the R and park either in
a layby here or at the far end of the
track. National Tree Week events
may take place in this wood during
late Nov-Dec, Please phone the
Woodland Trust for details in the
Autumn. Kingswood is situated on
the steep SW facing hillside of the
Pentewan Valley and according to
ancient maps has been in existence
since at least 1600AD. The slopes
above the valley bottom are
dominated by oak, beech and ash.
In spring bluebells appear on the
slope, as well as wood sorrel and
primroses. The wet valley bottom
provides an ideal habitat for alder,
sedge and gypsywort. You may spot

butterflies such as Holly Blue and Orange Tip along with many common woodland birds.

there are extensive mixed woodlands which are home to a herd of wild fallow deer.

Mount Edgcumbe Country Park
(Plymouth City Council & Cornwall County Council) F 350ha
O.S.S.201 - SX 453 533
☎0752 822236

From Plymouth, Cremyll Foot Ferry from Admirals Hard, Durnford Street. Vehicles, Torpoint Ferry. Follow A374 then B3247 to Mount Edgcumbe. From Cornwall A38 to Trerule Foot then A374 then B3247. Toilets including facilities for disabled by Orangery within the formal gardens at Cremyll.. No admission fee for formal gardens, woodland and parkland which are open all year. Mount Edgcumbe House and Earls Garden open April 1 until Oct 31, Wed to Sun, for which there is an admission charge. Car park with map and information boards located at Cremyll OS Ref. SX 453533 (three other car parks at Barrow Park OS Ref SX 450526, Maker OS Ref SX 446521 and Rame Head OS Ref. SX 420488). Mount Edgcumbe is a rare example of an intact 18th century landscape. Almost surrounded by Plymouth Sound and the sea. The opportunities for parkland and coastal walks are endless. There are gardens in the English, French and Italian styles which are over 200 years old. Tree species include gingkos, tulip trees, giant hedges of holm oak, and cork oaks, including the largest in Britain. In addition

★ Trelowarren
(The Vyvyan family, and the Trelowarren Woodlands Trust) A 117ha
O.S.S. 203 - SW 720 239
☎0736 731846

3 3/4 miles SE of Helston. Take the B3293 SE from Helston, turning L into the Trelowarren Estate at the village of Garras. There is parking for 20 cars and several coaches. There are some WC facilities on the site. In the central estate complex, close to the car park and WCs there is a bistro/cafe and small gift shop.Visits can be arranged but there must be a significant number of people booking for any one visit. All visits must be made by prior appointment only. For further information please write to Dr S P G Perry, Woodland Manager, Stile Cottage, Trevithal, Paul, Penzance, Cornwall, TR19 6UQ or ring the above number. Donations to the Forestry Trust.

CUMBRIA

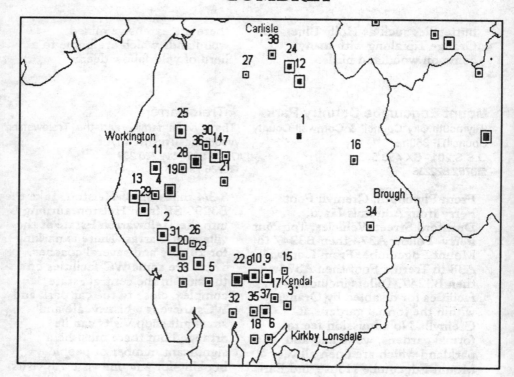

1. *Beacon Wood
2. Blengdale Forest
3. Brigsteer Park
4. Broadmoor
5. Broughton Moor
6. Brown Robin
7. *Brundholme
8. Bryerswood Woodlands
9. Chapel House
10. Claife Woods
11. Cogra
12. Coombs Wood
13. Dent Fell
14. Dodd Wood
15. Dorothy Farrers Spring Wood
16. Dufton Ghyll Wood
17. Durham Bridge Wood
18. Eggerslack Wood
19. Ennerdale Forest

20. Giggle Alley
21. Great Wood
22. *Grizedale Forest Park
23. Hardknott Forest
24. High Stand
25. Higham & Setmurthy
26. Hows Wood
27. Hutton-in-the-Forest Grove
28. Lanthwaite
29. Lowther Park & Sillathwaite
30. *Mirehouse & Catstocks Woods
31. Miterdale Forest
32. Old Hall Wood
33. Rainsbarrow
34. Smardale Gill
35. Thornphinsty & Crag Wood
36. *Whinlatter Forest Park
37. Witherslack Wood
38. Wreay Woods

★ Beacon Wood

(Lord Lonsdale) L 126ha
O.S.S. 90 - NY 520 311
☎0931 712577

Take the A6 through Penrith, turn
R towards Lazonby and R again
towards Langwathby past the
church and the path is on the L.
Limited parking. The permissive
path to Beacon Pike (open all year)
runs through productive woodland
where particular attention is paid
to the landscape value of this
prominent hillside. The view from
the Pike encompasses the town
itself., the Lakeland hills to the W
and the Eden Valley and Pennines
to the E. Predominantly coniferous. Beacon Wood contains trees
of all ages and plays host to a wide
variety of flora and fauna including
roe deer, badgers and red squirrels,
at the same time producing timber
for local sawmills.

Blengdale Forest

(Forest Enterprise) F 480ha
O.S.S. 89 - NY 109 059
☎0229 860373

Brigsteer Park

(National Trust) F 34ha
O.S.S. 97 - SD 489 877
☎05395 60723

Approach from the Levens village
to Brigsteer village road. Parking at
several lay-byes throughout the
wood. There is full free access.
Main access point "3 Beeches" at
the S end of the wood. Information
signs at various points. Ancient

semi-natural woodland. On ground
varying from limestone scree and
escarpment to peat moss. 16 ha
were cleared of hazel/ash coppice
in the late 1960/1970s and
replanted with a conifer/broadleaf
mixture. Remaining area was left as
old coppice with standards. At
present a long term plan to create
diversity and conserve species
through: (1) restoring mixed
plantations to ash/hazel dominated
woodland (2) restoring old coppice
to a small scale coppice cycle (3)
ride management (4) retaining
non-intervention areas, is being
carried out. The wood is rich in
invertebrates especially butterflies,
flowering plant species and native
shrubs.

Broadmoor

(Forest Enterprise) F 39ha
O.S.S. 89 - NY 082 159
☎0229 860373

Broughton Moor

(Forest Enterprise) F 79ha
O.S.S. 96 - SD 246 936
☎0229 860373

Brown Robin

(Cumbria Wildlife Trust) F 26ha
O.S.S. 97 - 411 792
☎05394 32476

From Grange BR station walk up
the drive of The Netherwood Hotel
taking farm track off to L.
Alternatively, park on B5271 at
above grid ref. and walk up slope.

Limited parking on roadside. A trail around the reserve is marked by white topped posts. A leaflet is also available from the above. The woodland contains some fine specimens of native and natural-ised trees with a ground flora including bluebell, violet, wild daffodil and primrose. A wide variety of woodland birds can be seen as can both red and grey squirrels. The woodland is being managed sustainably for timber and wildlife. Thinning, coppicing and deer fencing are being carried out at present.

★ Brundholme
(John Fryer-Spedding) F 34ha
O.S.S. 90 - NX 267 242
☎07687 72287

Follow Brundholme Road out of Keswick centre to car park at Briar Rigg. A leaflet will be available from National Park Information Offices. The woods are in the main ancient semi-natural but inter-spersed with young plantations of hybrid larch and sitka spruce landscaped with gean, ash and sessile oak. The ancient coppiced oak woods of the Manor of Brundholme provided bark for local tanneries. The Lake District National Park Authority has constructed a scenic walk through the woods from which exciting views of the northern fells can be enjoyed. The woods provide a habitat for badgers, red squirrels and many birds including fly catchers and, on the River Greta, river birds.

Bryerswood Woodlands
(Mrs P E Naylor) L 138ha
O.S.S. 97 - SD382 952
☎05394 43528

(a) From Windermere Ferry landing (W side) follow road B5285 to top of Ferry Hill and turn in at first gates on R, immediately turn R into woodyard. (b) From Hawkshead follow B5285 towards Ferry; after passing Far Sawrey (2.1/2 miles) entrance gates (black) are ahead; after entering gates immediately turn R into woodyard. There is parking for approximately 20 cars. There is one WC on site. Village shop and Sawrey Hotel nearby. Guided tour will be held on Sun 2 Oct 1994, start. 2pm (2 hours min.). Charges £2 per adult and £1 per child to be donated to the Forestry Trust. The Bry-erswood Estate Woodlands (300 to 700 feet above sea level) are managed as commercial woodland with main priorities: (1) Production of wood. (2) Conservation of woodland (some ancient woodland sites). (3) Enhancement of landscapes. (4) Maintaining a reserve of capital.. Provision of employment and creation of wildlife habitats are also important. 2/3 coniferous, mainly spruce and larch but also Scots pine and western hemlock. 1/3 broadleaved, mainly oak, but some beech, alder and birch. Good views. Mammals: red and roe deer, red squirrels. Birds: buzzards, ravens etc. SSSI. In the Lake District National Park.

Chapel House
(Forest Enterprise) F 333ha
O.S.S.96/97 - SD 393 858
☎0229 860373

Claife Woods
(National Trust) F 303ha
O.S.S. 97 - SD 388 954
☎05394 46534

Approach (S end) on the B5285 Hawkshead to Windermere Ferry road. National Trust car park at the foot of Ferry Hill. Claife Woods are mixed uneven aged woodlands stretching from near Ferry Nab on the W shore of Windermere to Wray Castle. The majority of the woodlands are on the steep slopes rising from the lake. There is an excellent network of footpaths, including a lakeside walk through the woods, plus splendid views of the Lakeland fells from the higher paths. The whole area is rich in wildlife including red and roe deer and red squirrel. National Trust policy is to ensure the continuity of the woodlands as an important backcloth to the lake. This involves continuous small scale timber operations which do not intrude on the landscape.

Cogra
(Forest Enterprise) F 192ha
O S.S. 89 - NY105 207
☎0229 860373

Coombs Wood
(Forest Enterprise) F 101ha
O.S.S. 86 - NY 511 449
☎0229 860373

Dent Fell
(Forest Enterprise) F 180ha
O.S.S. 89 - NY 042 136
☎0229 860373

Dodd Wood
(Managed by Forest Enterprise) F 260ha
O.S.S. 89/90 - NY 245 279
☎0229 860373

Dorothy Farrers Spring Wood
(Cumbria Wildlife Trust) F 2.6ha
O.S.S. 97 - GR 480 963
☎05394 32476

The reserve lies on a minor road between Staveley and Bowston. There are daily British Rail services to Burneside and Staveley. Parking is available where the public footpath leaves the road. This small area of ancient semi-natural woodland has been coppiced in the past to produce timber for bobbins, charcoal and basket making. Near the entrance the remains of a charcoal "pit" can be seen. Coppicing is currently being reinstated. By periodically opening up the canopy, the ground flora benefits from the increased amount of light available. In spring you can see early purple orchid, primrose, dog's mercury and bluebell. A variety of fungi inhabit the stacks of cut timber including black bulgur, many zoned polypore and honey fungus. Long tailed tit, goldcrest, treecreeper, great spotted woodpecker and sparrowhawk can be seen in the wood.

Dufton Ghyll Wood
(Woodland Trust) F 10.11ha
O.S.S. 91 - NH 687 250
☎0476 74297

Dufton Ghyll is situated 3.5 miles

N of Appleby on the western edge
of the Pennines. From the A66 and
B6542 in Appleby, follow the road
signs to Dufton village. It is best to
park at Dufton village green and
take the footpath signposted to
Ghyll, which leaves the village near
the post office. National Tree Week
events may take place in this wood
during late Nov-Dec. Please phone
the Woodland Trust for details in
the Autumn. Paths can be wet in
winter and stout footwear is
advisable. Dufton Ghyll is a
sheltered, steep-sided valley. The
ground flora is diverse and in
spring and summer an array of
various brightly coloured flowers
such as anemone, bluebell, pignut
and angelica carpet the ground. At
the E edge some large beech and
sweet chestnut can be seen which
may be up to 200 years old. 3,000
trees such as oak, hawthorn and
ash were planted by the Trust
between 1981 and 1983 to recreate
the woodland lost when many
mature trees were felled.

Durham Bridge Wood
(M S Argles) F 14ha
O.S.S. 97 - SD 449 895

From A590 (M6 to Barrow) turn
up Lyth Valley on A5074 at Gilpin
Bridge. After 3 miles turn L to
Row. Bear R at top of hamlet. Gate
into wood by house on right 700
yards. Parking for 2/3 cars at lane
side. The wood is always open and
there is a public footpath through
it. Other rides may be used. The
wood is part of the Whitbarrow
SSSI on limestone. Standards

(mainly oak) with ash and hazel
coppice. Unmanaged for 50 years.
Work started 1992/93 to attempt
coppice regeneration by cutting
overgrowth to stool, leaving young
maiden trees and shrub species. 6
hectares now attractive woodland.
Produce - hedging stakes, firewood
and charcoal burning on site.

Eggerslack Wood
(Forest Enterprise) F 47ha
O.S.S. 96/97 - SD 407 791
☎0229 860373

Ennerdale Forest
(Forest Enterprise) F 2603ha
O.S.S. 89 - NY110 153
☎0768 776880

Minor road from Ennerdale Bridge,
9 miles E of Whitehaven. Car park,
trails, toilets, refreshments - latter
two in summer only. No charges.
Enjoy the forests of the Ennerdale
Valley. Views of the Lakeland
peaks and Ennerdale Lake.
Abundant birdlife and botanical
interest. Marvellous autumn
colours from the varied tree
species.

Giggle Alley
(Forest Enterprise) F 10ha
O.S.S. 89 - NY 140 002
☎0229 860373

Great Wood
(National Trust) F 95.5 ha
O.S.S. 89 - NY 271 213
☎07687 73319

1 mile S of Keswick on the B5289 Borrowdale road is a large car park on the L (East) side of the road within the wood. Full open access to the wood although certain areas may be closed for safety reasons during timber operations over the winter months. This is a mixed wood on the W facing slopes of Walla Crag near Keswick. An important conservation area, 45 ha of the wood, is an SSSI due to the valuable bryophytes and lichens. Great Wood is part of the important group of woodlands in the Borrowdale valley. Being at the drier end of the valley it is markedly different to the woods further up the valley. The N end of the wood is predominantly conifer, planted in the 1930s and 1950s, while the S part has many native broadleaves of mixed ages.

★ Grizedale Forest Park
(Forest Enterprise) FC 2400ha
O.S.S. 96 - SD335945
☎0229 860010

3 miles S of Hawkshead and midway between Lake Windermere and Coniston Water, the Forest Park Centre is signposted off the A590 at Haverthwaite and the B5285 at Hawkshead. Visitor centre, tea room, toilets, exhibition, trails, sculpture, orienteering, art gallery, cycle hire, disabled access, education service. Main car parks £1. Visitor centre open Feb - mid Dec, 10am - 5pm. Educational groups please book in advance, coaches please telephone for access route. Grizedale is a

working forest with a history of supplying the needs of industry and communities for over 1000 years. Today the Forest Park is seen as a role model for others on how to successfully meet the challenges of multi-purpose management. Annually an estimated 300,000 visitors come to Grizedale whilst 25,000 tonnes of timber are sent to customers throughout the north of England and south Scotland. Conservation of wildlife and archaeological features is an important aspect of management, with Grizedale being home to the only native herd of woodland red deer in England and the site of numerous features which illustrate the long history of coppice management.

Hardknott Forest
(Forest Enterprise) F 629ha
O.S.S. 96 - SD 219 984
☎0229 860373

High Stand
(Forest Enterprise) F 261ha
O.S.S. 86 - NY 490 485
☎0229 860373

Higham and Setmurthy
(Forest Enterprise) F 159ha
O.S.S. 89 - NY 161 319
☎0229 86037

Hows Wood
(Friends of the Lake District) R 8ha
O.S.S. 89 - NY 180 010
☎0539 720788

On S edge of road between *Woolpack Inn* and Boot hamlet in Eskdale valley. Please do not park on the road. An ancient semi-natural woodland that was extensively re-planted in 1967 by the Forestry Commission. The FLD acquired the wood in 1987 to return it to a native woodland as the site forms an important visual element in the valley floor. Windblow of conifers has caused a change in the work programme and full access to the wood will be granted on completion of replanting.

Hutton-in-the-Forest Grove
(Lord Inglewood) R 4.6ha
O.S.S. 85 - NY 357 460
☎07684 84449

3 miles NW of junction 41 on the M6. On the B5306, Penrith to Wigton Road. WCs and tea room when house open. Open every day except Sat and Christmas day from 11am to 5pm. Hutton-in-the-Forest includes both ornamental and forest trees in a garden and forest setting. There are three generations of planting. First, a number of over-mature hardwoods planted by Henry Fletcher in the mid 18th century; secondly coniferous planting by Sir Henry Vane in the second part of the 19th century; and finally 20th century planting by the 1st Lord Inglewood.

Lanthwaite
(National Trust) F 28ha
O.S.S. 89 - NY 150 216
☎0900 85312

Take the B5289 from Cockermouth through Lorton towards Loweswater. Car park on L just past Scale Hill. The wood has full open access, but specific paths may be closed temporarily due to timber operations. Parts of the wood are accessible for wheelchairs. Lanthwaite is a mixed woodland on the N shore of Crummock Water. Chiefly uneven-aged mixed conifer with a significant broadleaf element. There is considerable natural regeneration of most species which is encouraged. Roe deer and red squirrel are present.

Lowther Park and Sillathwaite
(Forest Enterprise) F 156ha
O.S.S. 89 - NY 050 122
☎0229 860373

★ Mirehouse and Catstocks Woods
(John Fryer-Spedding) F 13ha
O.S.S. 90 - NY 236 282
☎07687 72287

From A66(T) Keswick Bypass follow historic house signs to Mirehouse car park. There is a tea room in an old sawmill. Car park, WCs, guide book. Full wheelchair access to woods. Adults £1, children 80p (includes access to Mirehouse grounds and adventure playground). Open 1st Apr to 31

Oct. Mirehouse Wood is made up of stands of Scots pine planted in 1784 and European larch planted in 1825, interspersed with sessile oak. There is a good population of red squirrels and badgers and a wide variety of birds especially woodpeckers, tree creepers and nuthatches. Catstocks Wood is an ancient semi-natural woodland on the lake shore, part SSSI. The wood consists of 200 year old sessile oak with younger planting of oak, beech, thuja and Norway spruce with a belt of hazel and alder scrub on the lake shore, widely used by water birds for nesting.

Miterdale Forest
(Forest Enterprise) F 336ha
O.S.S. 89 - NY 141 022
☎0229 860373

Old Hall Wood
(Forest Enterprise) F 36ha
O.S.S. 96/97 - SD 323 855
☎0229 860273

Rainsbarrow
(Forest Enterprise) F 50ha
O.S.S. 96 - SD 190 933
☎0229 860373

Smardale Gill
(Cumbria Wildlife Trust) R 40ha
O.S.S. 91 - 738 083
☎05394-32476

Take minor road from A685 signposted Waitby + Smardale. Go over railway line and disused line at Smardale Hall. Turn L by cottages to free car park (up to 10 cars). A permit is required to visit the sections of wood above and below the railway but these can be adequately viewed from the line. At Smardale, Scandal Beck has carved a deep gill through the Carboniferous limestone. Woodland covers much of the steep easterly slope of the gill but there are also important grasslands dominated by blue moor grass. Perched half-way up the slope is a disused railway line, once part of the Tebay - Darlington route, now a very pleasant path with fine views up and down the valley. The line crosses Scandal Beck on huge viaduct which has recently been renovated by the Northern Viaduct Trust. Over 20 species of butterfly have been seen on the reserve including the scotch argus which feeds on blue moor grass. Breeding birds include redstart, pied flycatcher, treecreeper and sparrowhawk.

Thornphinsty and Crag Wood
(C F M Rawlinson) R 20ha
O.S.S. 97 - SD 410 860
☎05242 72249

From A590 Barrow Road turn up through High Newton and take the Cartmel Fell Road. The wood is 2 miles along the road on the RH side. Car parking for 3 cars on timber loading lay by. Open at all times but the wood isused for shooting Oct/Feb and care should be taken during this period. The top of the wood is stocked with 30 year old spruce, Scots pine and larch. There is plenty of evidence of red and roe deer including wallows near the stream. The lower area, Crag Wood, has been deer fenced to allow regeneration of over mature hardwoods. Conifers have been planted in mixture but these will be removed as thinnings. The middle area has been planted with mixed hardwoods in tree shelters over the last seven years. There are signed public footpaths.

★ Whinlatter Forest Park

(Forest Enterprise) FE 1200ha
O.S.S. 89 - NY 206 245
☎0768 778469

4 miles W of Keswick on the B5292 between Braithwaite and Lorton. Visitor centre, tea rooms, toilets, trails, cycle hire, orienteering, education service; car parking £1. Visitor centre open Feb - mid Dec, 10am - 5pm. Educational groups please book in advance. Whinlatter is Englands only mountain forest with plantations extending to the 500 metre contour; the fertility of the soils varies greatly resulting in a wide variety of tree species and wildlife habitats. The numerous view points overlook the Northern Fells and are ideal locations for interpreting the effects of glaciation.

Witherslack Wood

(The Stanley Family) F 400ha
O.S.S. 97 - SD 433 862
☎05395 52252

Turn N off the A590 (M6 to Barrow in Furness) at Derby Arms. Go straight through Witherslack to Bowland Bridge. The woods surround Witherslack Hall school. There is access through the wood on rights of way, bridleways and a public road. Guided walks are occasionally held by the Lake District Rangers; contact them for details on above telephone number.

Wreay Woods

(Cumbria County Council) R 18ha
O.S.S. 85 - NY 435 513 or NY 450 497
☎05394 32476

On the A6 at Scalesceugh Hall, Wreay village, or from the N from the picnic area beside the M6. Open to the public at all times. A reserve leaflet can be obtained from the Cumbria Wildlife Trust. The W bank of the river is closed to all visitors. Wreay woods lies in a gorge formed by the River Petteril just S of Carlisle. Although it is a site of ancient woodland much of the old wood has been felled at some time in the past so there are not many mature trees in evidence. The ground flora, however, is of interest with species such as moschatel or "town hall clock", bluebell, wood sorrel, dog's mercury and ramsons. As well as woodland birds, river bank species such as dipper, grey wagtail, heron and even kingfisher can be seen.

DERBYSHIRE

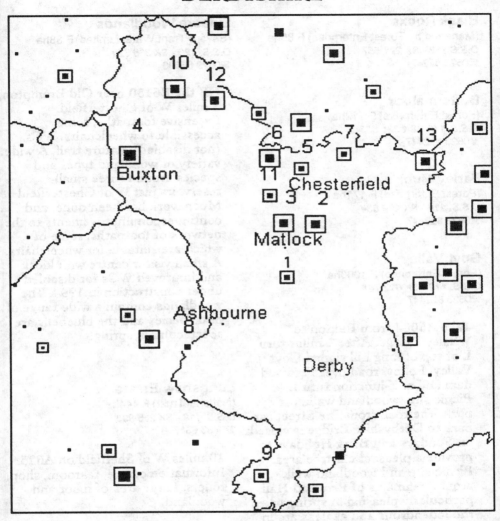

1. Black Rocks
2. Bottom Moor
3. Farley Moor
4. Goyt Valley
5. Linacre Woodlands
6. Longshaw Estate
7. Nor Wood, Cook Spring & Owler Wood

8. Norbury Estate Woodlands
9. Rosliston Farm Forest
10. Snake Plantation
11. *Stand Wood
12. Upper Derwent Woods
13. Whitwell Wood

Black Rocks

(Managed by Forest Enterprise) F 85ha
O.S.S 119 - SK 291 557
☎0623 82247

Bottom Moor

(Forest Enterprise) F 112ha
O.S.S. 119 - SK 321 633
☎0623 822447

Farley Moor

(Forest Enterprise) F 171ha
O.S.S. 119 - SK 299 634
☎0623 822447

Goyt Valley

(Forest Enterprise) F 1000ha
O.S.S. 119 - SK 012 748
☎0623 822447

Take A5004 from Buxton to Whaley Bridge. After 2 miles turn L at top of long hill signed Goyt Valley. Follow road over Errwood dam and at T-junction turn L. Picnic site, woodland walk, car park. The road from The Street car park to Derbyshire Bridge is closed on Sundays and Bank Holidays to provide a pleasant car free area. Picnic site and woodland walk around reamains of Errwood Hall particularly pleasing in spring when rhododendrons and azaleas are in bloom. The woodland comprises pine, larch, oak plantations (circa 1850) and remnant broadleaves in the numerous cloughs within the valley. Above the tree line lies large areas of heather moorland an acid grassland, most of which has been designated an SSSI.

Linacre Woodlands

(Severn Trent Water Limited) F 88ha
O.S.S. 120 - SK 336 729
☎0629 85696

Off the B6150 near Old Brampton, 3 miles W of Chesterfield. Extensive footpaths, some accessible to wheelchairs. WCs (not disabled), nature trail. A wide variety of woodland types and species around three small reservoirs just W of Chesterfield. Much work has been done, and continues, on improvements to the network of footpaths, some of which are suitable for wheelchairs. A small visitor centre with kiosk and improved WCs for disabled under construction in 1994. The woodlands contain a wide range of bird species and the bluebells are spectacular in spring.

Longshaw Estate

(National Trust) F 444ha
O.S.S. 119 - SK 266 800
☎0433 631708

10 miles W of Sheffield on A625. Information centre, tearoom, shop, toilets. Large area of moor and woodland.

Nor Wood, Cook Spring and Owler Wood

(Woodland Trust) F 30.75ha
O.S.S. 110 - SK 368 805
☎0476 74297

Take the A61 S from Sheffield for about 5 miles: then turn L onto the B6057 to Jordonthorpe. The woods are easily reached by footpaths from Jordonthorpe and Dronfield. National Tree Week events may take place in this wood during late Nov-Dec. Please phone the Woodland Trust for details in the Autumn. Some parts of these woods date back at least to the Middle Ages. The main tree species are oak, beech and ash, with understorey of hazel, cherry, aspen and alder. There is a rich vriety of flora to be found including creeping soft grass, buckler fern and dog's mercury. Fox and hare are also present. Look and listen for birds such as the great spotted woodpecker, cuckoo and tawny owl.

Norbury Estate Woodlands
(T W Clowes) A 22ha
O.S.S. 119/128 - SK 125 414
☎0335 324225

Meeting point is at Norbury Hall. Take A515 Ashbourne/Lichfield road. 3 miles out of Ashbourne turn sharp L down B5033 at signpost pointing to Norbury and Ellestone. After 2.5 miles from turning turn L after 2nd footbridge over road (5 miles SW Ashbourne). There is only a car park for about 12 cars or 1 coach only. No entrance fee but donations to local church and Forestry Trust welcomed. All visits by appointment between months Mar to Oct inclusive. Apply to owner giving 4 weeks notice. Strong footwear advised. Walking necessary. Duration of visit between 1 and 2 hours. About 55 acres of private woods varying in size from 1/2 acre to 12 acres. The woods are managed by the owner and his brother for amenity, sporting and commercial purposes. The commercial considerations are secondary. Age varies from 100 years to 1 year. The woods are mostly hardwood/softwood mixtures. Oak is the predominant hardwood. Birdlife is encouraged. The woods are regularly used by the local hunt. About 500 pheasants are reared yearly.

Rosliston Farm Forest
(Managed by the Forest Enterprise) R 56ha
O.S.S. 128 - SK 244 170
☎0889 - 586593

Rosliston Farm Forest is managed by Forest Enterprise in partnership with S Derbyshire District Council and the National Forest. Parking is in the village with access via the footpath through the churchyard at Rosliston. Rosliston Farm was acquired by the Forestry Commission in 1993 for planting as a community woodland under the National Forest initiative. The wood will be planted over the next 5 years in conjunction with the local community. This is a rare opportunity to follow the development of a wood from bare fields. Agricultural crops are still being grown and visitors are kindly requested to keep to the paths and headlands.

Snake Plantation
(Managed by Forest Enterprise) F 140ha
O.S.S. 110 - SK 109 915
☎0623 - 822447

★ Stand Wood
(Chatsworth House Trust) R 89ha
O.S.S. 119 - SK 263 705
☎0246 - 582204

From Rowsley, Baslow or Bakewell follow signs to Chatsworth. Park in the House car park where there is ample parking for cars and coaches. The visiting season is from Easter to the end of Oct, 1030-1630hrs. Cost for car £1. There are WC facilities, including disabled. The wood is adjacent to Chatsworth House, garden and farmyard. Shops and restaurant are open during the visitor season. There are marked trails through the wood (please keep to these). A limited number of guided visits can be arranged throughout the year. For details of these and to make group visit bookings please contact Mr S Seligman on the above telephone number. Stand Wood occupies a W facing escarpment in the Derwent Valley. It is the backdrop to Chatsworth House and prior to the first plantings of 1750 was a bare hillside. Some originally planted trees are still growing but there has been continuing felling and replanting by the Cavendish family since the early 19th century. This has produced an interesting mix of age class and species together with some exotics. It is a wood of great interest to people as well as wildlife. Timber production is a low priority. The surrounding commercial woodlands help to finance this conservation management.

Upper Derwent Woodlands
(Severn Trent Water Limited) FE 830ha
O.S.S. 110- SK 173 893
☎0629 - 85696

Off A57 Sheffield - Manchester Road. 12 miles W of Sheffield.Footpaths, horsetrails, information centre, toilets (incl.disabled), cycle hire (charge), way-marked walks, ranger service. Please keep to the extensive path network. Most of the forestry around the Upper Derwent Reservoirs is between 50 and 80 years old. Whilst the appearance is of extensive coniferous plantations, there are areas of mixed and ancient semi-natural woodland. Access is particularly encouraged on the extensive networks of footpaths and bridleways in the area, some leading to open moorland beyond. Road closures, and a minibus service on busy days, together wtih cycle hire facilities all add to visitors access opportunities and enjoyment. Wildlife includes goshawk, crossbills, herons and the occational red squirrel. An extensive programme of thinning and felling operations over the next few years will produce a more diverse and interesting forest that fits better into the landscape. A Centre of Excellence Award winner in 1993.

Whitwell Wood
(Managed by Forest Enterprise) F 171ha
O.S.S. 120 - SK 527 773
☎0623 822447

DEVON

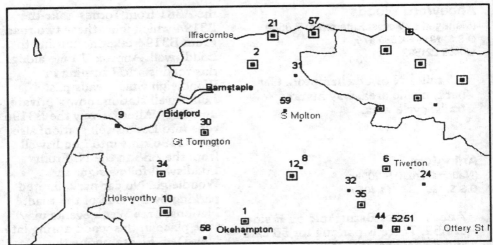

1 Abbeyford. 2 Arlington. 3 Avon. 4* Bovey Donn. 5 Burrator. 6 Buzzards. 7 Castle Drogo. 8
Chawleigh Barton. 9 Clovelly. 10 *Cookworthy. 11* Eastcottdown. 12 Eggesford. 13 Fernworthy.
14* Gatherley N. 15* Gatherley S. 16 Harcombe. 17 Hardwick. 18* Harpford. 19* Heath. 20*
Heathercombe. 21 Heddon Valley. 22 Hembury. 23 Higher Combe. 24* Hillersdon. 25 Hilltown.
26.Holne(1). 27 *Holne(2). 28 Holyford. 29 Hunting Park. 30* Huntshaw. 31* Kedworthy. 32*
Kennerleigh. 33 *Kiddens. 34* Knotts & Parsonage. 35 Lower Broxford 36 *Lukesland. 37 Lydford.
38 Manor. 39 Marridge. 40 Milber. 41 Occombe. 42 Parke. 43 *Pool Down. 44 *Quicke. 45 *Riding
Park. 46 Roadford. 47 Salcombe. 48 Scadson. 49 Shaptor. 50* Shute Hill. 51* Stoke(1). 52
Stoke(2). 53 *Tavistock. 54 Teign Valley. 55 Torquay. 56* Townleigh. 57 Watersmeet. 58* West
Bowerland. 59* Whitehills. 60 Whitleigh. 61 Wray Cleave.

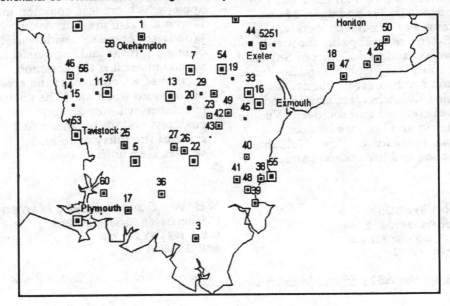

Abbeyford Woods
(Managed by Forest Enterprise) F 85ha
O.S.S. 191 - SX 589 975
☎0409 221692

1.5 miles N of Okehampton. Car park, picnic area, way marked trails, cycle area.

Arlington
(National Trust) F 200ha
O.S.S. 180 - SS 611 405

7 miles NE of Barnstaple on E side of A39. There is parking for 50 cars and 4 coaches. WC facilities on the site (summer only for disabled WC). All facilities at Arlington Court. No caravans. 1 April to 31 October. Extensive paths in the park and the wood are freely open all year. Arlington is a mixed woodland on valley sides surrounding the Arlington Court parkland. Managed on a sustained basis of mixed species and ages. Maintained as oak-beech woods. Extensive level paths through woods and park. Herd of Shetland ponies and Jacob sheep. Buzzards and ravens nest in woods. Also pied flycatcher, redstart, woodpeckers, red and roe deer. Wildlife haven and heronry by lake sanctuary for wildfowl. Valuable lichen and invertebrate site.

Avon Woods
(Woodland Trust) F 39ha
O.S.S. 202 - SX 732 486
☎0476 742970

From the A379 from Modbury or the A381 from Totnes, take the B3194 which joins these two roads. From B3194 take the turning to Loddiswell. Approx. 1 mile along this road is a RH turning to Woodleigh which leads past Loddiswell station (now a private dwelling). Alternatively the B3196 runs into Loddiswell station; also the B3196 runs into Loddiswell from the A38 to the N. From Loddiswell follow signs for Woodleigh. No car park, limited parking by the side of the road. National Tree Week events may take place in this wood during late Nov-Dec. Please phone the Woodland Trust for details. Woodland may well have existed on this site since the last ice age and has certainly been in existence for at least 300 years. Oak is the predominant tree species together with ash and hazel, much of which has been coppiced in the past. Field maple, spindle and crab apple, which are less common in Devon are also present. Avon Woods are home to a wide variety of insects, birds and mammals. Of special interest is the common dormouse which favours the areas of coppiced woodland. The spotted flycatcher, willow warbler, goldcrest and nuthatch are just some of the thirty or so bird species seen in this wood.

★ Bovey Donn & Bovey Warren
(Clinton Devon Estates) F 43ha
O.S.S. 192 - SY 203 912
☎0395 443881

Take A3052 Exeter/Lyme Regis

Road. Turn N at Hangman's Stone opposite B3174 to Beer. Parking in layby on A3052 at Hangman's Stone. 2 young commercial woodlands divided by public road running N/S. A SE border of hardwoods adjoins to an area of Japanese larch, Scots pine, Corsican pine and sitka spruce, giving an impressive array of colours during spring and autumn. Inhabited by many varieties of woodland wildlife including roe deer and badgers. Several rides suitable for walking.

Burrator Wood

(South West Water Services Ltd) F 392 ha
O.S.S 201/202 - SX 550 680
☎0822 852435

At the cross roads by the Burrator Inn in Dousland, take the road to Meavy. On the edge of the village fork L over cattle grid to Burrator Dam. There is informal car parking and picnic areas all round the reservoir and in the woods. WC facilities, including disabled, at Burrator Dam: these are, however, closed between October and March. Fishing is available at Burrator Reservoir (charges available on request), ice creams and refreshments are available from a vendor at the dam. Fully open access to the woods throughout the year, with permissive paths and a bridlepath. There are also byways, open to all traffic, through the wood. Guided walks and open days can be arranged by appointment. Contact John Griffiths, Head Forester on

the above telephone number. Burrator Woods, surrounded by hills and tors, has a centrepiece - Burrator Reservoir. The woodlands range from mature conifer plantations to newly planted broadleaved woods. A 40 acre arboretum is being established with special access for wheelchairs. Many walks in the woods and beside the reservoir. The interplay of woods, water and tors creates a magnificent natural setting.

Buzzards

(National Trust) F 67ha
O.S. S. 181/192 - SS 909 117

3 miles W of Tiverton on B3137. At far end of Withleigh take L fork with 'No through road' sign. Free car park at end of road. No other facilities. Good views of mid-Devon landscape. Quiet and isolated for those who wish to get away from it all. A network of paths freely open all year. Not for the faint-hearted. Steep climb to car park, otherwise fairly level paths. Mixed broadleaved woodland of varying ages. Some overgrown hazel coppice. Network of meadows in bottom of valley of Little Dart River, a tributary of the River Exe. Some broadleaved replanting took place in 1980s and is showing good growth. Plots of cherry and oak. Small plot of new hazel coppice being established. Called "Buzzards" because they can always be seen. Other woodland birds. Red and roe deer are resident.

Castle Drogo
(National Trust) F 329ha
O.S.S. 191 - SX 723 903

At Drewsteignton 4 miles S of A30, via Crockernwell. There is parking for 100 cars and 4 coaches. WC (including disabled), shop, information and tearoom in the castle. Extensive paths, rights of way and bridlepaths through the woods. Freely open all year. Castle open 1 April to 31 October. Pub and parking at Fingle Bridge all year round. Mixed conifer and broadleaved plantations of all ages. Straddles River Teign in the Dartmoor National Park. Extensive paths with marvellous views of the moor. Castle Drogo completed 1932. Ancient granite walled deer park with rare lichens and invertebrates. Some large areas of sessile oak woods derived from coppice system of last century. Prestonbury hill fort can be viewed from paths, also River Teign. Hunters' path and Fishermans' path are definitive public footpaths. Some paths are linked to woods at Steps Bridge (6 miles)

Chawleigh Barton Wood
(Mr J A Sibley) L 29ha
O.S.S. 180 - SS 714 126
☎0365 866305

The village of Chawleigh is on the B3042 which connects Eggesford Station (A3777) to Witheridge (on old A373). Park in the village, and walk 300m along the road leading NE out of the village towards the bridge over the Little Dart River.

The entrance gate is on the L. There are paths through the wood. Visits can be made on Sat and Sun, 0800-1800 hrs, between 4 April and 3 October. The Forest Manager is Mr W J C Blight and in the event of an emergency telephone the above number. This delightful mature oak woodland has a very good show of bluebells in the spring, when red deer can occasionally be seen in the fields across the Little Dart River. At the far end of the wood a magnificent mature crop of Douglas fir (120 - 130ft high at 65 years old) in a sheltered dingle was felled in 1988 and, hoping for a repeat performance the area was replanted with the same type of tree. As it is a dry, stony slope, Douglas fir was also planted on the old pasture next to the road. As spruce thrives on wetter sites this species was selected for planting in the two clay fields next to the river, which is a notable feature along the N boundary. This woodland provides a very pleasant walk with interesting variety.

Clovelly Wood
(John Rous) L 200ha
O.S.S. 180/190 - SS 315 245
☎0237 431200

Take the A39 to Clovelly Cross, then the B3237 to Clovelly. After <1 mile the road swings to the R, carry straight on through lodge gates to estate office by parish church. There is parking for 10 cars. For larger parties with coaches there is Clovelly's main car park. Facilities here include WC, coach park, cafeteria, film theatre, etc. There is a bridleway running through the wood. Visits are by appointment only. For further details please telephone the above number. Access is restricted during the period Oct/Jan, when there are shoots. An ancient semi-natural woodland fringing a NE facing coast. This woodland has early 19th century carriageways and paths through sessile oak, ash, beech and sycamore. The understorey includes hazel, holly and hawthorn.. Bridging streams with deeply incised valleys, the carriageway leads past vistas of Bideford Bay to the top of the famous cobbled street. From here it proceeds to dramatic headlands (350ft) and down to intimate valleys. There are abundant ferns including scaly male fern, male fern and broad buckler fern. 120 different lichen varieties thrive here which has resulted in the site being notified as an SSSI.

★ Cookworthy Forest
(Managed by Forest Enterprise) F 640ha
O.S S. 190 - SX 416 014
☎0409 221692

Signposted off the A3079 Oke-hampton to Holsworthy Road near Halwill junction. Car park, picnic area, forest walks, education facilities and all ability education trail. Please book educational visits at least 6 weeks in advance.

★ Eastcottdown Plantation
(Mr P T L Newman) A 50ha
O.S.S. 201 - SX 468 847
☎0566 83202

Approximately 8 miles from Tavistock via Chillaton (3 miles); 15 miles from Okehampton via Lewdown or Lydford (5 miles) and 9 miles from Launceston via Lewdown(3 miles). There is parking for 10 cars and 1 coach in the farmyard behind park cottage; a WC at the site, use by permission of the forge. The woods are open throughout the year. Visits to the wood are by appointment only. There are self guided trails and guided visits can be arranged. Guided visits will be charged for at £2 for adults and £1 for children. For appointments and further details please contact Mr Newman at the Manor House, Coryton, Okehampton, Devon EX20 4PG, or on the above telephone number. Donations to the Forestry Trust. The wood is located on a lower carboniferous chert ridge, with a steep southern escarpment. The site was planted in about 1840 with a mix of beech, oak, sweet chestnut, silver fir, larch, spruce and pine. This is now being felled and replanted over a 30 year period. Planting includes Douglas fir, larch, red cedar,grand fir, southern beech and cherry, with some natural regeneration of northern beech and chestnut. Rhododendron is rampant in parts of the wood. Old Manganese, slate and lime mines/quarries can be seen around the site.

Eggesford Woods
(Managed by Forest Enterprise) F 222ha
O.S.S. 191 - SS 694 106
☎0409 221692

Take the A377 N from Crediton, drive through Lapford, the forest car park is 2 miles further on to the R. Car parks, toilets, forest walks, cycle hire at the Eggesford Garden Centre. The Forestry Commission's first plantings in 1919 are commemorated. A beech avenue was planted after 50 years of Commission planting, Her Majesty the Queen and the Duke of Edinburgh helped to plant an oak grove when the Commission had planted over one million acres nationally. Walks lead through the arboretum and past a Norman motte and bailey castle. The picnic area is located under the towering Douglas fir. The woodland is a fine habitat for butterflies, deer and a host of birds of prey.

Fernworthy Wood
(Managed by Forest Enterprise) F 590ha
O.S.S. 191 - SX 668 838
☎0392 832262

From A382 take the road to Chagford. Turn R at the square in Chagford, follow signs to Fernworthy. Car parking, toilets, picnic area. Educational visits can be arranged in advance, please allow 6 weeks notice. This woodland is an excellent example of a commercial, timber producing forest within the Dartmoor National Park. Intensive work has been undertaken on landscape design, incorporating the management of the many ancient monuments, streams and open moor into one design plan. The proliferation of sitka spruce natural regeneration is of professional interest, and the tranquillity of the reservoir will ensure a relaxing visit.

★ Gatherley North
(JB Dyhouse, managed by Fountain Forestry) A 23ha
O.S.S. 201 - SX 384 836
☎0364-3316

From Launceston, through Lifton into Leat road. Go over river and take first R, signposted Gatherley, wood is 1 1/2 miles on the R. There is parking for 3 cars. All visits by appointment only. For further details and appointments please contact Fountain Forestry Ltd, Poundsgate, Newton Abbot, Devon TQ13 7PA or ring above number. Originally a broadleaved woodland, it was largely felled in World War Two. It is now predominantly conifer plantation with some broadleaf in retentions and new planting. Attractive views across Lyd Valley towards Launceston Castle. Roe and red deer. Main timber species are Douglas fir and Japanese larch.

★ Gatherley South
(J N Kirkman, managed by Fountain Forestry) A 22.5ha
O.S.S. 201 - SX 384 836
☎0364 3316

Launceston to Lifton (old A30) R turn after Arundel Arms into Leat Road. Take 1st R signposted Gatherley, wood is 1.5 miles on the R. Small parking area. Visits by appointment only. For further details and appointments please contact Fountain Forestry Ltd, Poundsgate, Newton Abbot, Devon TQ13 7PA or telephone above number. Bordered by the River Ramor. Good views over the neighbouring countryside. Young plantations of Douglas fir, Japanese larch and Sitka spruce. Ash retention blocks. New plantings of broadleaf varieties mainly oak. Roe and red deer have been seen.

Harcombe Estate
(Fire Services National Benevolent Fund)
RE 164ha
O.S.S. 192 - SX 888 818
☎0626 853639

From the N - leave S carriageway of A38 at top of Haldon Hill, turn L into lane 100 yds past Exeter racecourse. Approx. 1 mile down lane to main entrance. There is parking for 5 cars. No dogs on the estate please. Donations to Fire Services National Benevolent Fund and Forestry Trust. Access to the estate - check at reception. Open Mon, Tues and Wed 9am - 5pm. Closed mid Dec to mid Jan. There is a public right of way through the estate, also self guiding marked trails. Please keep to trails. Maps available. Mixed broadleaf woodland on the edge of Haldon Forest. Brought into production in 1987. The majority of the woodlands are now registered as an SSSI on which can be seen honey buzzards and other interesting birds of prey. The estate won the first Centre of Excellence award for Forest Practice in 1992. An extensive new plantation of mixed broadleaf trees established from 1985. With fishing lakes and rolling farm land. Woodland types include secondary ash, secondary birch and alder woods, mature English oak high forest, ash, sweet chestnut stands and beech hangers. There is extensive heathland on the upper edges of the estate, where a number of Bronze Age Tumuli can be seen.

Hardwick Wood
(Woodland Trust) F 21ha
O.S.S. 201 - SX 528 556
☎0476 74297

Hardwick Wood adjoins the Plympton to Plymstock road, which crosses the A38 to the E of Saltram House. There is limited parking at the wood but no other facilities. National Tree Week events may take place in this wood in late Nov-Dec, please phone the Woodland Trust for details in the autumn. Hardwick Wood covers an area of prominent hilltop on the edge of Plymouth, which has been covered by woodland for at least 300 years. It is one of the largest blocks of mature woodland in the area. The predominant tree species are oak, ash and beech with at least one small leaved lime tree, a rare native tree in this area. Hardwick is home for large numbers of plants and animals, including the bluebell, campion, creeping buttercup, wild garlic, woodpecker, goldcrest and fox.

★ Harpford Wood
(Clinton Devon Estates) F 63ha
O.S.S. 192 - SY 104 908
☎0395 443881

A3052 Exeter/Lyme Regis Road. Turn N at Bowd on B3176 Ottery St Mary road. Park 1/2 mile on L in layby beside recycling centre. 10 parking spaces. A most attractive mixed wood in two parts divided by former railway line. Very steep in parts. The wood contains oak, beech, chestnut and other broadleaves and some fine stands of Douglas fir, Japanese larch together with other softwoods including western hemlock, Norway and Sitka spruce ranging in age from 1812 to 1993. There are many rides throughout the wood and two routes, a short (red) and a green (long) are marked starting at the car park.

★ Heath Wood
(Mrs D Harper) A 40ha
O.S.S. 191 - SX 812 879
⬚Woodlands Farm, Bridford, Exeter, Devon
EX6 7EW

From Exeter take the B3212 towards Dunsford. After about 6 miles, at the bottom of a steep hill, turn L onto the B3193. Follow the river on the R. Cross the river and take the R turning as the road

bends to the L. Follow the road up the hill and take the first R. Carry on for 1 mile to the meeting point. There is parking for 4 cars. Guided visits can be arranged by appointment only. Please give 30 days notice for any visit. Charges for guided walks will be £2 for adults and £1.50 for children, group visits by negotiation. Donations to the Forestry Trust. For details contact Mrs Harper at the above address. There has been a wood on this site for over 600 years. The wood consists of a large and diverse range of habitats, from wetland to steep shaley slopes. At the highest point of the woodland there are commanding views over the upper River Teign. With so many different habitats there is a large bird and insect population, such as buzzards, sparrowhawks and woodcock. The flora in parts of the wood include rare species found in only a few localities in England. The wood has no defined paths or tracks, and as such suitable footwear should be worn. The wood is not suitable for visits by persons with limited mobility.

★ Heathercombe Wood
(C D Pike) A 150ha
O.S.S. 191 - SX 719 810
☎Weekend/064722 347

Through Manaton, Bovey Tracey - about 1 mile to 'T' junction (not L turn) turn L and keep straight on through Henttree Cross, signposts will then show Heathercombe. There is parking for 20 cars. Only medium size buses could be entertained. The meeting place is at Manwood, down the drive, as indicated by the signpost at the bottom of Heathercombe valley. Woodland paths and picnic area and limited WC facilities. There is one footpath and one bridleway through the wood. Visits by appointment 1 month in advance by contacting Mr Pike on above telephone number. Donations made to the Forestry Trust. Heathercombe is an estate in the woodland valley on the side of Dartmoor. It is dedicated to forestry, and contains an arboretum planted over the past 25 years. The forestry dates back about 100 years. There are some fine 100 year old trees but most of the planting has taken place since 1950. There are woodland rides and paths throughout the estate. The estate also includes Bronze Age settlements, a post war chalet bungalow and a medieval longhouse. Within the woodland snowdrops, daffodils, bluebells, rhododendrons and azaleas may be found. The estate is fully planted. During the next 20 years the development will take the form of thinning and main crop felling, mostly on a selective basis.

Heddon Valley
(National Trust) F 380ha
O.S.S. 180 - SS 655 481
☎0271 850560 (evenings)
Approximately 2.5 miles E of Blackmoor Gate (A39) turn L signed Heddon's Mouth and Hunter's Inn. Free car park in 1.25 miles. All in Exmoor National Park. Hunter's Inn public house open all year; in normal hours serves food and drink. Small souvenir and ice cream shop in summer months. Woodlands are predominantly sessile oak woods of coppice originally for charcoal, tanbark and lime burning in last century. Remains of lime kiln at Heddon's Mouth. Now being singled to high forest. Mostly timber goes for firewood, pulpwood or estate repairs. Many paths - open all year. Some suitable for wheelchairs. Woodlands on steep slopes but paths gentle. Good area for birds; flycatchers, treecreepers, buzzards and woodpeckers. Red deer, badgers and otters have been seen. Paths link to coastal path with spectacular views. Guided walks by arrangement with the Warden on the above telephone number.

Hembury Wood
(National Trust) FE 150ha
O.S.S. 202 - SX 729 680

The woodland is located 2 miles N of Buckfastleigh, 1 mile W of the A38. There is parking for 20 cars. Picnic area; level paths for the disabled and extensive paths through the woodlands by the River Dart. A mainly oak woodland with adjoining heathland. Managed in the last century for charcoal and tanbark; the trees have now been singled out to high forest. There are small areas of beech and mixed conifer. This woodland is an SSSI and within the Dartmoor National Park. An Iron Age hill fort on the crest of a hill gives good views of the surrounding area.

Higher Combe Wood
(Elliot Bialick) F 8ha
O.S.S 191 - SX 774 825
☎06477 257

Park in Lustleigh village as this is the nearest place to park. Follow public footpath through village orchard past Middle Combe. Higher Combe Woods are reached before Sanduck. Access is freely available under a voluntary access scheme promoted by the Countryside Commission and supported by the land-owner. One area of the wood is semi-ancient oak woodland with hazel coppice. The two further compartments were planted with a 'natural' mix of indigenous native deciduous species in 1992. These provide an interesting opportunity of seeing the development of a new woodland from its beginning.

★ Hillersdon Woods
(Mrs E N A Hadwen, managed by Fountain Forestry) A 23.6ha
O.S.S.192 - SS 984 078
☎03743 3316

From Cullompton take the minor road N towards Tiverton. After 2 miles at Butterleigh Cross turn L. Take next L at 'Birchen Oak'. After 1/2 mile entrance on L. There is parking for 5 cars. No WCs on site. Guided visits can be arranged at weekends between Mar and Oct. Please book at least 21 days in advance; contact Fountain Forestry on the above telephone number. Donations to the Forestry Trust. Hillersdon Woods are found on high ground overlooking Cullompton. There may have been woodland on this site for more than 400 years. The majority of the broadleaved woodland is dominated by beech dating from the 19th century and probably established for shooting purposes. Recent planting includes larch, fir and spruce. The woodlands are very diverse in species and ages and include examples of a number of trends in woodland management and establishment. There is also an archaeological site in the centre of the wood.

Hilltown and Quercus Walk
(Nicholas Collier) R 25ha
O.S.S.201 - SX 540 718
☎0822-852122

Woodtown is 4 1/2 miles from Tavistock and 2 miles from Horrabridge. Follow the signs to Sampford Spiney. It lies deep in the Walkham valley near Ward Bridge, and is signposted within the last mile. Continue through the entrance gate and down the drive to park in the estate yard. There is parking for 12 cars. The wood will be open to the public, throughout the week, between 1 April and 31 October, 10am - 5pm. All group visits are by appointment only and must be made at least 2 weeks in advance. Guided visits can be arranged and self guided trails are being developed, (please allow 1

1/2 hours to complete the woodland walk). There will be charges of £2 per car. Donations to the Forestry Trust. For further details and any enquiries please contact Nicholas Collier on the above number or at Woodtown, Sampford Spiney, Yelverton, Devon PL20 6LJ. Hilltown Wood stands at the centre of an important western oak wood system in the Walkham Valley, on the SW edge of Dartmoor. It is part of a major SSSI. The woodland character is predominantly high forest, dominated by pedunculate oak. Ash, alder and sycamore occur on the valley floor and there is some invasion of beech. The understorey contains abundant hazel, holly and sallow. Moss and fern communities are well developed in the more humid conditions by the streams. In response to the long history of woodland continuity and the pollution free oceanic climate, an interesting range of lichens have developed. The River Walkham, clean and well oxygenated, is a major spawning ground for salmon and sea trout; the site as a whole provides suitable habitat for a diverse bird community, and is rich in butterflies, flora and fauna. Badger setts and evidence of deer and otters are to be found. The Quercus Walk at Woodtown is an interesting Victorian perambulation of at least eight different species of mature oaks.

Holne Woods (1)
(National Trust) F 68ha
O.S.S. 191/202 - SX 702 703

3.5 miles W of Ashburton, S of B3357. Free car park at New Bridge. In Dartmoor National Park. No facilities, nearest 1 mile at Poundsgate - public house, shop and garage. Woodland on W side of picturesque River Dart. Predominantly oak woods of coppice origin for charcoal and tanbark in the last century - now cut for pulpwood to make cardboard and small timber for fencing and gates. Riverside path fairly level, with splendid views of Dartmoor. Paths extend 2 miles and out on to open moor. Small areas of semi-mature conifers grown for timber. Woodland birds - pied flycatchers, treecreepers, woodpeckers. Sea trout and salmon in river in due season.

★ Holne Woods (2)
(Dartmoor National Park) F 66ha
O.S.S 202 - SX 685 713
☎0626 832093

Take Princetown road out of Ashburton. Fork L on Newbridge Hill to Holne. Follow this road not turning off into Holne until you pass over Vennford Dam. Car park on R. S of wood (N of road). There is parking for 50 cars or 10 coaches. There are WCs (including disabled) but they are closed in winter. Please lock valuables out of sight in cars. Please do not climb over regeneration fences. Year round open access via common land. A guided visit will be held on 17 June 1994 at 1400-1700 hours (3hrs) costing £2 for adults and

50p for children. Donations to the Forestry Trust. Holne Woods are ancient oak woodlands of coppice origin with untouched areas and regeneration compartments. Woodland is well known for its bryophyte and lichen communities and upland birds including pied flycatchers, redstarts and many warblers. It is an SSSI.

Holyford Wood
(South West Water Services) F 25ha
O.S.S. 192 - SY 233 924
☎822 852435

From Exeter take the A3052 (or from Axminster take the A358 then turn R onto the A3052) towards Seaton. Turn N off the A3052 at Seaton for Holyford and then left at Holyford after 1/2 mile for Holyford Woods. There is limited parking. There is full open access to the wood with a public footpath crossing it from N to S. Requests for guided visits should be made to John Griffiths, Head Forester at Burrator Lodge, Sheepstor, Yelverton, Devon, or telephone above number. The woods form part of a water catchment leading to a small water treatment works. The N side of the valley contains ancient woodland with oaks.

Hunting Park and Sanduck
(Dartmoor National Park) A 18ha
O.S.S.191 - SX 772 842
☎0626 832093

1.4 miles S of Moretonhampstead

on A382, 400 yards S of Wray Barton layby (E side of road) almost opposite entrance to old railway. There is parking for 5 cars and 1 coach. No WCs. Guided visits can be arranged for groups of 10 or more, by appointment. Cost £2 for adults and 50p for children. Please give one month's notice to: Mr Lane,.Dartmoor National Park, Parke, Haytor Road, Bovey Tracey, Newton Abbot, Devon TQ13 91Q, or telephone the above number. Hunting Park and Sanduck are principally broadleaved woods. There is some sycamore which is being removed and the larch is gradually being felled. Mature oaks are retained to provide a rich habitat, in some cases until the trees die. The woods are being managed for butterflies and dragonflies in particular. Red and roe deer have been recorded in the woods as has the dormouse. There is an old ruined long house in Sanduck. The wood is prominent in the landscape and this is the principal object of management.

★ Huntshaw
(Clinton Devon Estates) F 84ha
O.S.S.180 - SS 503 224
☎0395 443881

B3232 from Great Torrington (3miles) turn L at Huntshaw Cross. Parking for up to 3 cars on public road at Foxes Cross. This group of commercial woodlands contains a variety of hardwoods and softwoods planted between 1874 to 1993. Near to the E perimeter is part of a scheduled

Ancient Monument known as Berry Camp. The wood is home to many varieties of typical woodland wildlife including roe and fallow deer. The wood contains many rides suitable for walking and a stream meanders E to W

★ Kedworthy Wood
(David Miller) L 17.7ha
O.S.S. 180 - SS 705 373
☎0271 860800

The wood is found 1.25 miles N of Brayford, off the A399. There is parking for 6 cars. Open Jan-May and Sept-Dec. Group/guided visits by appointment only. Please ring David Miller on the above telephone number. Please give one week's notice for visits. Donations to the Forestry Trust. Kedworthy Wood is a small mixed broadleaf and conifer woodland, just inside the Exmoor National Park. It has been a woodland site for at least 100 years. A delightful moorland stream runs the length of the wood. Main timber species are oak, alder, Douglas fir with some Japanese larch.

★ Kennerleigh Wood
(Paul Orchard-Lisle, managed by Fountain Forestry) A 45ha
O.S.S. 191 - SS 819 063
☎0364 3316

N from Crediton through Sandford on minor road. Approximately 3 miles on and 1/2 mile before Kennerleigh village the woods will be found, on the L with an open entrance/loading bay signposted `Kennerleigh Wood'. There is parking for 12 cars. Guided visits can be arranged for weekends except between 1 Nov and 1 Feb. All visits by appointment only, please give 2/3 weeks notice. For further details contact A J Sandels of Fountain Forestry, Poundsgate, Newton Abbot, Devon, TQ13 7PA, or telephone above number. Kennerleigh Woods are a very fine example of productive, high timber quality mixed conifer plantation. The wood is predominantly Douglas fir and larch but with some spruce and beech plantations. There are some very interesting areas of red oak. In addition there are stream habitats, hazel coppice, old oak coppice and young ash coppice, now thinned to single stems. A tour of Kennerleigh Wood gives a good insight into forest silviculture, woodland conservation and the use of woods for recreation and sport.

★ Kiddens Wood - (Bullers Hill)
(Managed by Forest Enterprise) Fc 500ha
O.S.S. 192 - SX 882 847
☎0392 832262

From Exeter take the A38 to the top of Haldon Hill. Take the exit signposted "Forest Walks". Car Park 1.5 miles from junction. As well as a car park there are toilets,forest trails (including disabled trail) butterfly trail, and the Bird of Prey Viewpoint where there is an honesty box. Educational visits can be arranged in advance. Please allow 6 weeks notice. Kiddens Wood is situated on the Haldon Hills, near Exeter. Tremendous views of the city, and Dartmoor make this forest an ideal place for bird watching. The Haldon Bird of Prey Viewpoint was created to provide birdwatchers with easy access to one of the best viewpoints, thereby reducing pressure on nesting raptors elsewhere in the forest. The most notable visitor to the forest is the honey buzzard, but sparrowhawks, goshawks and kestrels can also be sighted, along with 34 species of butterfly, 13 species of dragonfly - the list is endless. Part of the wood is a forest nature reserve, with SSSI status.

★ Knott's & Parsonage Woods
(Dr Derek A Wolfe) R 12.5ha
O.S.S. 190 - SS 407 112
0409 281454

Travelling SW along the A388 (main Torrington-Holsworthy road) from Woodford Bridge, take the road on the L just before the top of the hill, signposted Thornbury. The third lane to the L leads to Buttermoor Farm, where cars may be parked. For this the farmer may ask a small fee. Turning R from here on foot, the first farm gate on the L gives access to a cart track which after 260m stops at the boundary of two fields. Following this boundary for a further 160m it meets the boundary of Knott's Wood. The entrance gate is 75m along the side of the wood. Picnics are allowed by permission only. No

charges but donations are invited for the Forestry Trust. All year access, but limited to organised parties or groups, with prior permission, and a recognised individual fully responsible for all members of the group. A copy of Permission and Conditions for visit will be provided on request. Guides are available by arrangement. These ancient semi-natural woodlands include a derelict farm complex and a wet area where alder and goat willow were earlier coppiced. The stream which once supplied the farm now has a hydram pump to water cattle on the woodland fields. Changing seasons bring bluebell, blackberry and wild mushrooms. Wildlife includes fox, badger, red and roe deer and several species of bats. Kingfisher, dipper, woodcock and barn owl are all to be seen and there are butterflies, dragonflies, mosses and lichens. The woods border on a 7ha water meadow and the River Torridge with their own flora and fauna.

Lower Broxfords Wood
(Mr P Norman) F 24ha
O.S.S. 192 - SS 844 026
☎0363 866305

Take A3072 from Crediton to Tiverton. After about 1 mile cross over Creedy Bridge and then take first L to Upton Hellions. The entrance to the wood is on the R as the small village is approached. There are no facilities but the wood is open every day except Christmas Day. Tracks and paths will be closed for forestry operations. A working conifer woodland with crops dating from about 1960. Natural seedlings are appearing. Volunteer broadleaves have been nurtured. A very long wood that has many tracks suitable for walking. The woodland provides shelter for a range of wildlife in a predominantly fertile farming area.

★ Lukesland Cleave
(B N Howell) F 17ha
O.S.S. 202 - SX 640 575
☎0752 893390

The entrance is midway between Ivybridge and Harford. From the A38 exit on the W edge of Ivybridge, proceed up the main street and immediately after crossing the river turn L. Proceed up the hill (paper mill on the L) across the staggered cross roads. The Wood is on the left after Ermewood House. There is parking for 6 cars. There are no WC facilities on the site. There is fully open access to the wood on every day of the year except Saturdays. There are self-guided trails. Group visits by appointment only, rates by negotiation, please give one months notice. Donations to the Forestry Trust. For further details please contact Mr Howell on above telephone number. In Dartmoor National Park, the woodlands extend a mile along the river Erme. Mainly replanted 1954-1965 with Douglas fir, larch, western red cedar, beech and American oak. Some fine redwoods ("Wellingtoni-a"), of about 140ft, large Douglas

and noble firs and an incense cedar are left from a planting of 1880. Fallow deer, badgers, buzzards, ravens, woodcock, dippers and many other birds.

Lydford Wood
(Forest Enterprise) F 154ha
O.S.S.191/201 - SX 495 850
☎0409-221692

From Okehampton follow the A30, then A386 to Lydford. Turn as for Lydford and take first turning on R after the railway bridge. Follow the L hand fork 10m after the junction. Follow this road until you see the entrance sign for Lydford Woods on the L. There is fully open access to the wood for walkers, subject only to considerations of safety and conservation when areas may be closed off. Guided walks for groups are possible by prior arrangement for which a charge of between £20-£25 will be made, except for school parties which are free. More specialised forms of recreation are catered for by a permit system. For information leaflets and further details ring the Forest Enterprise District Office. Lydford was an oak coppice woodland until the 1920's. Under Forestry Commission management the woods have been converted, in the main, to conifers. Woodland walks lead through mature stands of larch, Douglas fir and Corsican pine, younger stands and a seed orchard. At several points walkers can enjoy beautiful vistas across the valley and may glimpse birds of prey. Management at Lydford is aimed particularly at increasing conservation value. The Forest Enterprise is working hand in hand with conservation organisations to further delevelop butterfly habitats, open space and water habitats. Two forts on site are scheduled ancient monuments.

Manor Woods

(Torbay Borough Council) F 15ha
O.S.S. 202 - SX 930 632 / 934 640
☎0803 218848

W entrance is off Hesketh Road, Torquay and the N entrance is off Lincombe Drive, Torquay. Two grid references are given for different entrances at either end of wood. Other public entrances also exist. There is a network of paths. Open all year, all day. The wood is on a steep coastal site, and includes a Victorian woodland garden with some impressive exotic tree specimens and an extensive footpath network. In addition there is a stand of naturally regenerated native hardwoods, partly second-ary, with an exceptionally fine pollard oak.

Marridge/Elberry/The Grove Woods

(Torbay Borough Council) F 46.5ha
O.S.S. 202 - SX 895 572 / 905 563
☎0803 218848

N entrance from Broadsands car park, go SE along Elberry Lane to junction with Churston golf course; entrance to wood is on L before golf course. S entrance is off Bascombe Road, Churston, at end of long stone-surfaced lane. Woodland is also on SW coast path. Two grid references are given for different entrances at either end of wood. Other public entrances also exist. Open all year, all day. A long relatively narrow coastal woodland on land sloping steeply down to cliffs, combes and beaches, with a magnificent series of long-abandoned quarries (the "seven quarries"), running into a large ancient semi-natural woodland (The Grove) partly replanted as a larch/sweet chestnut plantation in the 1930s. Good specimens of both larch and native broadleaved trees, some wonderful views and a very good variety of native species, including sorbus species with an extremely restricted distribution. An extensive footpath network crosses the site. Species include ash, sweet chestnut, beech, oak, extensive coastal sycamore, with a wide range of understorey/herb layer species including orchids and spurge laurel.

Milber Wood

(Teignbridge District Council) F 7.3ha
O.S.S. 202 - SX 875 705
☎0626 61101

1 mile E of Newton Abbot. Take road signposted "Milber" from Penn Inn roundabout on A380, then 1st R. Entrance on R after 100m. Open all year round. Occasional guided walks, picnic table, seats. Wood originally part of large estate owned by the Carew

family at nearby Haccombe House. Originally known as "Penninn Plantation" it was purchased as a local amenity in 1924. The higher land, including a public footpath, is dominated by mature oak, beech and Scots pine. The sloping land was planted by local children soon after clearance during the 1st World War. Species include larch, black and Scots pine, birch, spruce, sycamore and cherry. Management is designed to retain the visual quality and for nature conservation.

Occombe Wood

(Torbay Borough Council) F 27.5ha
O.S.S. 202 - SX 874 631 / SX 890 623
☎0803 218848

W entrance is off Preston Down Road, E entrance is off Langdon Road, Paignton. Open all year, all day. Two grid references are given for either end of wood; other public entrances exist. An ancient semi-natural woodland at its W end, merging into an oak/chestnut/pine plantation to the E. W section surrounds steep valleys with streams at foot, and has some very good native specimens and high quality wildlife habitat, a wide range of species. There is an extensive path network with good views of the sea and surrounding landscape from the E section. Tree species include oak (sessile and pedunculate) ash, beech, field maple, sycamore, hazel, with a native calcareous understorey/herb layer including viburnum, spindle, woodspurge, "town hall clock" and dog's mercury.

Parke Estate

(National Trust) F 36.9ha
O.S.S. 191 - SX 808 783

Take the A38 from Exeter to Plymouth Road. Turn off at Drumbridges Junction, 22km from Exeter onto the A382 to Bovey Tracey. Parke House is 1km W of Bovey Tracey. Parking for 20 cars and 3 coaches. There is an independently run shop, tea room, rare breeds centre and information centre. These are open between 1 Apr and 31 Oct. The woodlands are freely accessible all year round as is the picnic and play area. The wood is just outside the Dartmoor National Park. A selection of large old trees in the park. The woodland is predominantly broadleaves of mixed ages, although there are some fine Douglas fir. There is an extensive network of riverside woodland paths. One footpath follows the route of the old Moretonhampstead railway line. There is a variety of woodland birds. The house on the estate is the headquarters of the Dartmoor National Park Authority.

★ Pool Down Wood

(Mike Smith) A 7ha
O.S.S. 191 SX 799 755
☎0626 821465 (daytime)/0626 833099 (evenings)

Take the A382 W from Newton Abbot to Drumbridges roundabout over the A38. Take the second exit towards Liverton, Ilsington. After 300m turn R, pass through

Liverton, and Pool Farm is one third of a mile from the village centre. There is parking for 15 cars and 1 coach. There are WCs and a farm shop at the site. There are self guided trails through the woodland. Guided visits can be arranged but will need 3 weeks notice. Charges for visits are 50p for children and £1 for adults, non guided, and £1 for children and £2 for adults, guided. For further details please ring Mike Smith on the above number in the day or on 0626-833099 in the evenings. Thirty years ago the wood, a mixture of oak, ash and Scots pine, was clearfelled and replanted with Douglas fir, Japanese larch and western hemlock, with naturally regenerating birch, ash Scots pine and oak. The 1976 drought, plus intensive blackthorn competition, killed the larch in the central part, and this was replanted with Douglas fir and Corsican pine, with naturally invading ash also present. The current policy is to develop a high yielding temperate 'rainforest' with mixed species, varied ages, a high rate of carbon capture, yet with great wildlife value; in short, an example of woodland permaculture.

★ **Quicke Estate Woodlands**
(Dr J Quicke) Ac 375ha
O.S.S. 192 - SX 877 977
☎0392 851627

South of the A377 from Exeter. Limited car parking. Please do not obstruct roads or tracks. Visits by appointment only. Please ring above number or write to Dr J

Quicke at Venny Cleave, Newton St Cyres, Exeter, Devon EX5 5BT.

★ **Riding Parks and Lawelldown Woods**
(The Clifford Estate Co. Ltd) A 12.7ha
O.S.S.191/192 - SX 870 780
✉Clifford Estate Office, Ugbrooke Park, Chudleigh, Devon TQ13 0AD

From Chudleigh follow the signs to Ugbrooke Park. Go up Tower Hill and take the sharp R at Biddle-combe Cross. All visits must be arranged in writing to the above address. Riding Parks and Lawelldown Woods are of interest as a site in the national context. They have been classified by Dr Peterkin as an ash/wych elm woodland, of which ten were known to Dr Peterkin in 1983, Riding Parks being the most southerly example. The small leaved lime and the wild service tree regenerate naturally. As a diverse calcareous based woodland and for the quantity of lime trees present, it is unique in Devon and rare W of the Mendips. Much of the woodland is classified as ancient semi natural. The site is centred on an outcrop of Devonian limestone. Species include ash, small leaved lime, wych elm, field maple, pedunculate oak, some beech, sycamore and mountain ash with an underwood of hazel and hawthorn. The ground vegetation possesses a rich flora, characteristic of ancient woodland on base rich soils: dogs mercury, ransomes and wood anemone being abundant.

Roadford Lake Woods

(South West Water Services Ltd) F 62ha
O.S.S. 190 - SX 414 890
☎0822 852435

Follow the signs on A30 between Lewdown and Lifton. The site is to the N of the A30. There are some WC facilities at the site and parking for cars, for which a charge will be made at the main Roadford Dam car park. There is open access to the wood on permissive paths. Guided visits can be arranged. For further details contact John Griffiths, Head Forester at Burrator Lodge, Sheepstor, Yelverton, Devon on the above telephone number. This site is made up of three separate woods by the new Roadford Reservoir Slew Wood and East Banbury Wood and form a backdrop to the new dam. The woods are managed primarily for amenity and wildlife, the plan being ultimately to convert the whole wood to broadleaved trees.

Salcombe Hill

(National Trust) F 37ha
O.S.S. 192 - SY 140 882

1 mile E of Sidmouth. Free car park adjoining Norman Lockyer Observatory. No other facilities. Public houses, hotels and shops at Sidmouth one mile. AONB woodland on S side of road. Extensive network of paths - some level some steep - linked to coastal path with spectacular views from cliff tops over the whole of Lyme Bay. Some mixed broadleaves but larger area of mixed conifers planted in 1960s. Thinned out on a 4 year rotation and to be changed to broadleaves by about 55 years old. Some small areas blown down in 1990 storm already cleared and replanted with oak, ash, beech and sweet chestnut.

Scadson/Ten Acre Brake

(Torbay Borough Council) F 35ha
O.S.S 202 - SX 884 634/SX 895 627
☎0803 218848

NW entrance off Cockington Lane, Paignton, SE entrance off Old Paignton Rd. Grid references are given for entrances at either end of wood, other public entrances also exist.There is a footpath network which is open all year, all day. A long, linear woodland running down a steep sided valley with a stream in the bottom; part ancient semi-natural woodland, part plantation. Has some good specimen hardwood trees, extensive coppice with standards and a good range of native species. N compartments of the wood were severely storm damaged in 1990, and have been cleared and replanted; Aim is to improve the timber quality on site by an ongoing management programme; provide coppice underwood for the local thatching market, and maintain a valuable wildlife habitat. Trees include stands of oaks, ash, beech, a larch plantation, and sycamore, hazel with a herb layer including ivy and dog's mercury, with a good bryophyte/fern component.

Shaptor and Furzeleigh Wood

(Woodland Trust) F 78ha

O.S.S. 191 - SX 818 794

0476 74297

From Bovey Tracey take the A382 towards Moretonhampstead, then almost immediately turn R onto the steep minor road by the hospital. There is limited parking and no facilities. It is advisable to keep to the paths as unknown mine shafts may still be present. Fully open access. National Tree week events may take place in this wood in late Nov to early Dec. Please phone the Woodland Trust for details in the autumn. Shaptor and Furzeleigh Woods form an important woodland in the valley between Bovey Tracey and Moretonhampstead, with Shaptor Wood having had continuous cover for at least 300 years. Oak, ash and birch are the predominant tree species, with honeysuckle and spindle common in the understorey. These woods are particularly rich in plant life with a total of 92 woodland species recorded including wood anemone and epiphytic ferns. The wet areas support distinctive wetland plants. Spotted flycatchers, wood warblers, redstarts and foxes are among the wealth of animal life to be seen in the wood.

★ Shute Hill

(W A Nicholls & Sons, Managed by Fountain Forestry) R 47.6 ha

O.S.S 192 - SY 257 973

☎0626 834491

From Shute village take minor road leading up past church and school. The entrance and car park are on the left after 1/3 mile. Parking for 4 cars. Rights of way and permitted paths. Guided walks may be arranged. This woodland was damaged in the storms of 1989/90 and was largely replanted, with attention to environmental considerations as well as timber production. The exposed southern end of Shute Hill is planted with Corsican pine and a hardwood belt over the top of the hill will finally dominate the skyline. The other new planting is primarily Sitka spruce and Douglas fir with older mixed conifers which survived the storms.There is a stone Armada beacon on the property, and the surrounding area is being landscaped with funding assistance from Devon County Council and help from local community groups.

★ Stoke Woods (1)

(Dr S A Goulden) A 32ha

O.S.S. 192 - SX 930 961

☎0364 3316

From Exeter go N on A396. After 1.5 miles turn sharp R up Stoke Hill. After 500 yards the entrance is found on the L (just before a public car park on the R). No facilities on site. All visits by appointment only. For further details please contact Alastair Sandels, Fountain Forestry Ltd, Poundsgate, Newton Abbot, Devon, TW13 7PA or telephone the above number. Donations to the Forestry Trust. Stoke Woods is an SSSI and is noted as a fine example of western sessile oak woodland with a diversity of habitats and tree species. The woods are managed for the production of quality hardwood timber. Areas of mixed conifers provide further variety. Points of interest also include wetland flora, lichens, many species of bird. and management to promote the conservation value of the woodlands.

Stoke Woods (2)
(Managed by Forest Enterprise) F 45ha
O.S.S. 192 - SX 919 959
☎0392 832262

From Exeter take A396 Tiverton Road. Woods are situated on S side of road 1 mile Tiverton side of junction with A377. There are 3 car parks, picnic area and forest trail.

★ Tavistock Woodlands
(The Right Honourable The 7th Earl of Bradford) R 475 ha
O.S.S. 201 - SX 426 736
☎0822 832131

Find the Devon Great Consols Chimney Stack at grid reference SX 426736 (about 4 miles W of Tavistock). There is parking for 15 cars and 3 coaches. Visits will be possible on any day between 1700 hours to dusk (ie outside working hours) with prior permission being gained from Mr Timmis on the above telephone number. Group visits can also be arranged through the above contact, please give at least 8 weeks notice. Charges for guided visits will be £2 for adults, £1 for children; group charges by negotiation. Donations to the Forestry Trust. A unique block of woodland in the S Tamar and Tavy valleys with a forest cover that dates back to pre Domesday and which has been moulded by practical human requirements right up to the avant garde Bradford Plan continuous cover system of today. Extraordinary growth rates are displayed by both exotic conifers and broadleaves, such as Douglas fir and Nothofagus. There are some fine stands of beech and areas of ancient oak coppice. A truly diverse and functioning forest area supporting red and roe deer as well as most other British mammals There is a wide range of other fauna and flora.

Teign Valley Woods
(National Trust) F 129ha
O.S.S. 191 - SX 809 884

From Exeter take the B3212 Moretonhampstead Road W for 12km. Look for the Steps Bridge Hotel. There is parking for 30 cars and 3 coaches. During the summer months there is a private hotel, bar and tearoom. There is also a short path for the use of disabled visitors but most of the woodland is on hilly terrain. Open access and self guided trails. A spectacular hanging oakwood, consisting of mainly old oak coppice. The woodland is an SSSI in the Dartmoor National Park. The site is of high landscape value and famed for its profusion of daffodils. Birds found on the site include buzzards, pied flychatchers, marsh tits, three species of woodpeckers and dippers on the stream.

Torquay Coastal Woodlands

(Torbay Borough Council) F 108ha
O.S.S. 202 - SX 941 639 / SX 924 673
☎0803 218848

S entrance is off Ilsham Marine Drive, Torquay. N entrance is off Watcombe Beach Road. The SW Coastal footpath runs through the site end to end. Free access all year, all day. Footpath network. Grid references are given for different entrances at either end of wood, other public entrances also exist. An extensive stretch of coastal woodland, with outliers N and S of the listed section, comprising a mixture of ancient semi-natural, secondary semi-natural and a small amount of plantation woodland, interspersed with cliffs, beaches, narrow combes, and some open land. The area has no outstanding stands of timber, but is very rich in native species and in wildlife, especially birds. Tree species include ash, sycamore, elm, field maple, thorn, with occasional small-leaved lime, understorey/herb layer includes hazel, spindle, woodspurge, spurge laurel, butcher's broom, cowslips, and purple gromwell. There is a good population of raptors and other birds and fine displays of bluebells in spring.

★ Townleigh Wood

(R L Nicholson) A 14ha
O.S.S. 190 - SX 428 878
☎0566 83277

From Stowford Cross on A30 between Okehampton and Launceston take the road marked "Kennels". Visits by appointment. Townleigh Wood is part of a modern dairy farm where a lot of new planting has been done over the last 17 years to try and make the farm look attractive. New woods round the farm buildings join up with old woodland that goes down to the River Thrushel. There are also commercial woods of larch, Sitka, and Douglas fir in various states of management.

Watersmeet Wood

(National Trust) F 233ha
O.S.S. 180 - SS 744 486

The wood occupies both sides of the A29 SE of Lynmouth. Full access to the woodland paths throughout the year. Parking for 40 cars and 2 coaches at the car park above Watersmeet House, where between 1 Apr and 31 Oct the shop, tea room and picnic area are open. The paths by the river are not recommended for the disabled. The woodland clothes the steep valleys by E and W Lyn rivers. The wood is old coppice, once used by the tanning and charcoal industries. The extensive path system, which also links to open moorland, radiates from Watersmeet House. A point of interest is the Iron Age linear earthworks known as

Countisbury Camp. The wood is of great landscape and scenic value. Further information at Watersmeet House.

★ West Bowerland
(Mr A J Burgess, managed by Fountain Forestry) A 58.2 ha
O.S.S. 191 - SX 533 940
☎0364 3316

Take A3079 from Okehampton to Holsworthy. West Bowerland is 4 miles from Okehampton on left just after disused railway. Parking for 3 cars. This is an area of new woodland created in the early 1970s by planting some wet low grade agricultural land. A range of coniferous species were used with Sitka spruce being the dominant one. Other species include Japanese larch, Norway spruce and Corsican pine. Old hedgerows were retained to give diversity and two small ponds have been excavated and support rare species of dragonfly. The wood is thought to be the haunt of a black panther!

★ Whitehills Plantation
(Lady Margaret Fortescue) A 44ha
☎0598 760336

Directions on application. There are no facilities at the wood. Visits by appointment only. For further details and appointments please write to H R Thomas, resident land agent, Estate Office, Castle Hill Filleigh, Barnstaple, Devon EX32 0R4 or ring the above number.

School parties, one visit per term. Two weeks notice is required for group visits. Donations to the Forestry Trust.

Whitleigh Wood
(Woodland Trust) F 20ha
O.S.S.201 - SX 482 599
☎0476 74297

From the A38 follows signs for the A386 to Tavistock. From the A386 turn W towards the B3373 to Tamerton Foliot. After proceeding straight across at the next roundabout, turn R onto the Tamerton Foliot road. Whitleigh Wood is on the L a short way up the road, but it is better to continue as far as the island in the road centre and then turn L into Borrowdale Close. There is limited parking and no other facilities. Full open access to the wood. National Tree Week events may take place in this wood in late Nov to early Dec, please phone Woodland Trust for details. The site on which Whitleigh Wood stands has been tree covered for at least 150 years and has an important amenity value in an otherwise built up area. Oak, birch, field maple and sweet chestnut are the main tree species present along with hazel, blackthorn and young ash saplings making up the understorey. The wood suports a rich plant and animal community including grey wagtail and redpoll, heath speedwell, creeping jenny and harts tongue fern. Numerous fungi species including fly agaric and shaggy inkcap can be found in this wood.

Wray Cleave
(Dartmoor National Park) R 31ha
O.S.S. 191- SX 774 837

Half way between Moretonhampstead and Bovey Tracey on the
A382. Parking for 3 cars and 1
coach, but no other facilities.
Public rights of way link up with
permitted path to form circular
walk. Guided walk on 3 May 1994
at 1400 hours (2 1/2 hrs). Cost of
guided walks is £2 for adults and
50p for children. Donations to the
Forestry Trust. Wray Cleave is an
ancient and semi-natural wood.
There are micaceous haematite
mine workings in the wood which
were abandoned in 1926. Deer
frequent the site. Landscape,
wildlife and archaeological aspects
feature prominently in the
management plans. The principal
species being retained is oak.

DORSET

see map on p16

★ Belstone, Warren and Chaffins Copse

(WilliamCrutchley) A 7ha
O.S.S 194 - SY 530 943
⊡Mappercombe Manor, Powerstock, Bridport, Dorset DT6 3SS

Get to Powerstock 3 miles NE of Bridport. From Powerstock Church take S road to 'T' junction turn L towards Nettlecombe, passing Marquis of Lorne Inn. Leaving Nettlecombe on L. 1/4 mile to cross roads, turn L after 1/2 mile leave Marsh Farm on L. Further 1/2 mile up No Through Road to rendezvous. Park where conditions allow by road. Open on Thursdays, 7th and 21st April and 5 May 1994,from 1430 to 1730 hours. Groups of young people are especially welcome. Appointments by letter only. Donations to Farms for City Children and Forestry Trust. Three adjacent broadleaved woodlands totalling 7 hectares demonstrating three methods of attempting to establish viable crops. The plantings vary in age from 50 year sweet chestnut to current natural regeneration of ash and a planting saved late by Belgian thinning. Under western edge of Eggardon Hill, fine scenery, plenty of flora and fauna.

Duncliffe Wood

(Woodland Trust) F 86.19ha
O.S.S. 183 - ST 825 225
☎0476 74297

Take the A30 W from Shaftesbury towards E Stour. After about 3 miles turn L onto a minor road towards Stour Row. Duncliffe Wood is to the L of this road. 3/4 of a mile after turning on to the minor road a track leads off to the L into Duncliffe Wood. Park along this track. The wood is open at all times of the year but during National Tree Week events may take place during late Nov-Dec. Please phone the Woodland Trust for details in the autumn. Duncliffe Wood is one of the largest areas of woodland in N Dorset. It is set like a saddle on top of two hills and offers superb views of the surrounding area and contains a pollarded tree, which is perhaps the oldest living thing in Dorset. Oak and ash dominate the deciduous areas, but intermingled with them are wild cherry, rowan and hazel coppice. Butterflies, including white admiral, purple hairstreak and silver washed fritillaries, still breed in profusion in the wide rides of the wood, feeding on the sun-loving plants that grow here.

Garston Wood

(RSPB) R 34ha
O.S.S 184 - SU 004 194
☎0929 550969

The reserve is approached from the main Salisbury - Blandford Road (A354) 1 mile N of Sixpenny Handley on the road to Broad Chalke. Car parking for 14 cars. Leaflet available. No charges but donations welcome. Access at all times along woodland paths. Open days including free guided walks will be held on 8 May and 17 July 1994. Visitors are asked to stay on woodland paths and dogs must be kept under close control. Garston Wood is being managed traditionally by the RSPB as coppice with standards. Some 25 species of trees and shrub occur with standards mainly of oak and ash, and a hazel coppice layer. Fine examples of field maple, crab apple and whitebeam can also be seen. Cut areas are protected from deer by traditionally constructed brash and wattle fences. In spring the wood is alive with the song of breeding birds such as turtle dove and nightingale. Butterflies are represented by over 30 species including white admiral, purple hairstreak, silver washed and pearl bordered fritillary.

★ Hooke Park

(Parnham Trust) R 135ha
O.S.S. 194 - ST 526 002
☎0308 863130

From Beaminster take B3163 signed Dorchester, Maiden Newton, Evershot. After 2 miles turn R posted Hooke. After 1.1/2 miles turn R into Hooke Park through main entrance bounded by large wooden rings. There is parking for 30 cars and 3 coaches. The woodland is open 7 days a week throughout the year. There are rights of way and self guided trails - please keep to the marked trails. There is no charge to walk the woodland but there is a small charge for car parking. Guided,

specialist and educational tours of the woodland and of Hooke Park College's award winning buildings can be arranged by appointment during the period 1 Apr to 31 Oct 1994. Contact Marion Walbank on above telephone number for details and charges. Please book at least one month in advance. Hooke Park is situated on an ancient site. There is a network of old boundary banks with neglected pollards to be found throughout the Park. Replanted in the 1950s by the Forestry Commission after clearance of the then principal species of oak, ash and alder. Even age with a distribution of species, predominantly beech and Norway spruce and oak/Norway spruce mixtures. Resident population of roe and fallow deer.

Melcombe Park

(M C Woodhouse) A 60ha
O.S.S. 194 - ST 750 040
✉Higher Melcombe, Dorchester, Dorset DT2 7PB

From village of Melcombe Bingham, follow signpost to Melcombe Park Farm. Village 3 miles W of Milton Abbas in central Dorset. No facilities. Car parking limited to 6 cars or 1 coach. Public House, Fox Inn, Ansty, 1 mile. Written appointment only - for guided tour only, (May to August) please contact Lt Col J M Woodhouse, Estate Manager at above address. Charges £1 per head for adults (to Charity) children free. Replanted ancient woodland. Softwood planting 1946

- 60 being replaced now by hardwoods. Mainly oak and ash with varied softwoods remaining. Clay subsoil. Wildlife includes deer, and foxes.

★ Moors Valley Forest
(Managed by Forest Enterprise in conjunction with E Dorset District Council)
R 500ha
O.S.S. 195 - SU 110 045
☎0929 552074

From A31, Ringwood to West Moors Road, take the minor road to Horton at the A31/A338 roundabout. The Forest and Country Park are signposted on the R. Car park, toilets, forest walks, play trail, ranger service, all ability trails. Horse riding permits available. Car park £1. A productive woodland adjacent to Moors Valley Country Park which has a large visitor centre with exhibition, shop and refreshments.. Teeming with wildlife the forest is coming alive with people as well. A play trail with snakes and ladders, tree top trail and the Loggosaurus to name a few have been built from natural materials to entertain the children. All ability access is available to the Look Out, an observation platform for wildlife viewing, and may be an occasional outdoor concert. The forest is host to nightjars, goldcrests, sand lizards and adders amongst others.

Piddleswood
(G A Pitt-Rivers) F 71.2ha
O.S.S. 194 - ST 801 135

A357 Blandford - Sherborne road 2 miles E of Sturminster Newton. Car park 1/4mile N of main road signed Fiddleford Mill where there is car parking. There are no charges and access is unrestricted, except for camping which is not allowed. An SSSI, mainly oak with coppice, also larch and Douglas fir plantations. 16 hectares are managed by Dorset Trust for Nature Conservation as a nature reserve.

Ruins Plantation
(Ruins Plantation Trust) R 22ha
O.S.S. 194 - ST 790 023
✉Kitt Hill House, Sherborne, Dorset, DT9 3PL

From Milborne St Andrew on the A354 from Blandford to Dorchester take the road N to Milton Abbas. At the bottom of the village (just over 3 miles) take the road to Hilton past the Milton Abbey school for one mile and turn down the track through the beech avenue planted for Lady Caroline Sackville West.. There are no facilities and no charges. Open Saturdays and Sundays. Parking is sometimes allowed in the beech avenue but the land does not belong to the woodland. Educational visits should be arranged in writing to Mr M Gill at the above address. The wood was part of the Milton Abbey Estate which was once a favourite retreat for royalty. The beech woods on the steep N slope were felled during the war for making gliders and aeroplanes. The area was replanted mostly with beech between 1950 and 1965 but there

has been good regeneration of ash.
Grey squirrel damage has greatly
reduced the amount of beech.
Sycamore, oak,chestnut, horse
chestnut, Douglas fir, Thuja, Tsuga,
larch and Lawson cypress are also
present.

★ Slepe Wood
(W Bond) A 5ha
O.S.S. 195 - SY 961 871
☎0929 463301

The wood is off the unclassified
road from Stoborough, nr
Wareham to Arne. As it is part of a
nature reserve exact details will
only be given on application.
Limited roadside parking is
available. There are no charges.
This small but varied wood offers
examples of commercial timber
production, natural woodland and
conservation practice within the
RSPB reserve at Arne. The
sensitive nature of the wood makes
it especially suitable for education,
but inappropriate for informal
recreation.

★ Wareham Forest
(Managed by Forest Enterprise) F 2000ha
O.S.S. 194/195 - SY 890 920
☎0929 552074

Car parks are located along the
minor road between Wareham and
Bere Regis. Forest walks.
Sika deer trail. Forest classroom.
Education staff.

DURHAM

see map on p13

Carrickshill Wood

(Durham County Council) F 10.35ha
O.S.S. 88 - NZ 204 546
☎091 383 408

The wood is situated 1 mile to the N of Stanley at the western end of the Beamish Estate. It can be approached via minor roads leading from the A693 or A6076. Park at Beamish Burn picnic area and cross the bridge into the wood. There are no charges and the wood is open at all times. An ancient woodland site which is thought to have been continuously wooded since medieval times. The public footpath formed part of a "Ladies Drive" used for horse back riding in the last century. Comprising mixed deciduous woodland there is active regeneration and a well developed shrub and herb layer. A stand of mature birch, with abundant honeysuckle, is a particularly attractive feature at the western end of the wood. Growing in wet hollows are a range of herbs of interest including bugle, yellow pimpernel, valerian and water avens.

Cocken Wood Picnic Site

(Durham County Council) F 10.2ha
O.S.S. 88 - NZ 297 473
☎091 383 4028

The picnic site is 4 miles to the N of Durham City on the right bank of the River Wear. If travelling from Durham take the A690 N and turn L to Leamside village. There is a lay-by on the minor road on the N side of the river. Light refreshments are available at the (now ruined) Finchale Priory on the opposite side of the river. There is free and full access. The river cliffs are steep and dangerous in places and visitors should keep to approved paths. An area of ancient woodland and a designated County Wildlife Site comprising mixed deciduous woodland including oak, beech, ash, elm, sycamore and birch with an understorey of hawthorn, hazel, yew and holly. The ground flora is characteristic of acid woodland in the region with abundant giant woodrush. Species of interest include moschatel, toothwort and, where mineral rich flushes occur, opposite-leaved golden saxifrage. Roe deer and red squirrel are recorded from the wood. A footbridge across the river connects the site with Finchale Priory which was built in the 11th century and ruined at the time of the dissolution of the monasteries.

Durham Riverbanks

(The Dean & Chapter of Durham Cathedral, Durham University & Durham City Council)
F 20ha
O.S. S. 88 - NZ 277 423
☎091 384 1690

Several signed access points from the city direct you to these attractive wooded banks which clothe the riverside around the Cathedral and Castle in Durham. A leaflet and map are available from the SPCK Cathedral Bookshop and the local Tourist Information Centre. Facilities nearby in the City. Open all year round during daylight hours. A pleasant amble amongst mainly native broadleaved woodland planted some 200 years ago. Present management is endeavouring to achieve continuous cover forestry by a phased programme of felling and replanting. Sculpture of "The Upper Room" of elm trunks and Sir Walter Scott's musings of the view from Prebends' Bridge are worth seeing.

★ Hamsterley Forest
(Forest Enterprise) F 2500ha
O.S.S. 92 - NZ 092 313
☎0751-472771

Turn W off A68 between Toft Hill and Witton le Wear and follow signposts to Hamsterley. Follow brown signs from Hamsterley village to Hamsterley Forest. There is a small visitor centre selling leaflets, maps, books, and souvenirs. There are WCs with baby changing facilities and provision for the wheelchair user. There are also forest drives, picnic places, walks and cycle trails. Car parking charge is £1.50. Coaches, by appointment only, £15.00. Guided tours, also by appointment, are £10.00 per hour. The forest is open all year from 0730 to 2030 hours. Special provisions are made for school parties and educational groups. The largest forest block in County Durham, with attractive riverside car parks and picnic places. The forest drive enables the visitor to drive into the heart of the forest whilst waymarked walks, cycle and horse trails enable him to explore the woodlands which vary from old mature trees in the valley to newly replanted upland forest areas in the hinterland.

Hardwick Hall Fen Carr
(Durham County Council) F 2ha
O.S.S. 93 - NZ 346 292
☎091 383 4028

Part of Hardwick Hall Country Park, situated to the W of the A177, under 1 mile to the W of Sedgefield. From the car park cross the Serpentine Lake and follow the signs for the Nature Trail. Facilities include a boardwalk, interpretative signs and a resource pack for teachers available from Land and Property Dept, Durham County Council, County Hall, Durham DH1 5UH, price £2.75. Free and full access is available at all times. An area of willow and birch carr woodland with some ash with a ground flora including tussock sedge, the uncommon blunt flowered rush, and in the most marshy sections, plants such as bogbean, bottle sedge and ragged robin. A raised boardwalk, built by conservation volunteers in 1981, enables visitors to see the woodland and its wildlife without getting their feet wet and provides an excellent opportunity to view plant succession from marsh to mature woodland. A bird hide overlooks the carr from which many of the birds of interest, including warblers, tits, spotted flycatchers and woodcock, may be seen.

Pontburn Wood
(Woodland Trust) F 24.28ha
O.S.S. 81/88 - NZ 147 562
☎0476 74297

These woods are situated at
Hamsterley Mill, 7 miles SW of
Newcastle and 4 miles NE of
Consett, County Durham. Park at
Pontburn bridge on the B6310, or
on the A694 at the end of Mill
Farm road. There are no facilities.
No charge is made to walk in the
woods and it is open at all times of
the year. National Tree Week
events may take place during late
Nov-Dec. Please phone the
Woodland Trust for details in the
autumn. Pontburn Wood has an
interesting variety of wildlife. Red
squirrels are common in the wood,
but are shy and quite difficult to
spot. Look out for pine and spruce
cones nibbled to the stalk littering
the woodland floor. Sparrowhawk,
goldcrest and kestrel can also be
seen, along with bats in the
summer. Oak, silver birch, and
some fine old rowan are just some
of the trees found there. In
springtime the woodland has a
lovely cover of wild flowers,
including celandine, bluebell, wood
sorrel and wood sanicle.

ESSEX

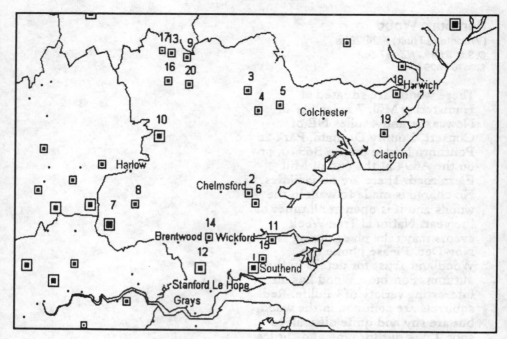

1. Belfairs
2. Blakes Wood
3. Broads Walk
4. Brookes Reserve
5. Chalkney Wood
6. Danbury Common
7. Epping Forest
8. Gernon Bushes
9. Great & Little Bendysh Wood
10. Hatfield Forest

11. *Hockley Woods
12. Langdon Reserve
13. Littlehales Wood
14. *Norsey Wood
15. Pound Wood
16. Rowney Wood
17. Shadwell Wood
18. *Stour Wood
19. Weeleyhall Wood
20. West Wood

Belfairs
(Southend-on-Sea Borough Council) F
121ha
O.S.S. 178 - TQ 834 876
☎0702 215618

Take the A127 towards Southend. On entering the signposted borough boundary, at the first set of traffic lights, turn R into The Fairway. Proceed to the next set of traffic lights and turn R into Eastwood Road. Entrance to park and car parks is approx. 100 yards on RH side. There are toilets and a cafe. Woodland open at all times, other facilities subject to Parks opening and closing times. The site comprises 85 ha of ancient woodland and parkland on which an 18 hole golf course has been laid out. Bowls, horse riding and field sports are all catered for and the woodland is used extensively for recreation. A further 36 ha (a designated SSSI) is actively managed as traditional coppice, with standards woodland. Over 400 species of flowering plants, 130 bird species and 500 fungi have been recorded. Wide rides provide easy access and support healthy butterfly populations.

Blakes Wood
(National Trust) F 43ha
O.S.S.167 - TL 775 065
☎0245.222669

SSSI and ASNW. Free access and parking. For further information telephone above number. Ancient semi-natural woodland.

Broads Walk
(Forest Enterprise) F 62ha
O.S.S. 167 - TL 784 316
☎0394 450164

The Brookes Reserve, Tumblers Green
(Essex Wildlife Trust) F 23.9ha
O.S.S. 168 - TL 813 267
☎0206 729678

Off the A120 take the road to Stisted and from there to Greenstead Green. The reserve is on the L after about 1 1/2 miles. Limited parking on this corner, but a small car park is planned. Free access. A varied reserve, comprising over 40 acres of SSSI ancient woodland and 18 acres of ex arable fields. The largely hazel woodland also has small leaved lime and hornbeam, numerous ponds and a network of historic green lanes one of which is a bridleway. Primrose and various orchids are found. The huge population of fallow deer will necessitate fencing or other protection once coppicing resumes. The outer fields are to be developed as woodland and the inner as a sheltered meadow.

Chalkney Wood
(Forest Enterprise) F 49ha
O.S.S. 168 - TL872 280
☎0394 450164

From A604 in Earls Colne turn southeast onto Tey Road (beside Coachman Inn) after 1/2 mile a sign to Chalkney Trail is on the left. Car park, way marked trail with interpretation. Open all year but some areas may occasionally be closed during forestry operations. For details of events and guided walks contact the above number. This ancient woodland site, SSSI and Forest Nature Reserve contains predominantly mixed broadleaved woodland and coniferous high forest planted by the Forestry Commission in the 1950s and 1960s In recent years the policy has been to revert to site native species through heavy thinning, ride widening and the reintroduction of coppice coupes. The wood is notable for a natural graduation from small leaved lime to hornbeam; wet flushes rich in bryophytes; diverse ancient woodland flora (best seen in spring); an intact boundary bank and a probably pre-Roman hollow-way. The wood features significantly in several publications by Oliver Rackham who opened the nature trail there in 1992.

Danbury Common
(National Trust) F 73ha
O.S.S. 168 - TL 781 045
☎0245 222669

SSSI and ASNW. Free access. 50p car parking. For further information telephone the above number. Ancient semi-natural woodland.

Epping Forest
(Corporation of London) F 2400ha
O.S.S. 167 - TQ 412 983
☎081 508 0028

Loughton (London Underground Central Line) 2 miles. Chingford (British Rail). WCs, information centre at High Beach. Disabled paths at High Beach and Connaught Water. Many parking areas. There is fully open access to the forest via rights of way. Guided visits can be arranged by contacting the Information Centre on the above number. Please book 4 weeks in advance. Charges are by negotiation. Bordered by undulating Essex farmland, Epping Forest enables visitors to contrast old pollarded trees with those growing in a small mixed plantation. Epping Forest contains the largest tract of ancient woodland in the Home Counties and its venerable pollards and maiden trees of beech, oak and hornbeam provide habitats for typical woodland birds as well as unique collections of fungi and beetles. Black fallow deer shelter in the holly undergrowth. Relict heathlands, grassy plains and ponds enhance this extensive area of public open space owned and managed by the Corporation of London.

Gernon Bushes
(Essex Wildlife Trust) F 32ha
O.S.S.167 - TL 478 030
☎081 508 1593

Turn off the B181 NE of Epping towards Coopersale. Turn L on to Garnon Mead 200m after passing under the railway bridge. There are no facilities. A leaflet is available from Epping District Council. A historic hornbeam pollard woodland with rich bogs and streams, whose notable plants include marsh fern, lady fern, bog bean, and kingcup. Re-pollarding is rejuvenating areas allowing natural regeneration. Gravel extraction in the N created Sphagnum bogs. Hawfinch and sparrowhawk are among the many species of birds recorded for the reserve. The Essex Way crosses the site.

Great and Little Bendysh Wood
(Forest Enterprise) F 92ha
O.S.S. 154 - TL 618 398
☎0394 450164

Hatfield Forest
(National Trust) F 240ha
O.S.S. 167 - TL 547 202
☎0279 870678

Off the M11 motorway take junction 8 the A120 Stansted exit. Follow A120 to Takeley village where Hatfield Forest is signposted - car park is 1 mile S of the village. There is a seasonal charge for the car park of £2.40 per car, between Easter and end of October when the cafe is also open. The wood, toilets and waymarked nature trail is open year round. There are two routes suitable for wheelchairs and an 18th century Shell House with information boards. Leaflets are available on sale for self guided routes around the property. Hatfield is the last surviving piece of medieval Royal Forest complete with its associated "plains" and coppices. The Forest is of national and international importance in terms of its biological interest and

historical ecology. It is listed as a Grade 2 Nature Conservation Review site, an SSSI and an ancient semi-natural woodland. The forest is particularly known for its pollards, dead wood invertebrates and coppiced areas.

★ Hockley Woods
(Rochford District Council) F 96ha
O.S.S. 178 - TQ 833 924
☎0752 546366

Leave A127 to Southend at Rayleigh Weir, follow signs to Hockley. Turn R at Bull public house, Main Road, Hockley. Facilities include WCs, Awareness Centre, nature trails, leaflets, rustic products, sculptures, and educational section. Access is free. Small areas are dead hedged to prevent access onto heath fritillary breeding areas. Hockley Woods has an ancient woodland flora and fauna, i.e. wild service trees, bluebells etc with cow wheat, heath fritillary butterflies, nightingales. There are self guided trails, permissive horse route, guided walks and talks each week. Annual Open Days. Volunteer work parties.

The Langdon Reserve
(Essex Wildlife Trust) F 186.3ha
O.S.S. 177 - TQ 659 874
☎0268 419095

Take the B1007 off the A127 nr Basildon, entrance is about 1/2mile on L after passing under railway bridge. Large car park. Visitor centre is planned. There is full access to the reserve. The Plotland Museum opens 1 Apr to end Sept, Sundays 2-5pm, Bank Holidays 10am-5pm. A huge reserve, divided into 4 main areas with their own character. Woods, plantations and scrub along with meadows and ponds form a rich mosaic. Woods are both ancient and secondary and are managed by coppicing and thinning. Miles of paths and bridleways cross the reserve, which was plotland from the turn of the century, reaching its heyday in the 1940s. No one has lived there since the 1970s and the reserve is an invaluable wildlife area on the urban fringe.

Littlehales Wood

(Forest Enterprise) F 16ha
O.S.S. 154 - TL 575 408
☎0394 450164

★ Norsey Wood

(Basildon District Council) F 75ha
O.S.S. 167 - TQ 680 951
☎0277 624553

The wood is located to the NE of Billericay via Norsey Road from the High Street. There is a car park which is always open, Information Centre (closed on Sundays), toilets, disabled facilities and guided walks. Norsey Wood is an ancient coppice woodland with the main species being sweet chestnut, hazel, oak, alder and larch. Coppicing is still being carried out with a patchwork of clearings being

created. The site is also a scheduled Ancient Monument containing Bronze Age tumulus, Roman industrial area and an extensive earthbank known as "Deerbank".

Pound Wood

(Essex Wildlife Trust) F 22.3ha
O.S.S. 178 - TQ 818 886
☎0206 729678

Take Daws Heath Road from the A129, S of Rayleigh Weir. Parking is limited on adjacent streets off Bramble Road. There are no facilities. A large wood with complex geology reflected in the mosaic of hornbeam and sweet chestnut woodland. Wild service tree is locally abundant and bluebells carpet large areas. Wood ants are noticeable. Several streams cross the wood and young coppice under a power cable shows how vibrant the wood can become with recoppicing. There are fine early medieval woodbanks , a dam, several ponds and dells.

Rowney Wood

(Forest Enterprise) F 84ha
O.S.S. 154 - TL 568 339
☎0394 450164

Shadwell Wood

(Essex Wildlife Trust) F 7.1ha
O.S.S. 154 - TL 573 412
☎0206 729678

The reserve is on the W of the road

from Saffron Walden to Ashdon, about 1 mile before Ashdon. Entrance is the track leading beside "Barleycroft". Limited parking at the side of the track on the opposite side of the road. There are no facilities. A small but rich ancient ash, maple, hazel wood, with a secondary oak woodland on old meadow, and rich ride flora. Now back in a coppice rotation, deer fencing is needed to exclude fallow deer. Oxlips are a feature, with orchids and bluebells. Cowslip, primrose and adders tongue fern are present in a glade in the old meadow. Dormice are present and many woodland butterflies.

★ Stour Wood
(Woodland Trust; leased to RSPB) F 54ha
O.S.S. 169 - TM 191 310
☎0255 886043

Approx. 5 miles W of Harwich on B1352 (Harwich to Manningtree Road), close to Wrabness village. Bold entrance sign. Car park, observation hides overlooking adjacent estuary, marked trails, entire reserve area totals 317ha. Access is free but a donation to RSPB would be appreciated. Regular guided walks - reserve leaflet available from warden 35p (telephone as above). Warden available for lectures. 1 mile wheelchair trail available in drier seasons of the year. Stour Wood is an extensive area of sweet chestnut with a long history of coppice management. In parts of the reserve woodland tumbles down to

the sea at Copperas Bay (Stour Estuary). The woodland supports a range of breeding birds including the nightingale, 25 species of butterfly, including the white admiral - its only site in Essex. Plants include the wild service tree, a wonderful showing of wood anemones and paths arched with pendulous sedge. The nearby estuarine sections of the reserve support large numbers of waterfowl between Aug and Apr. The woodland is very much a 'working' wood supplying timber needs for other RSPB reserves in the region.

Weeleyhall Wood
(Essex Wildlife Trust) F 31.6ha
O.S.S. 168 - TM 156 212
☎0206 729678

The reserve lies off a private road leading from the A133 SE of Weeley. Limited parking by the church. There are no facilities. A large non-intervention area has been left from the 1987 storm. It contains dangerous trees and must not be entered. One of the largest woods in Tendring, largely oak high forest with areas of sweet chestnut and hazel coppice, and a Scots and Corsican pine plantation. Also a stream with alder coppice and rich ground flora including moschatel. Bluebells carpet much of the wood which is visually at its best in May. Nightingales and dormice are recorded, other birds and woodland butterflies are well represented. Natural regeneration is rapidly healing the scars of the 1987 storm clearance. Coppicing and thinning are also carried out.

West Wood

(Essex Wildlife Trust) F 23.5ha
O.S.S. 167 - TL 624 332
☎0206 729678

The reserve is midway between
Thaxted and Great Sampsford off
the B1051. A track (bridleway)
leads from the road, 1 mile NE of
Thaxted. There is limited parking
but no other facilities, and no
charges. A wet ash, maple, hazel
wood on chalky boulder clay with
abundant oxlips and orchids.
Formerly extensively planted with
Norway spruce; remaining blocks
are being thinned. Recoppicing in
progress to rejuvenate hazel
coppice, involving brushwood deer
fencing to exclude fallow deer.
Dormice are present, and birds
include goldcrest, redpoll and
several species of warbler.

GLOUCESTERSHIRE

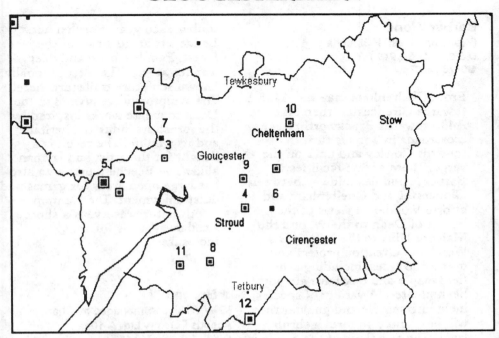

1. Barber Wood
2. *Beechenhurst
3. *Broomhill
4. Frith
5. High Meadow Woodlands
6. *Miserden Estate Woodlands
7. *Newent Woods
8. *Owlpen Estate
9. Popes Wood
10. *Queens Wood
11. Stancombe Wood
12. Westonbirt Arboretum

Barber Wood
(Woodland Trust) F 38.85ha
O.S.S. 163 - SO 946 164
☎0476 74297

From Cheltenham take the A435 S towards Cirencester, then take the A436 towards Brockworth. At the crossroads in 2 miles turn L towards Cowley and park on the verge. There are no facilities. Barber Wood lies midway between Gloucester and Cheltenham and affords wonderful views of the Forest of Dean to the W, and the Malvern Hills to the NW. It is a Woodland Creation project and over 2800 trees, including ash, field maple and oak have already been planted. A variety of species including spindle and guelder rose will be planted to form a shrub layer. The grassland at the S side is of importance for the conservation value of species such as devil's bit scabious and quaking grass.

★ Beechenhurst Forest of Dean
(Forest Enterprise) R 10ha
O.S.S.162 - SO 614 120
☎0594 833057

Beechenhurst Lodge is signposted off the B4226 between Coleford and Cinderford in the heart of the forest near the Speech House. Hotel. Car parking (£1), toilets with disabled access, forest cafe and shop, picnic area, barbecues, forest trails. The cafe is open 364 days per year. Educational groups should book well in advance. The Forest of Dean is a working forest producing 70,000 cubic metres of timber each year. Beechenhurst Lodge sits at the heart of the forest. People, sheep and deer wander at will. The internationally known sculpture trail starts here. The sculptors were invited to the Dean to create works inspired by the forest, its industrial heritage and its wildlife. The result is a delight for the artist and layman alike. The Beechenhurst area also has large open areas for games and quiet enjoyment. The Cannop Ponds nature reserve is a short stroll away, as is Russells Inclosure.

★ Broomhill
(S W Wilkinson, managed by Charlton Abbotts Forestry Ltd) A 10ha
O.S.S. 162 - SO 712 185
☎0285 831342/0249 750758

From Gloucester turn L off the A40 (T) Gloucester - Ross road (shortly after passing through the village of Huntley) on to the A4136 Monmouth Road. The wood is 1/2 mile down the road on the RH side. Parking for 6 cars. Teas in Huntley, public house in Blaisdon. No entrance fee; donations to the Forestry Trust. Open on 1st Sunday in October 1994, 1130am to 3.30pm. *Guided walks by Woodland Manager starting at 1130am and 2.00pm.* School visits (by appointment) will be welcomed. Broomhill Wood is an ancient, semi-natural woodland containing a wide range of crop types including stored coppice, chestnut coppice, larch, pine, coastal redwood stands, mature oak compartments, mid rotation oak and ash, areas of natural regeneration and a Christmas tree plantation.

Frith
(Gloucestershire Wildlife Trust) F 25ha
O.S. S. 162 - SO 878 088
☎0452 383333

Beside the B4070 at Bulls Cross between Stroud and Birdlip. Car parking for 20 cars or 2 coaches. No other facilities. There is fully open access to the wood via right of ways and bridleways. Guided visits can be arranged by contacting Dr McGlone on the above telephone number. Please book well in advance. A beautiful beech wood in spectacular Cotswold (AONB) country opposite Painswick and above the Slad Valley. Miles of good level tracks and views, an SSSI with a good range of wildlife associated with limestone habitat. Plants, including fungi, invertebrates and the usual range of animals.

High Meadow Woods: Forest of Dean/Wye Valley
(Forest Enterprise) F 1425ha
O.S.S. 162 - SO 563 160
☎0594 833057

Follow B4432 from Christchurch near Coleford. Facilities include car parking (Symonds Yat £1), toilets, orienteering course, disabled access, cafe, shop, forest trails. Please do not pass the fence in front of the cliff at Symonds Yat

Rock; the cliffs are dangerous. The ancient Forest of Dean is a working forest producing some 70,000 cubic metres of timber each year. High Meadow is a mixed broadleaved and conifer area alongside the River Wye. Symonds Yat Rock provides the focus with excellent views from the cliff tops. Peregrine falcons nest regularly on the cliffs adjacent to the rock. Forest trails wind through the forest offering the chance to spot a host of wild animals and plants.

★ Miserden Estate Woodlands
(Major M T N H Wills) AD 300ha
O.S.S. 163 -SO 938 088
☎0285 821303

Follow signs to Miserden off A417 Cirencester - Gloucester Road or off B4070 Stroud - Birdlip Road. There is parking for 20 cars , there are no WC facilities. The garden is open Tues, Wed and Thurs, 9.30 - 4.30, 1 Apr - 30 Sept. The garden nurseries are open daily, except Mon, There is access through the wood via rights of way, bridleways and a self guided trail (please keep to the marked trail). An illustrated pamphlet covering the trail is available at the estate office or from the village shop. Guided visits will be held on 10 April and 3 July 1994. All visits are by appointment only; please give 1 weeks notice for group visits. There will be a charge of £2 for guided visits (children free), £1.80 for group bookings. Donations to the Forestry Trust. For further details and bookings please contact the estate office at Miserden Park, Stroud Glos, GL6

7AJ, or telephone above number. The woodland straddles the banks of the River Frome, a tributary of the River Severn which runs N to S. All the woodland is on steep or sloping ground. The woodland, predominantly pure beech, was clear felled during World War 2. Pockets of mature trees still exist although 80% of the woodland has been planted post 1945, with planting continuing until 1967. Small areas have been planted more recently, principle species being beech, sycamore, ash, European larch, Norway spruce and Scots pine. Some fine Douglas fir are to be seen. The Estate won the Dulverton Flagon for best managed woodland in 1989.

★ Newent Woods
(Mrs Torill Freeman) A 280ha
O.S.S. 162 - SO 705 227
☎0452 830209

From Newent drive for 2 miles along the B4216 (signposted to Huntley) to take 3rd turning on R (signposted May Hill/Glasshouse). Drive for 1.1/2 miles to 'T' junction, turn R, carry on for 1/2 mile. There are rights of way through the wood and guided visits can be arranged by appointment with Mr Simons. Write to Huntley Estate, Woodend Farm, Huntley, Glos, GL19 3EY or telephone above number. (Alternative Numbers 0452 831349 and 0860 586418). Notice is required for visits. Newent Wood is approximately 10 miles W of Gloucester, on the NE slope of May Hill. The present mixed woodland rises from

the 250 ft contour to the 900 ft contour in its 1 1/2 mile length and occupies an ancient semi-natural woodland site. Its numerous springs and streams help to create many varied and interesting habitats for indigenous flora and fauna. Predominant tree species include oak, Douglas fir, sweet chestnut, and larch spp. Although a commercial woodland, compartments of different aged trees are undergoing various silvicultural treatments, including many acres of worked sweet chestnut coppice, to produce high quality timber and rich wildlife habitats.

★ Owlpen Estate
(C N Mander) R 55ha
O.S.S. 162 - ST 804 984
☎0453 860261

The hamlet of Owlpen is 1/2 mile E of Uley, off the B4066 3 miles E of Dursley. There is a licensed restaurant at the manor when the house is open. Adequate parking. 9 holiday cottages. Two public footpaths lead through the woods from the vicinity of the manor house. The manor is open to the public Apr - Sept, Sun, Tues, & Thurs and Bank Hol.Mons, also Wed in July and Aug. Information, educational materials and plans available at the manor. Stroud District Council publish maps with recommended walks through the woods. Traditional Cotswold edge beech woodland and associated limestone flora. The boundaries of the woodland today are much the same as in the earliest 18th century records, and they have been long managed for the production of quality beech and for conservation. After heavy felling during the two wars, there is good regeneration of mature beech in uneven-aged woods now being actively thinned to provide diverse habitats. There are a number of archaeological and historical features on this ancient estate centred on a celebrated Tudor manor house and its outbuildings in the Cotswold A.O.N.B. Small 1960s softwood plantations, and ash. Roe deer and badgers are prolific.

Popes Wood
(Mrs D D Walmsley) F 25ha
O.S.S. 162 - SO 875 126

Take lane off A46 behind "Royal William" public house, 2 miles W of Painswick. There are no facilities, but good tracks. Please keep to these tracks with dogs under control. Fine beech mixed natural regeneration. National Nature Reserve on Cotswold scarp.

★ Queen's Wood: Southam
(Mr & Mrs P G Adlard) A 23ha
O.S.S. 163 - SO 974 254
☎0242 579334

Park in layby near de la Bere Hotel. Walk 600m along bridle path to enter wood by stile on N side. There are no facilities and the wood is open only by appointment with the owners. There are no public rights of way within the wood. Queen's Wood is a semi-natural woodland of ash, oak and wych elm with 30 year old plantations of beech, larch and other

conifers. There are bluebells in season. Public footpaths adjoining wood lead to Cleeve Common.

Stancombe Wood
(N D Barlow) F 30ha
O.S.S. 162 - ST 741 979

Park in parking lot on Stinchcombe golf course. The wood is always open, there are no facilities and no charge is made for access. From the top of Stinchcombe Hill, there are spectacular views of the Severn Vale. The woods are made up of old established mixture of beech, larch and sycamore. Healthy growth of wild flowers.

Westonbirt Arboretum
(Forest Enterprise) R 240ha
O.S.S. 163 - ST 854 900
☎0666 880220
A433 3 miles S of Tetbury. Facilities include ample parking for cars and coaches, a visitor centre with gift shop, exhibition and video presentation, courtyard cafe and a plant centre specializing in trees and shrubs. There are 17 miles of waymarked trails and the grounds are open 365 days a year but the facilities are only fully open from Mar to Dec. Charges are £2.50 for adults, £1.50 for senior citizens and £1 for children. Educational visits by appointment. Westonbirt is the largest arbretum in the country and one of the most important in Europe. It is particularly renowned for its autumn colours and spring flowers.

GREATER LONDON

see map on p15

Chalk Wood
(London Borough of Bexley) F 26.3ha
O.S.S. 177- TQ 494 708
☎081 3096638

Off A223 heading S turn L into
Parsonage Lane. At top of lane dirt
track leads to Chalk Wood. Track
is not suitable for domestic
vehicles. The wood is open 24
hours daily. Ancient ash / maple
wood converted to sweet chestnut
coppice. Forty two ancient
woodland indicator species
including green hellebore and
solomon's seal. Winter roost of
long-eared bats. At least 265
species of invertebrates, only a
small number of total probably
present. Two acidic meadows, one
having Melampyrum pratense
(common cow-wheat), a rarity in
the London area. Hazel coppice
regime to start in 93/94.

★ Fryent Country Park
(Brent Council) F 100ha
O.S.176 - TQ 196 877
☎081 900 5659

Accessible on foot from either side
of Fryent Way and from roads
adjacent to the Country Park. By
car; as above, but a car park is
situated on the W side of Fryent
Way approximately in the centre of
the Country Park (i.e. at the above
grid reference). Kingsbury and
Wembley Park underground
stations are within walking
distance. There are many
footpaths. For leaflets and events

pro-
gramme telephone above number.
A deciduous community woodland.
Managed by Brent Council and
local volunteer groups. Woodland
includes a Humphrey Repton
woodland dating from 1793, 10 km
of hedgerows, scrub, oak coppice,
elm coppice and recently planted
woodlands (circa 15,000 trees
planted). Multi-purpose forestry is
practised: much of the woodland is
now being coppiced. The volunteers run a tree nursery, using local
seed and providing several hundred
trees a year. Wildlife of lowland
farm woodlands. Wild fruits,
meadows and over 20 ponds.

Hampstead Heath
(Corporation of London) F 272ha
O.S.S. 176 - TQ 260 850

Underground to Golders Green or
210 bus Hamstead (British Rail).
Gospel Oak area of heath has
children's play areas plus cafe.
Golders Hill Park has a children's
zoo. There are WCs, including for
the disabled. There is fully open
access to the heath with rights of
way on foot and horserides, not
bridleways. Undulating open space
including a small area of ancient
woodland at Kenwood. There is no
real heath left but 29 ponds,
including 2 at Kenwood, and some
acid grassland remain. Wildlife
ranges from grass snakes and slow
worms to purple hairstreak and
gatekeeper butterflies, plus nine
species of dragonfly.

Highgate Wood

(Corporation of London) F 28ha
O.S.S. 176 - TQ 280 870
☎081 444 6129

Nearest station is Highgate underground station, main entrance off Muswell Hill. WCs, including disabled. Chilren's playground, vegeterian cafe, pathways suitable for disabled access. No cycling allowed. Network of easily accessible pathways open 7.30 am to 30 minutes after sunset, 365 days a year. Guided visits can be arranged, contact Parks and Gardens Department on 081 472 3584, or Manager, Highgate Wood on the above number.Originally part of the old forest of Middlesex, Highgate Wood was dedicated as "an open space forever" in 1886 after being offered to the Corporation of London in 1885 by the Ecclesiastical Commission. Dominant tree species include oak, hornbeam and lime. There is also a diverse herbaceous understorey. A large variety of bird life has been recorded; 70 bird species, including nesting birds, which remain throughout the year and migratory birds which use the wood as a feeding station. Excavations of the site undertaken in 1962-74 led to discovery of kilns, pits and ditches and established it had been used by potters at about the time of the Roman conquest AD43.

Hockendon Wood

(Naturist Foundation) A 20ha
O.S.S.177

☎0689 871200

Write for appointment (week days in autumn and spring) and directions: Naturist HQ, Orpington, Kent, BR5 4ET. 50 acres of woodland/parkland including several acres of coppiced chestnut. Variety of specimen trees. Ancient woodland mentioned in Domesday Book. Extensive wild bird population. Wild flowers under woodland canopy. Fauna includes foxes, squirrels, voles, rabbits and badgers. Recreational facilities developed within the estate will not be in use at the time of visits, but the Foundation welcomes enquiries from those who wish to benefit and help their work.

Lesnes Abbey Woods

(London Borough of Bexley) F 88ha
O.S.S. 177 - TQ 478 787
☎0322 351150

By rail: Abbey Wood Station. By bus: London Transport routes 99 and 46A. Off-site parking available in Abbey Road and New Road. Facilities include information centre, toilets (including disabled). Access is free all year, 7.30am until dusk weekdays, 9.00am until dusk weekends and public holidays. Information Centre open 9.00am until dusk, every day. The display of wild daffodils in early spring is famous throughout SE England. Bluebells and other flowers also abound. The woods contain a Victorian ornamental woodland pond and a remnant of the heathland which once covered Bexleyheath. There are picnic areas beside the formal gardens, and the ruins of a 12th century Augustinian abbey attract many visitors. The woods contain deposits of tertiary age fossils, and digging for fossil sharks teeth can be arranged by appointment.

Petts Wood: Chislehurst
(National Trust) F 45 ha
O.S.S. 177 - TQ 450 687
☎0892 890651

The 45 hectares of Petts Wood includes Edlmann Wood, and is preserved as a public open space. Petts Wood is so called after the Pett family who were royal shipbuilders from the time of Henry VIII to Charles II. William Willett the founder of British Summer Time, who was an active Chislehurst resident, is commemorated in Willett Wood. It is an ancient, semi-natural wood with predominantly oak and birch.

Rookery Estate Woods
(Rookery Estates Co.) F 56ha
O.S.S. 177 - TQ 410 664
☎0981 2 40367

The woods lie 1 - 2 miles S of Bromley high street and are bounded by Hayes to the W, Bromley Common to the E and the Croydon Road to the S. Access is from any public road or path. Please keep dogs on a lead. This is ancient woodland all managed as coppice with standards. It is ecologically diverse, containing

about eight stand types with large areas of two rare categories, lowland sessile oakwood and plateau alder. The flora is superb including some 45 ancient woodland indicator species and 35 native trees and shrubs. There are woodbanks, old pollards and an intricate natural drainage pattern as well as three miles of old rides and a rich bird life.

Sheen Common
(London Borough of Richmond) F 21 ha
O.S. 176 - TQ 197 745
☎081 332 2184

Main entrance is off Fife Road, East Sheen - or go in from Bog Gate in Richmond Park - clearly marked on the "A to Z". Interpretive boards explain management. Pond dipping equipment/ranger service, nature trail. Open 24 hours. Toilets available during day and when pavilion is in use. To borrow a pond dipping pack, ring the ranger on 876 2382 or pick up a nature trail leaflet at the pavilion. Sheen Common has a fascinating history. Once a golf course and rifle range, it has now developed into a delightful woodland. Birch trees host nesting woodpeckers and a nature trail will lead you to the pond with its dipping platform. Watch out for conservation projects which you can join in with or book up to borrow the pond dipping/survey equipment to study the site. Don't miss the Woodland Open Day held in May each year.

Sydenham Hill Wood
(London Borough of Southwark) **F 9ha**
O.S.S. 177 - TQ 344 724
☎071 278 6612/3

The main entrance is in Crescent Wood Road, SE26, which is off Sydenham Hill - which can be reached from either the A212 to the S at Crystal Palace, at the South Circular (A205), to the N by the Horniman Gardens, Forest Hill, SE23. Self-guided trail, information leaflet available, numerous events. The wood is part of the largest surviving fragment of the historic Great North Wood - an economic resource for charcoal, timber and tanning - and today exhibits the results of varied recent history - old Victorian gardens and an old railway trackbed. Almost 200 species of flowering plants are present, together with a multitude of fungi, birds and insects - notable species include all 3 woodpeckers, chiff-chaff, tree-creeper, wild garlic and wood anemones under the dominant trees of oak, hornbeam, ash and yew. Declared a Local Nature Reserve in 1990.

GREATER MANCHESTER

see map on p14

Hulmes Wood

(Tameside Metropolitan Borough Council) F
10ha
O.S.S. 109 - SJ 923 937
☎061 342 3306

From Denton, take A6017
signposted Stockport. After 1.5
miles there is a lay-by, opposite a
sewage treatment plant. Entrance
to wood is via the gate/stile at this
lay-by. Bridlepaths, footpaths. Part
of Transpennine trail. A small piece
of ancient woodland bordering the
river Tame. The woodland was the
site of Hulmes mine, and industrial
archeology from the mine is still
visible. A small pond has been
created on the site of one area of
the mine, and this pond is a haven
for wildlife.

Tandle Hill Park

(Oldham Leisure Services) F 22ha
O.S.S. 109 - SD 907 087
☎061 627 2608

3 miles N of Oldham. Access is off
A671 Oldham to Rochdale Road;
turn into Tandle Hill Road.
Country Park is signed. The car
park is at the end of Tandle Hill
Road approximately 1/2 mile.
Access is free. Charges for other
facilities. There are toilets,
orienteering, pitch and putt golf. A
room is available for groups to use.
Contact the rangers who also run a
range of activities, for details. A
woodland open day will be held on
Sun 10 Jul 1994. Information
leaflet and map is also available.
There is full access for walkers;
dogs on lead please. No access for
bikes or horses. Tandle Hill Park is
a mature beech woodland with
more recent conifer planting
around the edge. Recent work has
concentrated on encouraging
natural regeneration. Guided visits
can be arranged for interested
groups. A nature trail has been
developed for junior schools who
wish to explore the wood. Please
ring the above number for further
details and bookings.

HAMPSHIRE & ISLE OF WIGHT

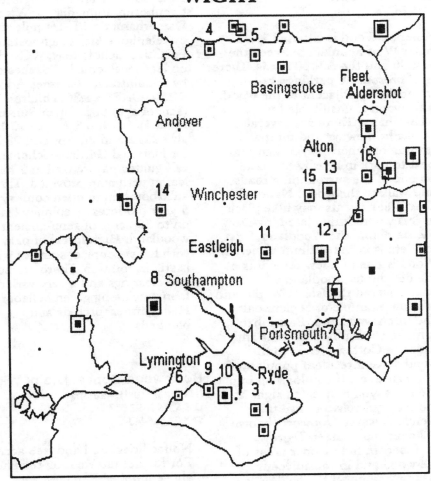

1. America Wood
2. *Ashridge
3. Borthwood Copse
4. The Chase
5. The Holt
6. Mill Copse
7. Morgaston Wood
8. *The New Forest
9. Newtown Woods
10. Parkway
11. *Phrympth Wood
12. *Queen Elizabeth Country Park
13. Selborne Common
14. Spearywell Woods
15. Stoney Brow
16. Waggoner's Wells

America Wood: Isle of Wight
(Woodland Trust) F 10.88ha
O.S.S 196 - SZ 568 819
☎0476 74297

America Wood is situated 1 1/2 miles W of Shanklin between the A3056 and the A3020 roads. There is at present no parking available immediately adjacent to the wood. This wood is unsuitable for wheelchairs. There are several public bridleways and footpaths leading to America Wood and it is best to park in nearby Shanklin or on one of the surrounding roads and walk to the wood. National Tree Week events may take place in this wood during late Nov-Dec. Please phone the Woodland Trust for details in the autumn. America Wood is one of a few remnants of the deciduous woodland which once covered the Isle of Wight, and is a fine example of ancient oak and birch woodland. Bats inhabit some of the old hollow trees and America Cottages, next to the wood, have a resident population of pipistrelles. If you look up into the trees, you may catch sight of the red squirrels that live there. Hemlock water dropwort (known as "deadmans fingers") grows profusely in the damper areas of the wood and in the adjacent meadow amongst the goat willow - A special warning - hemlock water dropwort is poisonous so *please do not pick it!*

★ Ashridge
(David J Dampney) L 30ha
O.S.S. 184 - SU 098 153

☎07253 200

Take B3078 from Fordingbridge to Cranborne. Immediately W of Damerham, turn L 1/4 mile, turn R by telephone kiosk signposted. Facilities include teas, WCs; dogs on leads welcomed. Coaches only by appointment. Charges Adults £1.50, OAPS £1.30, children (school age) 50p. Open Sun and Bank Hol., Mon 3 Apr to 13 Jul, also Sat 2 and 20 Apr and 28 May for National Gardens Scheme. A self guided nature trail of 2 miles, leaflet with map provided. Through an arboretum to open country with 5 year old forestry spinney leading on to 30 acres of semi-ancient woodland. High forest of oak, ash with hazel coppice, some of which is still in rotation. There are ponds and clearings and a very varied fauna including green hellebores, Helleborines, orchids and bluebells.

Borthwood Copse: Isle of Wight
(National Trust) F 23.3ha
O.S.S. 196- SZ 567 843
☎0983 526443

No facilities. Full and free access. For further information telephone above number.

The Chase
(National Trust) F 56.5ha
O.S.S 174 - SU 442 630
☎0372 453401

There is a car park. No facilities. Free and full access. Telephone above number for further information.

The Holt
(Major R A Colvile) F 68ha
O.S.S. 174 - SU 557 617

On the B3051 N of Kingsclere. The wood is mainly oak, fairly even aged. Worst areas were planted 1966-80 mainly with conifers, larch, Douglas fir, western hemlock and some poplar, red oak, cherry and notofagus. Some natural regeneration of sallow, alder and ash. Ashford Hill Nature Reserve (English Nature) adjoins on N side. Apart from trees felled as part of thinning regime it will be many years before timber is obtainable. As most of the wood is on clay, gum boots or strong boots are usually advisable.

Mill Copse: Isle of Wight
(Wight Nature Fund) R 5.6ha
O.S.S 196 - SZ 357 891

Park in local borough council car park off A3054 at Yarmouth. Walk along sea wall to old railway and then turn R then L onto footpath to wood. There are no facilities, nearest WC, Yarmouth, parking in council car park. A public footpath runs through the wood and there is no restriction on time of access. Please keep to obvious paths to prevent undue disturbance to wildlife. An ancient woodland site with small area of hazel coppice, home to bluebells, orchids,

dormice. Rest of wood is mixed conifer plantation including coastal redwood with clear felled areas being replanted with broadleaves. Paths allow views over Yar River and adjoining wet meadows. Only recently acquired. Management hopes to convert this plantation back to the splendour of a hazel coppice, typical of other West Wight woodlands.

Morgaston Wood - The Vyne
(National Trust) F 63.2ha
O.S.S. 175 - SU 625572
☎0372 453401

No facilities. Full and free access. Telephone above number for further information.

★ The New Forest
(The Forestry Commission) F 26500ha
O.S.S.196/195 - SU 300 080
☎0296-625825

Guided walks available. Contact the education officer at the Queen's House, Lyndhurst. The finest example of multi purpose forest management in the country catering for such diverse interests as the growing of trees for timber, the pasturing of commoners' stock, the safeguarding of a biologically diverse ecosystem and the provision of facilities for recreation and education.

Newtown Woods: Isle of Wight
(National Trust) F 21ha

111

O.S.S. 196 - SZ 430 905
0983 526443

No facilities. Full and free access
Telephone above number for
further information.

Parkway: Isle of Wight
(Managed by Forest Enterprise) F 390ha
O.S.S. 196 - SZ 473897
☎0420 23666

Parkhurst is signposted from the
A3054 Newport to Yarmouth,
about 2 miles from Newport.
Facilities include car park, toilets,
picnic area and educational
facilities. Parkhurst Forest is a
mixed broadleaved and conifer
woodland. The forest was
mentioned in the Domesday Book
in the 11th Century. The forest has
diverse habitats including mature
oak, plantation conifer, coppice,
heathland and wetlands. An
excellent education service has
been established to promote
understanding of woodland
management, conservation and
sustainability. This helps to meet
the requirements of the national
curriculum. in schools.

★Phrympth Wood
(Captain R F Phillimore RN (Ret'd)) F 22ha
O.S.S. 185 - SU 578 184
☎0730 265933

From the crossroads by the garage
on the A32 at the N end of
Droxford, take lane to Dundridge
(2 1/2 miles). From Winchester,
take the B3335 to Colden

Common, thence the B2177 to
Bishop's Waltham, leave this town
northwards on the B3035, turn R
for Dundridge (2 miles). *The
Hampshire Bowman* public house
permits use of car park. Bar meals
and WC available during licensing
hours. Access to the wood is via
signed footpath 100 yards S,
through farm. Small shoot uses the
wood, as do local foxhounds,
please respect these pursuits and
keep dogs on lead. Donations to
the Forestry Trust. Ancient
woodland site, natural regeneration
abundant, and now part of
management regime. Phrympth's
special character is the great
diversity of downland flora,
including toothwort, broomrape,
orchids including twayblades as
well as many ancient woodland
indicator species. Management
practices used to maintain this
diversity include biennial mowing
of rides and removal of sycamore.
Currently under about 50% conifer
cover from plantings in 1974.
Mentioned in 16th century tithe
records of Bishop of Winchester's
palace at Bishops Waltham. The
unusual name is of Saxon origin.

★Queen Elizabeth Country Park
(Managed by Forest Enterprise in
partnership with Hampshire County
Council) R 600ha
O.S.S. 197 - SU 718 185
☎0420 23666

The park is signposted from the A3
S of Petersfield. There is a car park
for which there is a charge. Other
facilities include a visitor centre

and cafe, toilets, with all ability access, forest walks, ranger service. The forest centre is open 1000 - 1630 hrs. The country park is located in the South Downs and is split between Butser Hill, an area on ancient downland, and War Down which is part of Buriton Woods. The woodland is predominantly beech, with a large range of flora and fauna. The park centre has education facilities and information, as well as a cafe and gift shop. The South Downs Way passes through the park as do a number of bridleways.

Selborne Common
(National Trust) F 108.6ha
O.S.S. 186 - SU 742 335
☎0428 683207

National Trust car park in village. No other facilities. Full and free access. Telephone above number for further information.

Spearywell Woods
(National Trust) F 52ha
O.S.S. 185 - SU 316276
☎0794 341257

Travelling N on the B 3084 from Awbridge to Broughton, cross level crossing at Dunbridge - 1 1/4 miles - Spearywell Wood and car park for 15 cars on left. There is a Tea Shop in village. Other woods on the estate also open to visitors. There is full and free access with a choice of waymarked walks. A mixture of managed plantations and

semi-natural woodland.

Stoney Brow
(Sir James Scott) F 72ha
O.S.S. 186 - SU 688 304
☎0420 588207

1 1/2 miles S of East Tisted on the A32, turn R for Ropley, the wood is immediately either side of the public road. There is full access but no facilities. There are no public rights of way through the woodland. Stony Brow is a semi mature oak and beech, sweet chestnut coppice growing on a 30 year rotation. 10 year old mixed hardwoods and conifers, 20 year old pure Norway spruce and western hemlock, 25 year old Douglas fir, 40 year old mixed larch, oak and beech, 2 year old European larch in tree shelters. Area of natural scrubland with groups of natural regeneration of ash and birch; area of old mature broadleaves.

Waggoner's Wells
(National Trust) F 29.1ha
O.S.S. - SU 863 344
☎0428 683207

There is a car park but no other facilities. Full and free access. Telephone above number for further information.

HEREFORD & WORCESTER

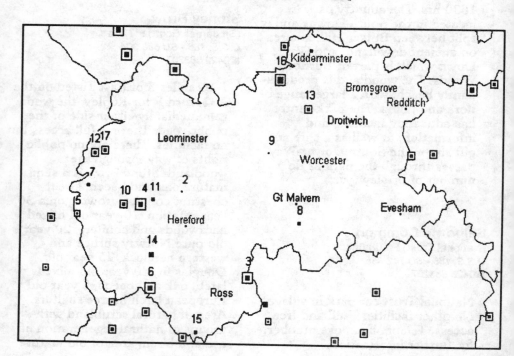

1. Bodenham Arboretum
2. Coedgwen
3. Dymock Wood
4. *Garnons Hill Wood
5. The Hills Wood
6. Kentchurch Deer Park
7. * Kiln Ground Wood
8. *Langdale Wood & the Lills

9. Longfield Coppice
10. *Monnington Wood
11. Nash Wood
12. Parkwood
13. Shrawley Wood
14. *Whitfield Woods
15. *Wolfwood
16. *Wyre Forest
17. Yeld Wood

Bodenham Arboretum

(Mr and Mrs J D Binnian) AE 17ha
O.S.. 138 - SO 808 815
☎0562 - 850382

Take the A442 from Kidderminster
1 1/2 miles towards Bridgnorth;
turn R onto B4189 for 3/4 mile; L
at crossroads; L at next junction
signed Bodenham. There is a car
park (not suitable for coaches) and
WC available. £2 donation to the
Forestry Trust. Visits arranged by
prior telephone call; parties require
14 days notice. The woodlands at
Bodenham Arboretum are planted
into a series of small valleys. Paths
guide the visitor alongside streams
and pools where the rare, unusual
and colourful trees and shrubs are
growing in young commercial
woodlands. Open areas among the
woods give views to the surrounding countryside. On the whole site
there is a blend of productive
farming, wildlife, good forestry and
the beauty of rare plants. The
Forestry Authority has presented a
full Centre of Excellence Award to
Bodenham Arboretum.

Coedgwen

(Jennie Guille) L 0.3ha
O.S.149 - SO 494 473
☎0432 - 830518

Off Hereford to Leominster road
A49, turn L into Wellington; in 1/2
mile turn L for Anberrow/Burghill;
in 1/2 mile turn L for Auberrow
Common. There are no charges
and no facilities. The wood is open
for the first two weeks of July. This
new little wood - planted in 1987

mainly with ash and alder - leads to
an ancient hay meadow enclosed
with tall hedges, which is in the
Countryside Commission
Stewardship Scheme, and looks
very colourful before it is cut for
hay. The wood is enriched with
Norway maple, hornbeam, lime,
cherry, walnut, wild service and a
few other interesting trees. It is
managed for growing veneer
quality or furniture timber for
future generations, so any likely
stems are pruned high. Others will
be coppiced for firewood for use in
the short term.

Dymock Wood

(Forest Enterprise) F 490ha
O.S.S. 149 - SO 679 285
☎0594 833057

From Gorsley on B4221, near
Junction 3 on M50, follow minor
road to Kempley village. There are
car parks, forest walks, fishing and
horse riding by permit from office.
The woodland is famouse for the
daffodils in spring.

★ Garnons Hill Wood

(H R G Cotterell) R 110ha
O.S.S. 149 - SO 394 448
☎098122 235

The only access is from village of
Mansell Gamage. Turn off road by
phone box. Small parking area at
above OS reference but parking is
entirely at own risk.. There are
marked trails and no charge is
made for access. The wood is open
from 1 Apr to 31 Oct during

daylight hours. No dogs, bikes, or horses. Please keep to the waymarked routes. Do not touch squirrel hoppers. Forestry trails for the enthusiast. Mixed woodland managed for production of quality timber. Beautiful views over Wye valley.

The Hills Wood
(The Penoyre Trust) F 6ha
O.S.S. 148 - SO 240 420

Take the B4347 from Hay on Wye towards Bredwardine. Approximately 3/4 mile outside the town limits a Public Footpath on the RH side of the road goes up into the wood on the far side of the hedge from a stone cottage. The wood is on a steeply sloping bank, the upper slope being planted with mature oak, larch and a few Spanish chestnut, and the lower slope with spruce. If visitors walk above the conifers to the edge of the wood they will see in the adjoining field a stone obelisk built in 1830 as an unemployment project and a memorial to her father by Anna Maria Brodbelt-Stalland-Penoyre. The wood adjoins Mousecastle Wood, now owned by the Woodland Trust, which is also open to the public.

Kentchurch Deer Park
(J E S Lucas-Scudamore) R 100ha
O.S.S. 162 - SO 422 258
☎0981 - 500291

From Pontrilas A465 turn SE

(B4347) to Kentchurch. Past church turn L up private drive to Kentchurch Court. There are no facilities. A charge of £1 will be made. Open on Sunday, 1 May. Guided tours starting at 2 pm and 3 pm. Dogs on leads welcome. Kentchurch Deer Park is one of three fully enclosed deer parks left in the county, with a herd of upwards of 200 fallow. Within the park and surrounding it are woods of oak and conifers. Typical landscape with fine views.

★ Kiln Ground Wood
(Lt Colonel E C Phillips) A 16.5ha
O.S.S.148 - SO 267 488
☎0981 500282

Take A438 from Hereford. Turn R past Whitney Church signposted Brilley. Pass Whitney Church on R. Turn R on top of hill. Gate and stacking area 1/2 mile on L. By appointment only but there is no charge. There are rough rides. Coppicing operation. Oak and cherry plantations '81/'86. Some larch and Norway spruce. Mid rotation oak and ash c.1971.

★ Langdale Wood & The Lills
(Three Counties Agricultural Society) A 25ha
O.S.S. 150 - SO 784 427
☎0684 892751

Follow Three Counties showground signs off motorway M5 and M50; B4208/4209 and road signs nr Malvern. Ample free parking.

Open all year. All visits by appointment, notice only required for guided visits: Adults £2, Children £1, self guided visits: Adults £1, Children 50p. Leaflets available for each participant which explains various stops. Planted in about 1890, Langdale Wood has a remarkably interesting and varied history. The wood was originally part of the Blackmore Estate and was probably planted to increase the shooting potential of the estate. During the last 80 years over 15 different timber species have been planted in blocks to increase the income from the wood. Good stands of oak, Douglas fir, western hemlock and western red cedar occur in the wood, although the storms of January 1990 inflicted much damage. Despite being only 100 years old, the wood has developed a remarkable variety of plants, birds and insects. Throughout the year some 38 different species of birds use the wood and in the summer 16 species of butterfly may be seen. These are largely dependent on the well developed layer of shrubs and bramble that occurs in the wood.

Longfield Coppice
(E W Evans) A 9.4ha
O.S.S.150 - SO 705 564
☎0886 21431

Take gated road off A44 c.11 miles W of Worcester, 4 miles E of Bromyard. Call at first farm on R (Longlands). Longfield coppice is approx 1/2 mile from farm. As you come from Worcester on the A44,

the turning onto the gated road is to the R, about 300 yards beyond the Whitborne turn at the Wheatsheaf Inn. As you come from Bromyard the turning L is very tight and it is safer to go past it to the Wheatsheaf, turn round in the car park and come back towards Bromyard in order to make the turn. Car parking is in wood (dry weather only). Network of rides cut annually. Open all the year round by appointment, subject to timber operations. Please give as much notice as possible. Longfield contains a great variety of woodland both in age and species. It grows exceptionally high quality oak, some of which has been harvested over the last 20 years. These felling areas, now restocked, illustrate different methods of establishing oak woodland. There are several stands of conifer, mature oak, ash, and many other species amongst the main crop trees. Longfield offers a picture of an evolving, uneven aged productive wood, with a wide range of wildlife habitats.

★ Monnington Wood
(H R G Cotterell) R 30ha
O.S.S. 148/149 - SO 351 445
☎098122 - 235

Turn off A438 (SO 357451) heading SW. Entrance to wood at above O.S. reference. Access and parking is entirely at own risk. Open from 1 Mar to 1 Aug during daylight hours. No dogs, bikes or horses. Please keep to the waymarked routes. Mixed forestry.

Lovely views over the River Wye from the Scar SSSI. Monnington walk and Wye Valley walk.

Nash Wood
(David Davenport) L 54ha
O.S.S 149 - SO 426 456
☎098122 224

The rendezvous will be signposted from Mansel Lacy Church (OS Ref as above). Mansel Lacy is 7 miles W of Hereford on the A480. A guided walk lasting some 3 hours will be lead personally by the owner starting at 2.30pm on Sunday, 3 July 1994. Plenty of hard standing for parking. No WCs. Dogs on lead only. Donations of £2 a person (children under 18 free) to the Forestry Trust. Nash Wood is on the Foxley Estate which was landscaped some 200 years ago by Sir Uvedale Price. The landscape is listed Grade II. Mature groups or individual trees of oak, sweet chestnut, lime, Lebanon cedar, holm oak, beech, yew, acacia. Discussions will take place along the route on forestry, timber production, the landscape and flora and fauna.

Parkwood
(R A Banks) R 16ha
O.S.S.148 - SO 280 563

Kington is on A44 27 miles W of Worcester and 60 miles E of Aberystwyth (though by-passed). From Kington take Hergest Road (signed Brilley etc), then first R

Cutterbach Lane (very narrow) 1/4 mile to Haywood Common. Parking on common for 10 cars. Entrance Adults £1, children 50p. There are two public rights of way running through the wood, other paths through rhododendrons and ornamental trees open to paying visitors to Hergest Croft garden from Easter to end Oct and to others at all times, except weekends Oct - Jan - payment in box near cottage. All dogs mut be kept on lead and please keep to paths and tracks. About 7 hectares are planted with rhododendrons and exotic trees and shrubs which are exceptionally beautiful from Mar to Jun and again in autumn. The main wood consists of mixed age oak with understorey of beech and some conifers. It is a habitat for buzzards, ravens and badgers.

Shrawley Wood
(Managed by Forest Enterprise) F 85ha
O.S.S. 150 - SO 800 665
☎0584 - 874542

The landlady of the New Inn on the B4196 one mile N of Shrawley has kindly agreed to allow parking behind the New Inn public house. Please patronise the pub. Informal walks only.

★ Whitfield Woods
(G M Clive) A 400ha
O.S.149 - SO 423 335
☎098121 - 375

Whitfield entrance is 8 miles from Hereford on A465. Turn R from

Hereford. Meeting point 2 miles up drive. There are no facilities. The wood is open by appointment and charges are by arrangement. Educational parties are not usually charged. Mixed woodlands surrounding parkland. Landscaped woodland walk, including pinetum with 1851 grove of Sequoia sempervirens (coast redwood). Old oak woodland, many 1960s onwards plantations, including oak, ash, softwoods. Many ornamental trees, including 1780 gingko, 1982 maple walk. Mixed plantations being converted to broadleaves. Native species such as wild service tree and small-leaved lime.

★ Wolfwood
(Charles Griffin and Major Ralph Griffin) A 40ha
O.S.S.162 - SO 535 160
☎0600 - 712992

From Monmouth take the A40 N. Turn left for Newton Court half a mile after the Dixton roundabout. There is one right of way on foot and one bridleway through the wood. All visits to be by apppointment only, guided group visits (maximum 30) can be arranged, please contact Mr C Griffin on the above telephone number. Donations made to the Forestry Trust. Bought about 1980 by family trust for Major Ralph Griffin. Species include: Douglas fir, European larch, sweet chestnut, America red oak, Norway spruce, Tsuga,cherry and ash. Layout for game and timber. The pond in Wolfwood is used by ducks and

also contains newts and dragon-flies.

★ Wyre Forest
(Managed by Forest Enterprise) R 1,000 ha
O.S.S. 138 - SO 753 740
☎0584 874542

3 miles W of Bewdley on A456. Visitor centre, forest shop, refreshment bar, forest walks, car park - charge 80p. Visitor centre open 11.00 - 16.00 hrs. Forest events programme with 35 annual events available from district forest office. Wyre is a very attractive ancient royal hunting forest which now has an exciting visitor centre and varied woodland walks, including an all ability trail. The visitor centre has a fascinating display on the history, wildlife and management of Wyre, including a living wood ants nest. A leaflet illustrating the walks is available from the visitor centre, price 50p. The all ability trail is designed for families with pushchairs, and for people with walking difficulties or in a wheelchair.

Yeld Wood
(W L Banks) R 49ha
O.S.S. 148 - SO 284 568
☎0544-230160

Off A44 W of Kington, follow signs to Hergest Croft Gardens. Garden car park may be used by visitors to the wood between Oct and Mar only. Footpaths signposted. There are no facilities and there is no

entrance fee. The wood is open
daily all year round. A footpath
runs the length of the wood -
visitors may use the main rides
only. Dogs on leads. There is a fine
stand of oak and beech about 200
years old at the E end of the wood.
There are good stands of Douglas
fir dating back to the 1860s and
1890s. Much of the wood was
replanted following an ice storm in
1941. Wildlife includes buzzards,
ravens and sparrowhawks and a
good variety of smaller birds.

HERTFORDSHIRE

see map on p11

★ Broxbourne and Bencroft Woods

(Hertfordshire County Council) F 60ha
O.S.S. 166 - TL 328 069
☎0992 555257

The woods are near the village of Brickenden, 3 miles S of Hertford. The location of small car parks in the wood is shown on the Ordnance Survey Landranger Map 166. Telephone the Countryside Management Service on above number if in doubt about how to drive to the woods. Alternatively, the woods are only a one mile walk away from Bayford railway station, to which there is a regular train service from London (Moorgate) and Stevenage. (Telephone 071 278 2477 for timetable). There is parking for a total of approximately 50 cars in 4 separate car parks, where picnic tables are also provided. There are no other facilities in the woods, but refreshments and toilets are available in pubs in the nearby villages of Brickendon, Bayford and Wormley West End. There is a network of footpaths including public rights of way and other waymarked routes along which the public are permitted to walk. These and other County Council woods feature in the "Stepping Out" programme of guided walks which is organised by the Countryside Management Service. Other guided visits for parties of 20 or more can also be arranged with David Dench, Countryside Management Service Manager, Planning and

Environment Dept, Hertfordshire County Council, County Hall, Hertford, SG13 8DN, (Telephone: Hertford (0992)555257. These ancient woodland sites are part of an extensive and spectacular tract of densely wooded countryside Hertfordshire's distinctive "wild wood" scenery close to London. Broxbourne Wood comprises mixed broadleaf and conifer areas where work to protect and enhance wildlife habitats and the landscape is being successfully integrated with timber production. Bencroft Wood is a superb example of semi-natural oak, hornbeam and birch woodland which continues to be managed by traditional coppicing, perpetuating a varied woodland structure rich in wildlife.

★ Bullens Green Wood

(Hertfordshire County Council) F 17ha
O.S.S. 166 - TL 214 065
☎0992 555234

Turn S off the A414 into the village of Colney Heath which is situated between St Albans and Hatfield. After 2/3 mile through the village, turn L at a roundabout on to Roestock Lane and drive 2/3 mile to the end of the lane. There is parking for cars and coaches along the roadside at the end of Roestock Lane. There are no facilities in the wood, but refreshments and toilets are available in nearby pubs in Colney Heath and Roestock. There is a network of footpaths including public rights of way and other waymarked routes along which the public are permitted to walk. This and other County Council woods feature in the "Stepping Out" programme of guided walks which is organised by the Countryside Management Service. Telephone above number for information. Other guided visits for parties of 20 or more can also be arranged throughout the year by prior arrangement with Julian Pitt, Forestry Officer. Telephone Hertford (0992) 555234 or write to him at Planning & Environment Dept, Hertfordshire County Council, County Hall, Hertford, SG13 8DN. This is the first large new broadleaved woodland to have been created in Watling Chase Community Forest. The planting is already transforming a damaged urban fringe landscape next to the A1(M) motorway. A good place to see silvicultural practices used to establish trees and how new woods can be designed successfully to integrate environmental objectives with timber production.

Hardings

(Richard Mabey) R 7ha
O.S.S. 165 - SP 946 095

The wood is in Crawleys Lane, Wigginton. There are no facilities and visitors are welcome at all times, but there are only permissive footpaths so please keep to them. No horses. Dogs on leads please. A mixed deciduous ancient wood. Run as a community wood since 1981, with special attention to wildlife conservation. Very rich range of ancient woodland indicator plants and semi-natural

stand - types unusual for the Chilterns.

Northaw Great Wood

(Welwyn Hatfield Council) F 117ha
O.S.S. 166 - TL 284 043
☎0707 872213

Entrance off the Ridgeway Cuffley on the B1057. 2 miles from Cuffley Railway Station towards Hatfield. Car park (£1), toilets, including disabled, information centre, picnic areas. Car park closes 6.00pm in summer, 4.30pm in winter. Wood open 8am to sunset all year round. No vehicles allowed in wood. Northaw Great Wood is a remnant of the extensive forest that covered much of Hertfordshire and Essex before the Norman Conquest Declared an SSSI in 1953 and obtained Country Park status in 1968. Sessile oak and hornbeam predominate the area and provide cover for a range of interesting flora and fauna. There is a warden on site, telephone number above.

Post Wood

(East Herts District Council) F 22ha
O.S.S.166 - TL 359 129
☎0279 655261 ext 485

Exit off A10 at Hertford A414 junction and take road off roundabout signposted to Gt Amwell. Take first exit off Gt Amwell road over A10 and first R down single track road. Car park 400m down track on L. The wood is across the playing field. There are no charges for entrance to the wood which is open daily all year round. The car park is also free, which is open from dawn till dusk. No WCs. Oak/hornbeam ancient woodland on glacial gravels, dissected by three dry valleys. Good displays of bluebells in spring. The wood was cleared of sycamore in 1991 and restocked with oak, hornbeam and cherry. The eastern dry valley is managed and cut annually as a glade. It has a rich ground flora and a few very large specimens of wild cherry on the lower slopes. A good wood to see hawfinches.

Sherrardspark Woods
(Welwyn Hatfield Council) F 74.6ha
O.S.S.166 - TL 228 138
☎0707 339211 ext 137

(1) Rectory Road Reservoir car park via Great North Road, B197, E of Ayot Green, or (2) Campus West car park, access via old railway line footpath. Entry is free and the wood is open all year round. Facilities include public footpaths, bridleways, display boards. Designated an SSI in 1986, because it isone of the larger remnants of ancient semi-natural sessile oak/hornbeam woodlands with associated flora in lowland England. Managed for recreation and conservation. Active woodland management taking place throughout winter periods. Voluntary wardens patrol the wood daily.

★ Tring Park Estate
(Lady Weiss) F 165ha
O.S.S.165 - SU 942 089
☎071 371 8500

Off A41 on minor road through Wigginton Bottom. There are no facilities but there is free and full access at all times by means of the many public footpaths that cross the property. For educational visits contact the agent on the above number. A former Rothschild property, the woods contain some fine large beech, typical of the Chilterns and now being felled at the end of its rotation. Natural regeneration of beech, oak and birch is encouraged. Conifers, particularly larch, grow well, though they have been severely attacked by the edible doormouse, Glis Glis. Numerous nesting boxes have been installed by the Natural History Museum now housed in the former Rothschild mansion in Tring.

★ Wall Hall Estate Woods
(Hertfordshire County Council) F 52ha
O.S.S.166 - TQ 139 985
☎0992 55234

The woods can be reached easily via public footpaths from the nearby village of Aldenham, which is situated just off the B462 midway between Radlett and Watford. Alternatively, the Ver-Colne Valley walk leads out of Watford to the other side of the woods. Watford is easily accessible by train from London. A leaflet for the Ver-Colne Valley walk can be obtained by telephoning Hertford (0992) 555257. There is roadside parking for cars in Aldenham, especially near the church and village green. There are no facilities in the woods, but refreshments and toilets are available in nearby pubs at Round Bush and Patchetts Green. There is a network of footpaths including public rights of way and other waymarked routes along which the public are permitted to walk. An interpretative woodland trail leaflet will be available in 1994, to be produced in conjunction with Watling Chase. This, and other County Council woods, feature in the "Stepping Out" programme of guided walks which is organised by the Countryside Management Service. Telephone Hertford (0992) 555257 for information. Guided visits for parties of 20 or more can also be arranged with Julian Pitt, Forestry Officer, telephone number above, or write to him at Planning and Environment Dept, Hertfordshire County Council, County Hall, Hertford, SG13 8DN. These woods are some of the most varied and interesting woodlands in Watling Chase Community Forest. The woods are partially ancient and semi-natural but are mostly mixed plantations, some of which are mature 'estate' planting dating from the 19th and 20th centuries. Many broadleaf and conifer species are present in these uneven aged woods where silviculture for high quality timber production is being successfully combined with wildlife and landscape conservation.

Wormley Wood

(Woodland Trust) F 137.7ha
O.S.S.166 - TQ 330 060
☎0476 74297

From the A1(M) going S take the A414 road to Hertford and turn S towards Bayford before reaching the town, then follow signs to Wormley. There is a car park in the adjacent county council property of Bencroft Wood (the western car park) which via track No.1 gives access to Wormley Wood. There are no facilities and the wood is open at all times of the year. National Tree Week events may take place in this wood during late Nov-Dec. Please telephone the Woodland Trust for details in the autumn. Wormley is a magnificent wood with a feeling of wildness and seclusion. The bird life of Wormley is one of its most notable features, with hawfinch, redstart and, if you are lucky, you might spot the green and great and lesser spotted woodpecker. Wormley Wood is almost entirely ancient woodland; both native oaks as well as hornbeam are present. You will see many different plants as you walk through the wood including sweet woodruff, bluebell and honey-suckle.

see map on p13

Allerthorpe Wood
(Forest Enterprise) F 150ha
O.S.S. 105/106 - SE 753 479
☎0751 72771

The Arboretum
(P W J Carver) A 0.5ha
O.S.S.106 - SE893 323
☎0430 422203

The Arboretum is situated in North Cave which is 1 1/2 miles from Junction 38 M62, 15 miles W of Hull. Entrance through oak handgate, east end of churchyard. Park on roadside. The Arboretum is strictly by appointment at any visiting time. A small arboretum planted in 1990. Approximately 80 species in attractive setting adjacent to 12th century parish church. Mown paths meander round the planting which was laid out by David Garnett to replace early 19th century woodland. An encouragement to all who want to see "The glades be grown anew".

The Avenue
(Sir Tatton Sykes Bt) R 14ha
O.S.S. 101 - SE 938 647
☎0377 236221

Take the B1252 just SE of Sledmere village and follow Humberside County Council permissive footpath signs. There is no parking space on highway adjacent to wood. There is no entrance fee and facilities include toilets, cafe, exhibition at Sledmere House (in season only). Open when not closed by Humberside County Council "No Entry" signs - but mostly open throughout year except in shooting season. Dogs on lead only (HCC bye law) This is a permissive footpath only and not a bridleway. The Avenue has mature hardwoods forming S boundary to Sledmere park - landscaped by Capability Brown circa 1780 - with recent replanting following gale damage with aim to restore landscape feature. Forest Condition Monitoring plot (Forest Authority) at eastern end. The outward route is through an avenue of beech circa 1750 and return through Sledmere deer park. This latter requires agility over ladder stiles to deer fence.

KENT

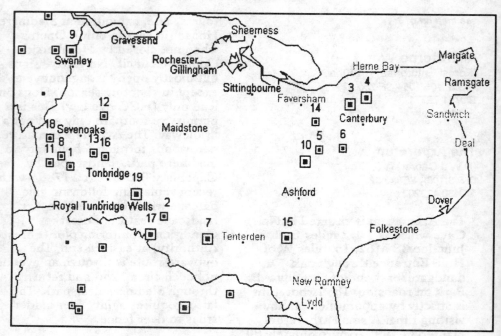

1. *Batfold, Bushy and Kilnhouse Woods
2. Bedgebury Pinetum
3. *Blean Woods Nature Reserve
4. Clowes Wood
5. Cutlers Wood
6. Denge & Pennypot Wood
7. *Hemsted Forest
8. Ide Hill
9. Joydens Wood
10. Kings Wood

11. Octavia Hill Woodlands
12. Oldbury Hill & Styants Wood
13. One Tree Hill
14. Perry Wood
15. Orlestone Forest
16. Scathes Wood
17. Scotney Estate
18. Toys Hill
19. *Tudeley Woods

★ Batfold, Bushy & Kilnhouse Woods: Bore Place
(The Neil Wates Charitable Trust Commonwork) F 30ha
O.S.S. 188 - TQ 490 506
☎0732 463255

Bore Place is SW of Sevenoaks, near Bough Beech reservoir. Take the B2027 which runs between Edenbridge and Tonbridge and follow the signposts to Bore Place. There is a free car park. Field Trail leaflet (30p). The woods are included in the Field Trail (total time needed at a leisurely pace: up to 2 1/2 hours). Bushy Wood has been designated SNCI and with Batfold Wood is partly ancient woodland. Many examples of woodland flora and fauna including orchids, wild service trees, dormice, roe deer. The ancient practice of coppicing has been reintroduced and the woodlands are managed to provide a variety of economic uses as well as to maintain wildlife. Examples of environmental sculpture are also visible. The Field Trail also includes other copses and some interesting woodland ponds. Educational visits to Bushy Wood only can be arranged.

Bedgebury Pinetum
(Managed by Forest Enterprise) F 60ha
O.S.S. 188 - TQ 715 388
☎0580 211044

Take the A21 N from Flimwell and after about a mile turn R on the B2079 to Goudhurst. The Pinetum is an attractive place to visit at all times of year. In spring there are rhododen- drons and azaleas in bloom and in September and October there are varied autumn colours. National collection of coniferous trees. There is a great variety of fungi (protected) which are particularly abundant in autumn and uncommon birds such as hawfinch and crossbill are regular visitors.

★ Blean Woods Nature Reserve
(RSPB) F 310ha
O.S.S. 179 - TR 122 594
☎0227 462491

Take A290 Whitstable Road out of Canterbury, turn L after 1 1/2 miles into Rough Common, R after 500 yards, following stone track for 500 yards to car park where information leaflets are on sale. The car park is open from 7 am to one hour after sunset, but the reserve open to walkers at all times. There is no entrance fee. If you must bring a dog, please keep it on a lead. 63 hectares of the reserve are leased from three local authorities. There are three waymarked trails - 1 1/2; 1 3/4 and 2 1/2 miles. The reserve is one of the largest semi-natural, broad-leaved woodland reserves in southern England, with extensive mature oakwood, plus managed coppice, rides, glades and heath.. The wide range of breeding birds includes nightingale (about 30 pairs), redstart, wood warbler, tree pipit, kingfisher, and nightjar. One of the few remaining sites for the endangered heath fritillary

butterfly. Management includes
conversion of some of the sweet
chestnut coppice (poor in wildlife)
to mixed coppice or high forest;
and limited felling of mature oaks
to break up the uniform age
structure. Production of quality
timber is not a priority objective,
but timber and coppice are
harvested regularly in order to
improve the reserve for wildlife.
Reserve warden would be happy to
show groups the extent to which
these two aims are seen as being
compatible at Blean Woods.

Clowes Wood

(Forest Enterprise) F 236ha
O.S.S. 179 - TR 137 629
☎0580-211044

From the A2 roundabout in
Chestfield take the minor road
through Radfall towards Tyler Hill.
The car park can be found on the R
50 yards after a sharp L hand
bend.

★ Cutlers Wood

(TW Reed) A 56ha
O.S.S. 179/189 - TR 043 523
☎0227-730330

8 miles SW of Canterbury on
A252, 2.5 miles from junction with
A28. The first visit per family or
group, with conducted tour, will be
charged at £25, with 4 free visits
within one year.Visits can be
arranged at any time after sunrise
until one hour before sunset all
year round. These times can be

extended for badger watching. No
dogs are allowed. An ancient mixed
woodland and undulating
topography, with some planting but
also long periods of neglect, have
produced a wide range of trees,
shrubs and ground flora. The
mammals, which include dormice
and badgers, are equally diverse. A
"no burning" policy to increase the
humus content of the soil has
increased fungal and insect
diversity. These in turn have
encouraged insectivorous birds.
Prime timber and care for the
environment are the present
objectives

Denge and Pennypot Wood

(Woodland Trust) F 49.8ha
O.S.S. 179/189 - TR 105 525
☎0476-74297

Turn off the A28 Ashford to
Canterbury road to Shalmsford
Street and Chartham. Follow the
road through the village and take
the right hand turning towards
Thruxted. After 3/4 mile turn left
into Pennypot Lane towards
Thruxted. Pennypot Wood is on the
L of this lane after about 1 mile.
National Tree Week events may
take place in this wood during late
Nov-Dec. Please phone for details.
The structure of Denge Wood is
varied, with a large area of sweet
chestnut coppice. In other parts of
the wood you will find a mixture of
hazel and hornbeam coppice along
with some fine yew and beech
trees. Due to the mixture of
habitats the wildflowers of Denge
Wood, including bluebell, are a

picture in spring and summer. The Warren, which is an area of shrubby grassland in the east of the wood, is one of the few places in Kent which supports a colony of Duke of Burgundy Fritillary butterflies. Also around the area of the Warren you may hear the beautiful song of the nightingale.

★ Hemsted Forest
(Forest Enterprise) F 404ha
O.S.S. 188 - TQ 813 344
☎0580 211044

From the cross roads at the W end of Benenden village turn N towards Sissinghurst. Take the next R turn opposite the entrance to Benenden School. The entrance to the car park is on the left after about 500 yards.

Ide Hill
(National Trust) R 13ha
O.S.S. 188 - TQ 485 515
☎0892 896651

1 mile E of Toys Hill and 2 1/2 miles S of Brasted. Wooded hillside overlooking the Weald.

Joydens Wood
(Woodland Trust) F 137.50ha
O.S.S. 177 - TQ 507 715
☎0476 74297

Travelling N on the M25, leave at junction 3 and go through Swanley on the B2173. Turn into Birch-wood Road on the NW side of

Swanley. Then turn L into Summerhouse Drive. Park in Summerhouse Drive, with due regard to local residents. There is no fee for entrance to the wood and there are no facilities. The wood is accessible to pushchairs. National Tree Week events may take place in this wood during late Nov-Dec. Please phone the Woodland Trust for details in the autumn. Joydens Wood contains a number of interesting archaeological features; perhaps the most significant is Faesten Dic (Dyke), which is referred to in a Saxon boundary survey of AD814. The ground is rich in flowers, over 300 species have been counted, and honeysuckle and wild clematis are found among the trees. Many native trees have survived and these support a varied population of woodland birds. Redpoll, jay and bullfinch are present in large numbers and turtle doves are summer visitors to the wood.

Kings Wood
(Forest Enterprise) F 514ha
O.S.S. 189 - TR 025 500
☎0580 211044

From the junction of the A251 and A252 in Challock village take the A251 towards Ashford. Take the next L (1/2 mile). The car park can be found on the L some 400 yards distant. The wood is permanently open and entrance is free. There are waymarked walks.

Octavia Hill Woodlands: Toys Hill
(National Trust) R 41.8ha
O.S.S. 188 - TQ 465 512
☎0982 890651

Oldbury Hill and Styants Wood: Wrotham
(National Trust) F 61.5ha
O.S.S. 188 - TQ 582 561
☎0892 890651

Car Park.

One Tree Hill: Sevenoaks
(National Trust) R 13.8ha
O.S.S. 188 - TQ 560 532
☎0892 890651

Car Park.

Perry Wood
(Smale Borough Council) F 59ha
O.S.S. 179 - TQ 045 558
☎0795 424341

From the A2 passing Faversham, turn towards Selling at the Macknade Garden Centre. Follow the road past the *Sondes Arms*. Take the 3rd L turn. Perry Wood is signposted. There is a free car park for 40 cars. The wood is open 24 hours a day all the year. Perry Wood provides only for informal recreation - walking and horseriding. No other activities are permitted. Perry Wood consists of several blocks of varied trees separated by bridle and footpaths. The largest blocks are sweet chestnut coppice stands felled on a 15 year cycle. Other areas include plantations of Scots pine, European larch and mixed native hardwoods.

Due to the 1987 storm large areas of very young native trees now exist, particularly on the higher ground. The wood provides some very attractive walks detailed on the car park information board. There is also an excellent viewpoint looking over the canopy of the wood to the adjoining hop fields and orchards.

Orlestone Forest
(Forest Enterprise) F 451ha
O.S.S. 189 - TQ 986 348
☎0580 211044

From Ham Street village take the A2070 towards Ashford. At the next crossroads (1 1/2 miles) turn L and then L again. The car park is on the R 50 yards beyond this junction. The wood is permanently open and entrance is free. There is a waymarked walk.

Scathes Wood
(National Trust) F 16ha
O.S.S.188 - TQ 585 535
☎0892 890651

A broadleaved woodland, with disabled access via a circular walk, which was funded by Rotary International, District 112, Kent and East Sussex. Access for the disabled is through a locked gate, the combination for which can be obtained from the ticket hut in the car park. The woodland is abundant in wild flowers and birds.

Scotney Estate

(National Trust) R 316.5ha
O.S.S. 188 - TQ 688 353
☎0892 890651

Woodland surrounding Scotney Castle Garden, a famous landscape garden (admission fee for entrance to garden). Many defined public footpaths.

Toys Hill

(National Trust) F 81ha
O.S.S. 188 - TQ 465 517
☎0892 890651

Much of this woodland is recognised as Grade 1 site of national importance for nature conservation. Free car park with information board. Many marked footpaths including a disabled route.

★ Tudeley Woods

(RSPB under management agreement with the Trustees of the Goldsmid Estate) F 708ha
O.S.S. 188 - TQ 616 433
✉Crown House, Petteridge Lane, Mayfield, Tonbridge, Kent TN12 7LT

Lying beside the A21 Tonbridge to Hastings road and entered off the minor road to Capel, 2 miles S of Tonbridge. There is a car park but no other facilities. Entrance is free and the wood is open at all times. No dogs are allowed on the Reserve. Please keep to way-marked trails. Deciduous woodland on Tunbridge Wells sand and Wealden clay comprising mature

oaks with sweet chestnut and mixed coppice; also some grazing pasture. Green, greater-spotted and lesser-spotted woodpeckers are common and nuthatches are abundant. Blackcap, garden warbler, willow warbler and whitethroat inhabit the coppice. Tree pipit and hawfinch occur annually while hobby, nightjar, crossbill, siskin and long eared owl may breed occasionally. In springtime carpets of bluebell and primrose can be impressive. Seven species of orchid including greater butterfly, bird's nest and violet helleborine are found in the woodland. For educational visits write to the RSPB warden, Martin Allison at the above address.

LANCASHIRE

see map on p14

Gisburn Forest
(Forest Enterprise) F 1200ha
O.S.S.103 - SD 746 551
☎0200 448256

N of the B6478 midway between Slaidburn and Long Preston, the Cocklet Hill car park and picnic area is signposted at the Stephen Moor crossroads. Forest trails, no charges. This, the largest area of woodland in Lancashire, was first planted immediately following the second world war. It has recently undergone extensive clearfelling and is being replanted to cater for the multi-purpose needs of the 21st century. The forest now ably demonstrates the way in which Forest Enterprise manages a second rotation forest, by building in open space and broadleaves and providing opportunities for public access and wildlife conservation.

Longridge Fell
(Tilhill Economic Forestry) F 322ha
O.S.S. 102/103 - SD 663 396/687 406
☎0524 272249

Take the Longridge to Clitheroe "Fell Road" ie NOT the B6243. Two miles E of the New Drop Inn on the L is the main entrance. The other entrance is at Kemple End approximately one mile W of the Hodder Bridge Inn. From the top of the wood there are impressive views out towards the Trough of Bowland to the N and Pendle Hill to the S. Scattered groups of Scots pine and larch up to 200 years old have been retained amongst the commercial conifer crops planted 25 years ago. Both Sika and roe deer are present in the forest.

Lords Lot
(Forest Enterprise) F 71ha
O.S.S. 97 - SD 549 706
☎0229 860373

Witchwood
(Lytham St Annes Civic Society) F 4ha
O.S.S. 102- SD 365 274
☎0253 736397

Train to Lytham, entrance W side of N side of railway bridge, or A584 to Lytham along Beach Road to main car park on the green, S side of road. Turn N 400 yards to railway bridge as above. The wood is permanently open, and there are no facilities and no charges. A pleasant walk is to go one mile through the wood, turn S over the railway and return along the promenade to Lytham with views over estuary and sea. Witchwood is a mixed broadleaf woodland, mainly sycamore, beech, oak, willow, and chestnut. Wildlife includes tree creeper, wren, blue tit, woodpecker and grey squirrel. In the middle of the wood there is a gravestone which states "The Witch 1888". Also a favourite horse of Squire Clifton is buried there, when the Cliftons owned all the land.

LEICESTERSHIRE

see map on p12

Burbage Wood and Sheepy Wood

(Hinckley & Bosworth Borough Council) F
40ha
O.S.S. 140 - SP 445 953
☎0455 633712

One mile from Hinckley on the A47 turn R into a lay-by and then R up Burbage Common road, the Visitor Centre is 100 yards up road. Toilets available. There are footpaths, horse routes, and refreshments at Woodhouse Farm. Group bookings; rates on application; school groups, etc. please get in touch for details of activities , work sheets, etc. Visitor Centre open 6 days in summer, 4 days in winter (ring for details). This is some of the richest coppice woodland in Leicestershire. Known for its spring flowers and birds, this area of ancient woodland is part designated an SSSI in recognition of its conservation value. Although wildlife is the priority for the site, the area is open to the public at all times with a network of paths covering several miles. The woodlands adjoin Burbage Common, 50 hectares of unspoiled meadows. Leaflets available.

Land at Willesley

(Woodland Trust) F 40ha
O.S.S. 128 - SK 335 142
☎0476 74297

Access is from the A42, S of Ashby de la Zouch. Take the turning signed B5006 and follow the signs to Willesley. On approaching Ashby, turn sharp L on the bend after the golf course, continue for 1 mile to the first crossroads. Turn L onto Willesley Wood side and the site is 150 yards on the RH side. There is limited parking. There is full access. National Tree Week events may take place in this wood during late Nov-Dec. Please phone the Woodland Trust for details in the autumn. Over the past two centuries this site in the National Forest has been closely associated with the coal mining industry. It is composed of 4 hectares of broadleaved woodland, a lake fed by Saltersford Brook and a large area of open land. Over the last two years much of the open land has been planted with native trees and shrubs including oak, ash, silver birch and wild cherry, which in time will complement the existing area of woodland. The sparrowhawk, vole and tawny owl are among the more recent inhabitants of this new woodland. The lake also attracts many visitors including the heron, Canada goose and pochard.

Martinshaw Wood

(Woodland Trust) F 99.30ha
O.S.S. 140 - SK 510 073
☎0476 74297

From the N and Leicester take the main A50 road and turn off at Groby, then follow signs towards Ratby. From S, leave the A47 towards Kirby Muxloe and then Desford along the B5380. Turn off R to Ratby and continue through the village in the direction of

Groby. Limited parking space is available in both Groby and Ratby. There is an especially constructed wheelchair trail in parts of Martinshaw Wood. Stout footwear is advisable due to the wood's heavy clay soil. National Tree Week events may take place in this wood during late Nov-Dec. Please phone the above number for details in the autumn. Martinshaw Wood is a haven for wildlife. Despite coniferisation, patches of original woodland survive. Oak and hazel can still be found along with aspen, holly and the unusual eared willow. The Toothills area supports a rich variety of flora, with broadleaved helleborine, primrose and wood sanicle of special interest. Also interesting botanically, is a boggy area near Well Finish Crossroads where bogmoss, which is uncommon in Leicestershire, and two rare willow herbs are found.

★ Red Lodge Wood
(Mr D N Duxbury) A 12 ha
O S S. 141- SK 753 073
☎0533 605533

Take the B6047 to Tilton on the Hill, then Marefield Lane to Red Lodge Lane. There are no facilities. By appointment only. This is an opportunity to see a wood in the making and may well appeal to those who could be tempted to create a wood of their own. First planting took place in 1988 and for the subsequent four years and consists of 12 hectares of broadleaf hardwoods grown on a commercial basis on former arable land in accordance with the requirements of the Forestry Commissions woodland grant scheme.

★ Staunton Harold Estate Woodlands.
(John Blunt) L 110ha
O.S.S. 128 - SK 378 210
☎0332 863337

Meeting point is the courtyard of the Ferrers Centre behind Staunton Harold Hall (Ryder Mission) amd 3 miles from Melbourne, Derbyshire on B587. There is ample parking, a large craft centre with tearooms, toilets (facilities for the disabled). Charages are Adults £2 ; children £1. The woods are open on 8 May, 12 Jun, 10 Jul, 14 Aug, 11 Sept at 11 o'clock. Arrangements can be made for parties at other times. Visitors will go by car to the woods which are within 1 1/2 miles of meeting point. These mixed woodlands, the largest private ownership within the new National Forest, are managed for timber production with conservation as a natural concomitant. Species include oak, ash, sycamore, larch and Scots pine. Much of the conifer is in mid-rotation but overall there is a constant programme from planting, brashing and thinning through to final felling. The estate is unusual in that it processes much of its produce through to end user and interested parties can inspect the saw mill, drying sheds and sales outlets; even some of the furniture made from home-grown hardwoods.

LINCOLNSHIRE

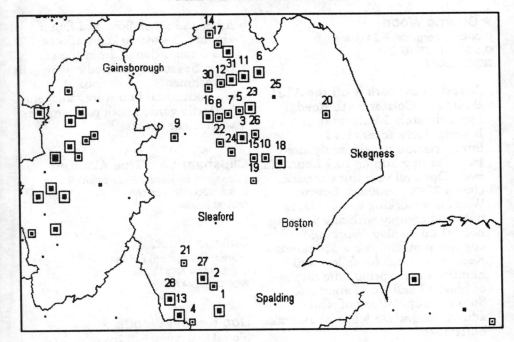

Gainsborough

Skegness

Sleaford

Boston

Spalding

1. *Bourne Wood
2. Callans Lane Wood
3. *Chambers Farm Wood
4. Clipsham Yew Tree Avenue
5. College Wood
6. Dog Kennel Woods
7. Great West Wood
8. Hardy Gang Wood
9. Hartsholme Country Park
10. Kirkby Moor
11. Legsby Woods
12. Linwood
13. Morkery
14. Nettleton Woods
15. New Park Wood
16. Newball Wood
17. Osgodby Wood
18. Ostlers Plantation
19. The Pinewoods
20. Rigsby
21. Ropsley Rise Wood
22. Scotgrove Wood
23. Sotby Wood

24. Southrey Wood
25. *Stenigot Woods
26. Stixwould & Horsington
27. Temple Wood
28. Twyford
29. Wallesby Woods
30. Wickenby Wood
31. WillinghamWoods

★ Bourne Wood
(Forest Enterprise) F 217ha
O.S.S. 130 - TF079 204
☎0780 83394

Access to car park is off the A151 Bourne to Colsterworth Road, approximately 1 mile west of Bourne. Easy access trail, interpretation panels, sculpture trail. Parking 30p up to 2 hours, £1 over. Open all year but car park closed 2200 -0800hrs. Bourne Wood is a working wood: please note and comply with any warning notices on display. Working coppice plot, Bourne wood ponds. Keep an eye out for fallow and muntjac deer. Spring time displays of bluebell and wood anemone. Summer populations of white admiral and white letter hairstreak butterflies.

Callans Lane Wood
(Forest Enterprise) F 59ha
O.S.S. 130 - TF 061 271
☎0780 83394

★ Chambers Farm Wood
(Forest Enterprise) F 350ha
O.S.S. 121 - TF 148 739
☎0623 822447

Clearly signposted from Wragby, Chambers is located 3 miles south, just off the B1202 Bardney road. Seasonal refreshments and information, 3 waymarked walks. This is the largest, most varied and important habitat in the area with extensive areas of semi-natural woodland interspersed with broadleaved and conifer plantations on old farmland. Butterflies, fungi and other flora and fauna abound. 3 waymarked walks of 1, 2 and 3 miles depart from the car park. Seasonally staffed centre sells refreshments and various environmental literature, adjacent butterfly garden with path enables wheelchair access.

Clipsham Yew Tree Avenue
(Managed by Forest Enterprise) R 1ha
O.S.S. 130 - SK 981 169
☎0780 83394

College Wood
(Forest Enterprise) F 64ha
O.S.S. 121 - TF 119 754
☎0623 822447

Dog Kennel Woods
(Forest Enterprise) F 162ha
O.S.S. 113 - TF 144 885
☎0623 822447

Great West Wood
(Forest Enterprise) F 70ha
O.S.S. 121 - TF114 764
☎0623 822447

Hardy Gang Wood
(Forest Enterprise) F 36ha
O.S.S. 121 - TF 095 753
☎0623 822447

Hartsholme Country Park
(Lincoln City Council) F 40ha
O.S.S. 121 - SK 945 698
0522 686264

Signposted from A46 Lincoln bypass, 2 miles SW from centre of

Lincoln. Free access all year round. Facilities include visitor centre, toilets, cafe, camp site (for which there are charges), ranger service. Mixed woodland areas, remnants of formal landscaping scheme planted in 1860s. Good specimens of sweet chestnut, cedar of Lebanon, redwood, Wellingtonia and swamp cypress. Fine areas of oak/birch woodland. Demonstration coppice areas. Variety of birds, plants and fungi. Guided walks for parties, including schools, by arrangement. Good footpath network.

Kirkby Moor
(Forest Enterprise) F 33ha
O.S.S. 122 - TF 213 639
☎0623 822447

Legsby Woods
(Forestry Enterprise) F 120ha
O.S.S. 113 - TF 141 873
☎0623 822447

Linwood
(Forest Enterprise) F 41ha
O.S.S. 112 - TF 088 002
☎0623 822447

Morkery
(Forest Enterprise) F 157ha
O.S.S. 130 - SK 955 193
☎0780 83394

Nettleton Woods
(Forest Enterprise) F 79ha
O.S.S. 112 - TF 088 995
☎0623 822447

New Park Wood
(Forest Enterprise) F 33ha
O.S.S. 122 - TF 213 639
☎0623 822447

Newball Wood
(Forest Enterprise) F 103ha
O.S.S. 121 - TF 083 758
☎0623 822447

Osgodby Wood
(Forest Enterprise) F 69ha
O.S.S. 112 - TF 094 926
☎0623 822447

Ostlers Plantation
(Forest Enterprise) F 101ha
O.S.S. 122 - TF 215 629
☎0623 822447

The Pinewoods
(Woodland Trust) F 7.8ha
O.S.S. 122 - TF 193 633
☎0476 74297

From Lincoln, to the NW, it is just a 20 minute drive along B1188 and the B1191, which runs through Woodhall Spa to Horncastle. From Sleaford, take the A153 towards Horncastle and turn L in Tattershall on to the B1192 to Woodhall Spa. There are no facilities, no charges and the wood is open all year. National Tree Week events may take place in this wood during late Nov-Dec. Please phone the Woodland Trust for details in the autumn. The Pinewoods were once an almost pure pine plantation; now they have a much greater variety of species. Many native trees grow in the wood, especially birch, oak, ash and willow in the wetter spots, with rows of elegant limes along the wood's borders. Bracken and bramble are common in the wood and these also attract many birds and animals. Gatekeeper butterflies, in particular, seek out the nectar from the bramble flowers. There is a wealth of fungi in the pinewoods, with numerous interesting species such as sulphur tuft and shaggy inkcap.

Rigsby
(Lincolnshire Trust for Nature Conservation) F 15ha
O.S.S. 122 - TF 421 762
☎0507 526667

The wood lies at the foot of the Wolds some 1 3/4 miles W of Alford. Turn N towards South Thoresby at the crossroads on the A1104 road halfway between Ulceby Cross and Alford. Entrance 1 1/4 miles along road on R. There is no charge but a donation by post to the Trust would be appreciated. There are no facilities. There are waymarked footpaths which we would ask visitors to keep to. Please keep dogs on leads. The wood is open only in daylight hours. Rigsby is an ancient wood, managed by a traditional coppice system. It is mainly oak, ash and hazel with bluebells, wood anemone, etc. Birds include blackcap, tawny owl, and in winter redpoll and woodcock.

Ropsley Rise Wood
(Managed Forest Enterprise) R 0.8ha
O.S.S. 130 - SK 972 337
☎0780 833394

Scotgrove Wood
(Forest Enterprise) F 45ha
O.S.S. 121 - TF 126 703
☎0623 822447

Sotby Wood
(Forest Enterprise) F 115ha
O.S.S. 122 - TF 185 782
☎0623 822447

Southrey Wood
(Forest Enterprise) F 83ha
O.S.S. 121 - TF 133 686

★ Stenigot Woods
(Peter Dennis) AC 10ha
O.S.S. 122- TF 258 811
☎0507 343225

Meet at Moses Farm Yard, Stenigot - one mile S of Donington-on-Bain which is 7 miles SW of Louth. There is car parking for 10 cars or 2 coaches. Pub lunches can be had in nearby villages of Donington-on-Bain and Goulceby. There are no charges but donations would be welcomed and shared by the Forestry Trust and St Nicholas Church, Stenigot. Visits by groups of four or more, and by schools and societies, are welcome between 1 Apr and 1 Jul, and are by appointment only. Dogs on leads please. Write for bookings 3 weeks in advance to: The Manager, Estate Office, Stenigot, Nr Louth, Lincs,

LN11 92SL, or telephone the
above number. Three woods total
approximately 25 acres, consisting
of mixed hard and soft woods with
oak as the final crop. They were
planted between 1958 and 1978 to
provide timber for estate use and
for sale. Sport and all forms of
wildlife are given consideration and
encouragement. Tree species are
labelled and visitors will be guided
whenever possible.

Stixwould and Horsington
(Forest Enterprise) F 95ha
O.S.S. 122 - TF 186 665
☎0623 822447

Temple Wood
(Forest Enterprise) F 242ha
O.S.S. 130 - TF0 058 299
☎0780 83394

Twyford
(Managed by Forest Enterprise) R 195ha
O.S.S. 130 - SK 946 238
☎0780 83394

Wallesby Woods
(Forest Enterprise) F 237ha
O.S.S. 113 - TF 117 906
☎0623 822417

Wickenby Wood
(Forest Enterprise) F 46ha
O.S.S. 121 - TF 084 828
☎0623 822417

Willingham Woods
(Forest Enterprise) F 293ha
O.S.S. 121 - TF 138 884
☎0623 822417

MERSEYSIDE

see map on p14

Acornfield Plantation
(Knowsley Metropolitan Borough) F 10ha
O.S.S 108 - SJ 437 976
☎051 443 3682

At SE end of Knowsley Industrial Estate (N). From East Lancs Road (A580) turn N along Coopers Lane, R into Molly's Lane, L into Penneter Road and L into Spinney Road where there is a small car park on your R. A leaflet available from Ranger Service and programme of events. There is no charge for access and the wood is open at all reasonable times. Acornfield is one of the few original Kirkby woods remaining, and has been restored since 1983 when the closure of a chemical works removed a chronic pollution problem. A remarkable transformation now sees seventy species of birds and all the common small mammals. At the centre of the site is a sphagnum bog hidden by rhododendron. A pond is much used by local schools and anglers. Part the Mersey Forest.

Formby
(National Trust) F 209ha
O.S. S. 108 - SD 275 082
☎0704 878591

15 miles N of Liverpool, 2 miles W of Formby, 2 miles off the A565. 209 hectares of dune, foreshore and pinewood between the sea and the town of Formby. The woodlands are dominated by large areas of Corsican and Scots pine with some areas of maritime and lodgepole pine. Red squirrels can frequently be seen in the pine trees and the shoreline attracts waders such as oystercatchers and sanderlings. Wheelchair access along hard surface paths to the red squirrel reserve and Cornerstone Walk.

Halewood Triangle Country Park
(Knowsley Metropolitan Borough) F 28ha
O.S.S. 108 - SJ 442 859
☎051 443 2277

Very easy to reach from Halewood station which has a half-hourly service on the Liverpool-Warrington line. Walk from station. 1/2 mile along cycle way to visitor centre. From M57/62 junction follow signs to Halewood village, past church, L into Okell Drive. Car park 1/2 mile on L. There is no charge for access and the park is open at all reasonable times. A leaflet and events programme is available. A visitor centre is under construction. Once a busy railway junction and sidings, the Triangle has returned to nature with oak and birch woodland covering about half of the park. Newts and dragonflies can be found in ponds. Wildflowers including orchids, centuary and ox-eye daisy provide an attractive summer spectacle. The Trans-Pennine trail passes through the park which also caters for BMX/Mountain biking, fishing and orienteering. Part of the Mersey Community Forest.

Littlewood Community Wood
(Knowsley Metropolitan Borough) F 8ha
O.S.S 108 - SJ 428 943
☎051 443 3682

M57 Junction 2, N along Knowsley Lane, L into Stockbridge Lane, across roundabout to Waterpark Drive, across two further roundabouts and turn L into Hollow Croft. Path adjacent to wood, or in Ninetrees School (need to ask permission). There is a leaflet and occasional events. There is no charge for access, and the wood is open at all reasonable times. Evening/night visits are not advised. Special care is needed to secure your car and belongings to avoid damage or theft. One of the best woods is Knowsley, with oaks and sweet chestnuts, planted by Napoleonic prisoners of war in the early 1800s. There are several ditches, streams and ponds together with a rich woodland flora. A coach road links the wood to Croxteth Country Park with numerous attractions. The wood has been restored by the local community in partnership with the council to form part of the Mersey Community Forest.

NORFOLK

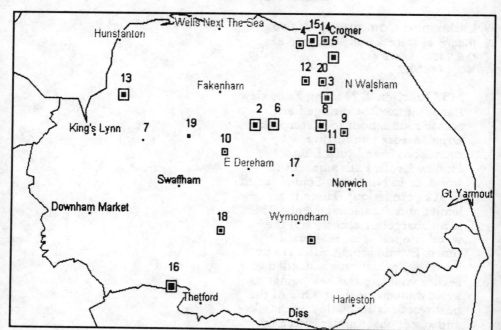

1 Ashwellthorpe Wood
2 Bintree
3 Bickling Woods
4 Bodham
5 Felbrigg Great Wood
6 Foxley Wood
7 Gayton Thorpe Wood
8 Haveringland
9 Hevingham Park
10 Honeypot Wood

11 Horsford Wood
12 Mannington Wood
13 *Sandringham Country Park
14 Sheringham Old Wood
15 Sheringham Park
16 *Thetford Forest Park
17 *Warren
18 Wayland Wood
19 *Weasingham Azalea Wood
20 Wolterton

Ashwellthorpe Wood
(Norfolk Naturalists Trust) **F** 37ha
O.S.S. 144 - TM 140 980
☎0603 625540

From A11 in Wymondham. take B1135 to Ashwellthorpe Village, entrance to wood just before entering village, opposite road to Tacolneston. There is a car park with visitor interpretation. A leaflet is available from Norfolk Naturalists Trust on above telephone number. There is free access on all days, 10 am to 5 pm. No dogs allowed, except guide dogs. Alder, ash, oak, hazel and hornbeam coppice, with field maple, holly, elm, hawthorn and blackthorn. Guelder rose and spindle with their attractive winter berries and dogwood are also present. Ramsons, bluebells, dog's mercury, wood spurge, and early purple orchids in spring, followed by hairy st john's wort and herb paris. Butterflies abundant including white admiral.

Bintree
(Forest Enterprise) **F** 122ha
O.S.S. 133 - TG 004 227
☎0842 810271

Blickling Woods
(National Trust) **F** 245ha
O.S.S. 133 - TG 176 286
☎0263 733471

Aylsham 1 1/2 miles. Free access. Four free car parks. Main car park at Blickling Hall.

Bodham
(Forest Enterprise) **F** 39ha
O.S.S. 133 - TG107 400
☎0842 810271

Felbrigg Great Wood
(National Trust) **F** 165ha
O.S.S. 133 - TG 190 400
☎0263 734924

The estate is 1 1/2 miles due S of Cromer on the B1436. There are 3 car parks and a picnic area. The main car park in front of the house has an information board. Paths are extensive with some way-marked. There are WCs, leaflets, shop and tearooms available every weekend all year round and on advertised open days Apr-Oct. Most of this wood is SSSI and adjoins an historic Park which also has SSSI status. The woods are approximately 70% hardwood. The conifer areas were planted after World War 2. There is a Bronze Age burial mound in the woods and an 18th century ice house. The woods are particularly noted for the large number of lichens and fungi (160 species) and the ancient beech pollards.

Foxley Wood
(Norfolk Naturalists Trust) **F** 120ha
O.S.S 133 - TG 049 229
☎0362 88I706

From Norwich take the A1067, Fakenham Road. Foxley Wood is situated about 1/2 mile beyond

Foxley village. From A1067 follow brown tourist signs. Access is free Fri to Wed, 10 am to 5pm (closed Thurs) - open all year. No dogs allowed, except guide dogs. There is a car park and on-site interpretative information. Traditionally coppice with oak standards so there is a large diversity of ground flora - herb paris, bluebells, primroses and violets. Ride flora includes bog stitchwort, bugle, water avens, and tufted hair grass. Coppice was largely hazel although small-leaved lime, midland hawthorn and wild service tree are also present.

Gayton Thorpe Wood
(Julian Marsham) A 3.8ha
O.S.S.. 132 - TF 736 188
☎0553 636 292

Take B1153 N from A47. 50 m N of crossroads signpost Gayton Thorpe to R turn into field entrance on L 200 m on R. There are no charges and no facilities. The wood is open by appointment - please telephone estate office on the above number. Main wood mature ash, over hazel coppice, brought into production over last 10 years. Ponds and ornamental planting. Small hardwood stand planted in 1986. Primrose carpet in spring. Interesting dish excavations.

Haveringland
(Forest Enterprise) F 113ha
O.S.S. 133 - TG 162 226
☎0842 810271

Hevingham Park
(Forest Enterprise) F 92ha
O.S.S. 133 - TG 196 210
☎0842 810271

Honeypot Wood
(Norfolk Naturalists Trust) F 9.5ha
O.S.S. 132 - TF 934 143
☎0603 6255540

From A47, through Wendling Village, head towards Hall Green. There is a car park inside gate - concrete rides suitable for disabled visitors. There are no charges and the wood is open every day from 10am to 5pm. No dogs allowed, except guide dogs. Coppicing has allowed a wide diversity of ground flora to develop - wood anemone, twayblade, bluebells, herb Paris and marsh helleborine. Also supports an abundance of fungi including candle-snuff fungus, coral spot fungus and jew's ear.

Horsford Heath
(Forest Enterprise) F 82ha
O.S.S. 133 - TG 185 175
☎0842 810271

Mannington Woods
(Lord Walpole) RE 80ha
O.S.S. 133 - TG 142 321
☎0263 87 4175

1 1/2 miles from Saxthorpe. (Brown signs from Saxthorpe).

B1149 Norwich - Holt Road and B1354 Fakenham - Aylsham Road. The woods are open all year round 9am to 5pm or dusk if earlier. There is a car park (£1), WCs, including disabled. Information Centre/Board, waymarked walks and trails - leaflet available. Boardwalk for wheelchairs. Guided visits for schools and societies are arranged. Education materials to illustrate all aspects of wild life will be provided for which a charge will be made. Preliminary visit recommended. Always consult notice board at Information Centre to see if any restrictions apply. Dogs must be on leads at all times except in the car park. Walks take you round a series of woods with their own individual characters on gently undulating ground to the N of the upper reaches of the River Bure and along one of its tributaries. At least three are ancient woodlands, most woods had been established by 1742. The woods have recently obtained a Forestry Award of Excellence for access, wildlife habitats and environmentally friendly timber production.

the country park. However, if you follow this road for approximately three quarters of a mile you will find car parks, a cafeteria, shops and toilets on your left. Tractor and trailer tours. Parking for 500 cars and 60 coaches. Facilities open Easter Sunday until begining of October. Picnic areas, nature trails, andventure playground open all year. There are also two caravan sites. Management of the park started in 1862 when the Estate was purchased by Prince Albert for Edward Prince of Wales. Prior to this it was an area of open heathland with few trees. The woods are managed commercially to produce timber, as well as for public recreation and conservation. They contain a wide variety of conifer and broadleaf trees which provide a habitat for many acid loving plants and fungi. The woods are also home to many birds, small mammals and a few deer. A natural history guide and other books are available from the Rangers Room.

★ Sandringham Country Park
(Her Majesty the Queen) F 270ha
O.S.S. 132- TF 690 290
☎0553 772675

From the Knights Hill roundabout on the eastern side of Kings Lynn, take the A149 to Dersingham and Hunstanton. Take the fifth turning on the right signposted Sandringham Country Park: you are now in

Sheringham Old Wood
(Forest Enterprise) F 23ha
O.S.S. 133 - TG 158 410
☎0842 810271

Sheringham Park
(National Trust) F 126ha
O.S.S. 133 - TG 139 412
☎0263 823778

Sheringham 2 miles. The woods were laid out by Humphrey Repton. There is free access. A car park is provided and the charge is £2.30 per car. Further information from the above telephone number.

★ Thetford Forest Park

(Forest Enterprise) FE 20,000ha
O.S.S.144 - TL 811 852
☎0842 810271

High Lodge Visitor Centre, off B1107 between Brandon and Thetford, up Forest Drive to the south (about 1 mile).Visitor centre and shop, toilets and cafeteria, open play area, childrens play furniture, squirrel maze, cycle hire, wildlife hide, disabled walk and facilities. Parking: £1.50 cars, £3 coaches (£15 over 2 hours). Open Easter weekend until first week in October. Special Christmas opening with seasonal programme of events. Numerous other facilities throughout the forest, including picnic sites, walks, cycle trails, arboretum, caravan site, youth canpsites, horse trails (permit). 25 events held each year from fun to conservation to wildlife safaris. School visits catered for, teachers packs provided.

★ Warren

(R W Meynell) A 7ha
O.S.S. 130 - TG 095 115
☎0603 880215

10 miles W of Norwich - directions given when making appointment to visit. There are no charges, and no facilities. Visitors will be taken round the wood by the owner - appointments can be made at any time except during March,

September and December. Uneven aged mixed woodland managed for the production of high quality timber, wildlife and aesthetic aspects, demonstrating that these objectives are complementary.

Wayland Wood

(Norfolk Naturalists Trust) F 34ha
O.S.S. 144 - TL 924 995
☎0603 625540

Between Watton and Thetford on the A1075. There is a car park but no other facilities. Access is free and the wood is open everyday from 10 am to 5pm. No dogs allowed (except guide dogs). Said to be the setting for the Babes in the Wood tale, Wayland is still managed on a rotational basis, as coppice with standards. Bird cherry, field maple and hazel are all cut allowing large diversity of ground flora. In spring, swathes of bluebells and
dog's mercury carpet the floor along with wood anemone, yellow star of Bethlehem growing here in its only Norfolk locality. Coppicing also benefits birds, including woodcock and the exotic golden pheasants which breed on the woodland floor.

★ Weasenham Azalea Wood

(Major R L Coke) L 22.2ha
O.S.S. 132 - TF 847 199
☎0328 74288

Midway between Swaffham and Fakenham on the A1065. Free car

parking on side of minor public road. No other facilities. Entrance charges Adults £2, Children under 12 years 50p. Open from 2pm to 5pm on 29 May, 30 May, 5 Jun for general public. Parties at other times by arrangement. Dogs allowed only if kept on leads. People expected to keep to paths. Flowers not to be picked. No smoking inside wood. A wood situated on old heathland and managed since 1907 on an uneven aged system with no clear felling with the combined objectives of high quality timber production, amenity and conservation. It is mainly mixed conifers with some hardwoods. The tallest trees up to 140 feet. It also contains flowering shrubs e.g. rhododendrons (not ponticum), azaleas, magnolias etc. and also specimens of some of the rarer trees.

a Forestry Award of Excellence for access, wildlife habitats and environmentally friendly timber production.

Wolterton

(Lord Walpole) RE 60ha
O.S.133 - TG 163 320
☎0263 874175

A140 Norwich to Cromer Road. 2 miles N of Aylsham turn L for Erpingham. Follow brown signs. There is a car park (£2), WCs, Information Centre. Always consult notice board at Information Centre to see if any restrictions apply. Dogs must be on leads at all times except in car park. Open all year round, 9 am to 5pm, or dusk if earlier. 18th and 19th century parkland, woods varying from near arboretum type stands to aldercarr. The woods have recently obtained

NORTHAMPTONSHIRE

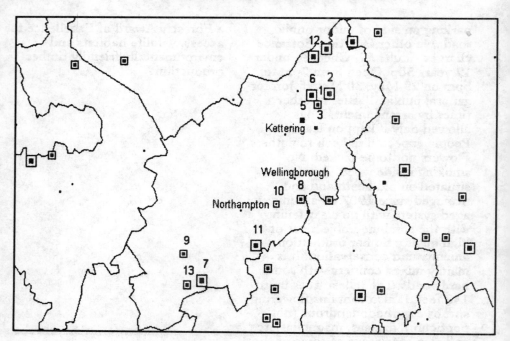

1 Brigstock
2 Cherry Lap/Mounterley
3 Drayton Estate Woodlands
4 *Fineshade Wood
5 * Grafton Park
6 Harry's Park
7 Hazelborough
8 *Irchester Country Park
9 Plumpton
10 Rotary Wildlife Corridor
11 *Salcey Forest
12 Wakerley Great Wood
13 Whistley Wood

Brigstock
(Forest Enterprise) F 35ha
O.S.S. *141 - SP 953 850*
☎0780 83394

Cherry Lap/Mounterley
(Forest Enterprise) F 124ha
O.S.S. *141 - SP 965 859*
☎0780 83394

Drayton Estate Woodlands
(LG Stopford Sackville Esq) L 40ha
O.S.S. *141 - SP 950 794*
☎0832 732405

A14 (M1/A1 Link) to Islip, near Kettering, then proceed to village of Slipton. There is limited parking at the Slipton Grange chip store. Please contact Edwin de Lisle on above number. No dogs. The Biomass trial plots at Slipton, on the Drayton Estate, were established in the mid 1980's for cuttings to fuel the large (1 million BTU) wood boiler in Drayton House. To fuel the boiler, the Estate is restarting the ancient practice of harvesting coppice with standards in some of the semi-natural ancient woodlands. There will be two guided visits to look both at the woods and at the Biomass wood chip store and boiler. The first on 10 March at 1100 hours, organised by the Forestry Authority will study "Grey Squirrel Control", the second at 1400 hours on 19 May will look at "Biomass Fuel - how to grow and harvest it" Both visits are by appointment only.

★ Fineshade Wood
(Forest Enterprise) F 475ha
O.S.S. *141 - SP 978 985*
☎0780 83394

★ Grafton Park
(His Grace the Duke of Buccleuch) A
110ha
O.S.S. *141 - SP 935 814*
☎0536 515731

1 mile N of Grafton Underwood on the Cranford to Brigstock road, on RH side of road. There is car parking for 10 cars. Other facilities include a picnic area and permitted ways on foot through the wood. The wood is open from 1 Jan to 31 Dec, 0830 to 1800 hours or sunset if earlier. All visits by appointment only, in case the wood is being used for forestry or sporting operations. All group visits require 7 days notice, please contact Mr. G Fitzpatrick, The Living Landscape Trust, Boughton House, Geddington, Northants on the above telephone number. A commercially managed woodland, with diverse broadleaved and coniferous tree species, incorporating a previous American Air Force Base dating from World War 2. Typical woodland fauna and flora are in evidence.

Harry's Park
(Forest Enterprise) F 186ha
O.S.S. *141 - SP 948 865*
☎0780 83394

Hazelborough

(Forest Enterprise) F 407ha
O.S.S. 152 - SP 655 428
☎0780 83394

(Forest Enterprise) F 54ha
O.S.S. 152 - SP 605 490
☎0780 83394

★ Irchester Country Park

(Northamptonshire County Council) FE
81ha
O.S.S. 152 - SP 910 660
☎0933 276866

The park is off the B570 Irchester to Lt Irchester Road 1/3 mile from the Junction with A509. Facilities include a visitors centre, railway museum, ranger service, and ample parking. The park is open from 8.30am to 5pm in winter, and 8.30am to 6.00pm in summer. The park facilities are closed on Xmas Day and New Years Day, although out of hours parking is available and the Park itself is open to the public. Irchester country park has been developed on the site of a former ironstone quarry the remains of which can be seen in the hill and dale landscape upon which the trees were planted. The 81 hectares offer plenty of opportunity for quiet strolls and nature watching. The ranger service can assist you when you visit and guide books are available, events through the year include guided walks, talks, school visits and special events. A visitor centre is open Sun afternoons and by appointment and a railway museum is open Sun and Bank Hols. Free entry

Plumpton

Rotary Wildlife Corridor

(The Marquess of Northampton) F 4ha
O.S.S. 152 - SP 849 610
☎0604 696839

From A45 trunk dual carriageway between Northampton and Wellingborough turn southwards opposite Earls Barton, signed to Grendon and Castle Ashby. Proceed southwards for about 1 mile along Station Road. At Cogenhoe to Grendon Road junction turn W towards Cogenhoe to car park about 1 mile opposite to Whiston. There are no facilities other than a free car park. Free access to the central public footpath linked to the Nene Way etc. Walkers are asked to keep all dogs on leads to protect wildlife. A belt of roadside trees over 1 mile long planted Sun, 29 Nov 1992 by Rotary International; Lord Northampton; and some 400 members of the public with support from Northamptonshire County Council, Nene valley project and South Northamptonshire Council. Species: all native to Nene valley, 600 ash, 280 field maple, 250 oak, 175 birch, crab apple, hazel, alder, cherry and 3,000 quickthorn as roadside hedge. Also 40 beech trees as Queens Coronation Stand and many shrubs to encourage wildlife. Succesful growth 1993, main interest to watch these young trees growing.

★ Salcey Forest
(Forest Enterprise) F 500ha
O.S.S. 152 - 795 515
☎0604 696239

Leave M1 at junction 15 and head for Quinton. Salcey Forest is located 2 miles from Quinton on the Hanslope Road. Parking, picnic tables, toilets, childrens play area, disabled walk, orienteering. Educational visits for schools can be arranged. Mixed woodland which takes in an area of oak planted in 1847. Wildlife includes fallow and muntjac deer, great spotted woodpecker, sparrowhawk and nightingales which can be heard singing in early summer. Salcey is also home to 30 species of butterfly including the wood white and rare black hairstreak. The bird tables in the picnic site are visited by over 20 different species over winter months.

Wakerley Great Wood
(Forest Enterprise & Marquis of Exeter) F 361ha
O.S.S. 141 - 962 987
☎0780 83394

From A47/A43 roundabout go south on A43 towards Corby. Wakerley Woods is signposted about 2 miles on right. Toilets (including disabled), picnic sites, barbeques, car park. Over winter there may be restrictions due to shooting activities. Dogs must be kept off the picnic sites. Riding is by permit only. Organized events must be booked in advnace at the main office. An attractive mixed species multipurpose woodland.

The full range of forest operations can usually be seen throughout the year. The woodland is also very rich botanically due to its ancient woodland background. It is well known and used for its public recreation.

Whistley Wood
(Forest Enterprise) F 64ha
O.S.S. 152 - SP 615 415
☎0780 83394

NORTHUMBERLAND

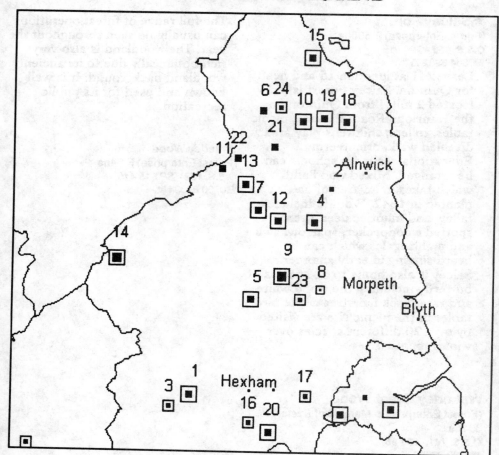

1 Allen Banks/Staward Gorge
2 Birsley Wood
3 Briarwood Banks
4 Cragside
5 Fourlaws
6 Fredden Hills
7 Harbottle
8 Hartburn Glebe Woods
9 *Harwood
10 Hepburn
11 Hepden Burn
12 Holystone
13 Kidland
14 *Kielder
15 *Kyloe
16 Letah Wood
17 Priestclose Wood
18 Quarry House
19 Ros Hill
20 Slaley
21 Threestoneburn
22 Uswayford
23 Wallington, East & West Woods
24 Wooler Common

Allen Banks/Staward Gorge
(National Trust) F 200ha
O.S.S. 87 - NY 799 630
☎0434 344218

Access is from the A69 approaching Bardon Mill. Car parking provision at Allen Banks only. The woodland is open to the public all year round. Facilities include WCs and picnic site at Allen Banks. The woodland covers the valley sides of the River Allen and stretches from Allen Banks picnic site to Cupola Bridge at its southernmost point. The valley sides are very steep and, as a result, provide some breathtaking views, particularly during the autumn. At the southern end of the valley are the remains of Staward Pele. There are several footpaths leading from the Allen Banks car park, along the riverside and across a suspension bridge. There is a tarn to visit, and for the more energetic, footpaths lead from one end of this woodland to the other.

Birsley Wood
(Forest Enterprise) A 36ha
O.S.S. 81 - NU 111 094
☎0669 20569

Briarwood Banks
(Northumberland Wildlife Trust) F 11.7ha
O.S.S. 87 - NY 791 620
☎0912 846884

Turn L off the A69 W of Haydon Bridge towards Ridley Hall, go under the railway bridge, taking the L fork and park at the National Trust car park (30p) at Allen Banks (WCs available). Follow the public footpath beside the River Allen until you come to Briarwood Banks. Alternatively go past the NT car park and continue on minor roads to Plankey Mill, where parking is available. In summer the farmer makes a small charge. Cross the suspension bridge, turn R up the steps and follow the path until the footbridge takes you across Kingswood Burn. Briarwood Banks is reached by the footpath on your L. Access is full and free all year round. Briarwood Banks nature reserve is part of the once extensive area of ancient woodland growing along the Allen river and the Kingswood burn. It is an SSSI and was bought by Northumberland Wildlife Trust in 1988. The most common trees are ash and wych elm, sessile oak and birch. The shrub layer is made up of holly, bird cherry, blackthorn, honeysuckle, guelder rose and a few clumps of old hazel coppice. Spring is the best time to enjoy the wild flowers: wild garlic, sweet woodruff, giant bellflower, wood sorel, wood sanicle and toothwort. Roe deer and red squirrel are both found here. Pied flycatcher and wood warbler, treecreeper, great spotted woodpecker as well as a number of common species.

Cragside
(National Trust) R 350ha
O.S.S.81 - NU 073 022
☎Rothbury 0669

Cragside is situated on the B6341

Rothbury - Alnwick road, just N of Rothbury itself. There are several car parks at the main visitor centre and around the particularly scenic areas of the estate. A restaurant, shop, the Armstrong energy centre and WCs are situated at the visitor centre and there is fishing available. Cragside is open from 1 Apr to end of Oct. There are several footpaths along the Debdon Valley and around the lake shores and through the pinetum where many of the specimen trees are labelled for easy identification. The woodland withing Cragside Estate was planted between 1860 and 1880 by the first Lord Armstrong to transform the bare Northumbrian moorland. There is an arboretum immediately around and below the House, containing many specimen trees.

Fourlaws
(Forest Enterprise) L 352ha
O.S.S. 80 - NY 934 844
☎0669 20569

Fredden Hill
(Forest Enterprise) A 230ha
O.S.S. 75 - NT 955 270
☎0669 20569

Harbottle
(Forest Enterprise) F 599ha
O.S.S. 80 - NT 927 048
☎0669 20569

Hartburn Glebe Woods
(Woodland Trust) F 3ha
O.S.S. 81 - NZ 088 864

☎0476 74297

Hartburn is situated on the B6343 road running from Morpeth to Cambo. Roadside parking adjacent to the wood is possible but please park carefully since traffic can be travelling fast along the lane. There are no facilities and free and full access is available. Some paths are muddy at times and stout footwear is advisable. National Tree Week events may take place in this wood during late Nov-Dec. Please phone the Woodland Trust for details in the autumn. Hartburn Glebe contains a number of features of considerable historic interest, including Roman earthworks and some very unusual 19th century architecture. A very striking plant in this wood is wild garlic, or ramsons. Also numbers of great woodrush and yellow pimpernel can be found. There is a rich variety of wildlife; red squirrel and roe deer are just some of the species you will see. Wildlife in Hartburn Glebe is enhanced by the adjacent stream, where pied and grey wagtails and dippers can be seen. Red-breasted mergansers have also been known to nest here.

★ Harwood
(Forest Enterprise) F 2954ha
O.S.S. 81 - NZ 003 898
☎0669 20569

Hepburn
(Forest Enterprise) F 102ha
O.S.S. 75 - NU 073 248
☎0669 20569

From A697 at Wooperton turn east onto B6346, after about 2 miles turn L for Chatton. After further 2 1/2 miles turn R for Hepburn. Forest walks, picnic site. Woodland walks in thinned semi-mature conifers and some broadleaves. From high ground there are excellent views on a clear day.

Hepden Burn
(Forest Enterprise) L 101ha
O.S.S. 80 - NT 874 139
☎0669 20569

Holystone
(Forest Enterprise) F 209ha
O.S.S. 80/81 - NT 950 024
☎0669 20569

From Rothbury head W towards Otterburn on B6341. Ater 4 miles turn R for Harbottle and Alwinton. Follow through Sharperton over the bridge and turn L for Holystone. The picnic site is signposted in the village. Open all year round. Forest nature reserve, forest walks, picnic place. Holystone Burn, oak woodland and mixed confers.

Kidland
(Forest Enterprise) F 113ha
O.S.S. 80 - NT 917 105
0669 20569

★ Kielder Forest
(Forest Enterprise) FE 60000ha
O.S.S. - NY 633 935
0434 220242

Recommend starting at Kielder Castle Visitor Centre (open Easter - end October and winter weekends), which is in Kielder village, off C200. 17 miles W of Bellingham and 3 miles S of Scottish border. Numerous walks, cycle trails, toilets, car parks, forest drive, raptor viewpoint. Car park £1 at visitor centre, otherwise free. Cyclists are asked to keep to waymarked cycle routes. Kielder is a working forest so please obey all signing. Kielder is Britains largest manmade forest, surrounding Kielder Water. Forest Drive (12 miles) crosses some of Englands most isolated moorlands between Kielder Castle and A68. Numerous easy access waymarked trails plus 3 long distance "strenuous" walks. Wide range of cycle routes for all abilities. Raptor viewpoint at Bakethin provides opportunity to see goshawks and other birds of prey. Exhibitions and forest recreation information in Kielder Castle, which also features a restaurant. Guided walks programme. The Archercleugh area of Kielder Forest recently received a Centre of Excellence Award.

★ Kyloe
(Robin Fleming) A 391ha
O.S.S. 75 - NU 062 392
0295 688100

From Berwick on Tweed take the A1 S for 9 miles. Turn R on to the B 6353 into Fenwick. Turn L at the telephone and drive up the hill for 1000 yards. The entrance to the wood is at the end of the road. Follow signs for the gate to the car park and meeting point. There is parking for 15 cars and 1 coach. All visits should be arranged by appointment by contacting Peter Hale on the above telephone number. The forest was established by C J Leyland of Haggerston Castle in about 1880 as a repository for his collection of exotic species. The wood gives a rare opportunity to view stands of fully mature large conifers. The forest is broken up into valleys by outcrops of rock forming crags. There are red squirrel, roe deer and badgers. Fulmars nest on Kyloe Crag which is about 120 feet tall. Adders are frequently seen.

Letah Wood

(Woodland Trust) F 13.35ha
O.S.S. 87 - NY 940 607
☎0476 74297

Take the B6306 S of Hexham, turn first R after about 300 yards signposted to Slaley and Blanch-land, and first L signposted to Ordley, Dye House and Whitley Chapel. Drive past a small crossroads and down the hill to Newbiggin. Turn R here towards Newbiggin Hill and park on the roadside. There are no facilities. There is free and full access. National Tree Week events may take place in this wood during late Nov-Dec. Please phone the Woodland Trust for details in the autumn. Some of the paths within the woods can be muddy and they take you across the stream in Letah

Wood. Stout shoes or wellingtons are advised. The wild daffodils make this a very special place to visit in early springtime. It is a quiet, sheltered haven for wildlife and is particularly rich in bird life, including pied flycatcher, blackcap and garden warbler. At the crossroads, oak trees dominate. The ground flora changes here both above and below the path, from a carpet of great woodrush, bracken and honeysuckle, to a mixture of flowers which include sweet woodruff, wood sanicle and dog's mercury. North of the burn, on the S facing sunny slopes, the wild daffodils are abundant in April.

Priestclose Wood

(Northumberland Wildlife Trust) F 15.4ha
O.S.S. 88 - NZ 107 627
☎0912 846884

Little of the ancient woodland character remains unchanged at Priestclose. In the 1930s, a large part of it was destroyed by fire, after which more trees were felled to supply a nearby sawmill. Dominant among the trees now is the native oak. Birch and rowan are common. Ash, sycamore, Norway maple and beech also occur and a large black poplar grows close to the pond. Holly and elder are found throughout the wood. Bird cherry is found at the northern edge of the wood. Patches of woodanemone and celandine appear in spring followed by greater and wood stitchwort, wood sorrel and bluebells and in a few places the greater woodrush. Brambles, honeysuckle and bracken provide abundant ground cover together with male fern. A good variety of birds is found in the reserve throughout the year. Roe deer occasionally visit the wood though they are seldom seen, also foxes and badgers. A leaflet is available from the above telephone number.

Quarry House
(Forest Enterprise) F 150ha
O.S.S. 75 - NU 110 247
☎0669 20569

Ros Hill
(Forest Enterprise) F 163ha
O.S.S. 75 - NU 091 254
☎0669 20569

Slaley
(Forest Enterprise) F 511ha
O.S.S. 87 - NY 979 548
☎0669 20569

Threestoneburn
(Forest Enterprise) A 711ha
O.S.S. 75/81 - NT 980 198
☎0669 20569

Uswayford
(Forest Enterprise) L 761ha
O.S.S. 80 - NT 880 143
☎0669 20569

Wallington, East and West Woods
(National Trust) F 14.9ha
O.S.S. 81 - NZ 030 843
☎0670 74283

Wallington is situated 12 miles W of Morpeth (B6343), 6 miles NW of Belsay (A696) - take B 6342 towards Cambo. There are car parking facilities, picnic areas, WCs, mansion, shop, restaurant available during opening times, from 1 Apr to end of Oct. Reduced opening hours for the shop and restaurant from 1 Nov to 19 Dec. Free access to the woodland all year round. Most of the woodland walks are accessible to wheelchair users. Wheelchairs and electric scooter available by prior arrangement with the Administrator. Amenity woodland situated around Wallington mansion and along the banks of River Wansbeck. Planted mainly over 200 years ago the woods are predominantly beech, but considerable felling and replanting has taken place in the last 20 years. There are extensive linked footpaths in both the East and West woods and along the River Wansbeck.

Wooler Common
(Forest Enterprise) F 81ha
O.S.S. 75 - NT 980 277
☎0669 20569

NOTTINGHAMSHIRE

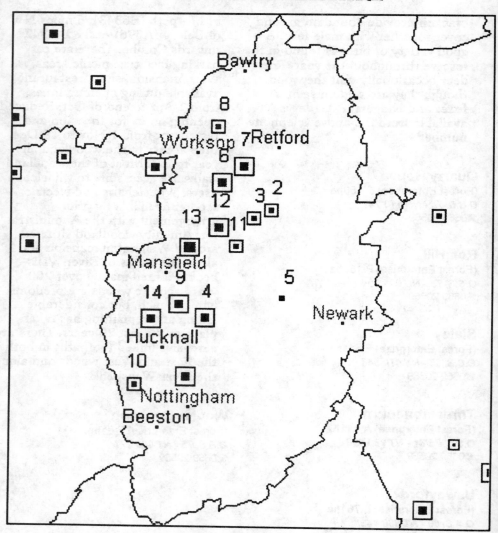

1 Bestwood Country Park
2 Bevercotes Park
3 Boughton Brake
4 Blidworth Woods Complex
5 Chevral Wood
6 Clumber (part)
7 Clumber Park
8 Forest Plantation

9 Harlow Wood
10 Oldmoor Wood
11 Rufford Country Park & Abbey
12 Sherwood Forest Country Park
13 *Sherwood Pines Forest Park
14 Thieves Wood

Bestwood Country Park
(Nottinghamshire County Council
and Gedling Borough Council) F 164ha
O.S.S. 129 - SK 573 463
☎0602 670042

Approximately 5 miles N of
Nottingham, take the A60 out of
the City, L into the B6004, first R
into Queen's Bower Road and first
R again into Bestwood Lodge
Drive. Car park approximately 3/4
mile on the R. The country park is
free for all to enjoy throughout the
year with an adventure playground,
picnic sites and countryside
rangers on hand to advise and
assist visitors. A year round
programme of public events is
organised, all with a natural history
theme. You are welcome to join
any of the public events, or if you
would like to have a special event
organised for you and a group of
friends, please do not hesitate to
contact the above number.

Bevercotes Park
(Managed by Forest Enterprise) F 92ha
O.S.S. 120 - SK 696 705
☎0623 822447

Boughton Brake
(Forest Enterprise) F 47ha
O.S.S. 120 - SK 669 692
☎0623 822447

Blidworth Woods Complex
(Forest Enterprise) F 488ha
O.S.S.120 - SK 592 524
☎0623 822447

Along Longdale Lane situated

between A60 and A614. Car parks,
waymarked trails, bridle trails,
toilets. This complex includes
Sansom and Haywood Oaks as well
as Blidworth. Sansom and
Blidworth comprise mainly of
conifer with areas of broadleaves.
Haywood Oaks contains some
ancient oak trees which are the
remnants of the ancient Sherwood
Forest. A number of waymarked
walks weave through all the woods,
affording interesting views and
providing a pleasant walk.

Chevral Wood
(Mr and Mrs D C Herbert) A 32ha
O.S.S. 120 - SK 715 565
☎0636 812335

Drive to Hockerton, 2 miles N of
Southwell and park in car park of
Spread Eagle public house in
Hockerton (O.S.Ref above) - from
there by convoy. There are no
facilities and the wood is only open
by ringing or writing for an
appointment. Please book two
weeks in advance. Adults £2 and
Children 50p.. Chevral Wood is an
ancient woodland situated 1 mile N
of the Nottinghamshire cathedral
town of Southwell. When Southwell
was granted its Royal Charter in
780 AD Chevral Wood was
described in great detail as forming
the northern boundary of
Southwell. It is a broadleaved wood
being mainly oak and ash. The ash
has been coppiced for hundreds of
years and many of the ash stools
are very old. There are plenty of
other trees such as "midland"
hawthorn, hazel, willow, sycamore

and horse chestnut. There is a duck flight pond and a large release pen for pheasant, 1500 pheasants being released yearly. It is also a source of many edible fungi - morels, chanterelles, blue stalks and parasol mushrooms. It is rich in bird life. 4 miles SE of Worksop, 6 miles SW of Retford. Signposted off A1. Facilities include restaurant, tearoom, shop, toilets.

Clumber (part)
(Managed by Forest Enterprise) F 539ha
O.S.S. 120 - SK 645 773
☎0623 822447

Clumber Park
(National Trust) R 400ha
O.S.S 120 - SK 645 774
☎0909 476653

4 miles SE of Worksop, 6 miles SW of Retford. Signposted off A1. Facilities include restaurant, tearoom, shop, WC.

Forest Plantation: Hodsock Priory Estate
(Sir Andrew Buchanan) F 14.5ha
O.S.S. 120 - SK 616 834
☎0909 591204

1 3/4 miles from Blyth on B6045 to Worksop. Sign by entrance says Hodsock Farms. Wood is adjacent to road and cars can be parked at side of track. There are no facilities and free access is available at all times. This irregularly shaped wood on well drained sandland, has a wide variety of species and ages of timber. There are some very fine beech, chestnut and oak planted about 100 years ago. The present owner is attempting to combine commercial forestry with amenity and insists on having wide rides. He replanted a two hectare block in 1970 and is currently restocking, with a mixture of replanting in tree shelters and natural regeneration.

Harlow Wood
(Managed by Forest Enterprise) F 147ha
O.S.S. 120 - SK 552 567
☎0623 822447

Oldmoor Wood
(Woodland Trust) F 15.37ha
O.S.S. 129 - SK 497 428
☎0476 74297

Leave the M1 at Exit 26 and take the A610 towards Nottingham. After 1 mile turn R onto the B6004, signposted to Stapleford and Bilborough. Continue on the B6004 for approximatel y 2 miles until Strelley is signposted to the R. Park in Strelley village, on the roadside to the S of the church. Full and free access. Stout footwear is advisable on the woods heavy clay soils. National Tree Week events may take place in this wood during late Nov-Dec. Please phone Woodland Trust for details in the autumn. Oldmoor Wood has an attractive combination of high forest and open glades, with dense scrub along the SW boundary. There are many large mature trees in the wood, which can provide roosts for wren, tree-creeper and other small birds. Although ground flora in many parts of the wood is sparse there are abundant bluebells in spring, along with lesser celandine and common hemp-nettle. In more open areas bracken and bramble predominate.

Rufford Country Park and Abbey
(Nottinghamshire County Council Leisure Services) F 69ha
O.S.S.120 - SK 645 647
☎0623 824153

Situated on the A614, 17 miles N of Nottingham and 2 miles S of Ollerton, Rufford Country Park comprises a 25 acre lake, woodland walks and delightful formal gardens, including sculpture and herb gardens. In the heart of the park stands the impressive remains of a 12th century Cistercian abbey with exhibitions on life as a Cistercian monk and Rufford as a country house during the time of the Savile family. The facilities include a craft centre, restaurants, and Nottinghamshire heritage exhibition. The rangers run a programme of special events and activities details of which are available from Rufford Country Park, Ollerton, Notts NG22 9DF or telephone the above number. The country park is open all year from dawn to dusk and admission is free although there may be a charge for some events and there is a car parking charge at weekends and Bank Hols from Apr to Oct. Abbey, craft centre and heritage centre open 10am to 5pm Apr to Oct, 10am to 4pm Nov to Mar..

Sherwood Forest Country Park
(Nottinghamshire County Council Leisure Services) F 182ha
O.S.S. 120 - SK 626 678
☎0623 823202

Situated on the B6034 N of the village of Edwinstowe, between A6075 and A616, 20 miles N of Nottingham. Sherwood is one of the most famous oak woodlands in the world. The name Sherwood means "wood of the Shire" and in the days of the Norman kings, Sherwood was a royal hunting forest covering one fifth of Nottinghamshire. Today you can follow the woodland paths through 450 acres of old Sherwood Forest to the mighty Major oak, reputed to have been Robin Hood's favourite hideout. Situated on the edge of Sherwood Forest Country Park is a visitor centre with a range of facilities, including a Tourist Information Centre, site information and ranger's office, gift shop and colour exhibition and Robin Hood's larder which serves snacks and refreshments. Sherwood is forever linked to the legend of Robin Hood but it is also a rare woodland habitat famed for its wealth of ancient oaks and insect fauna. The importance of this unique environment has been recognised with the area being designated an SSSI. Twice yearly events leaflets, details of which can be obtained from Ranger's Office, Sherwood Forest Visitor Centre, Edwinstone, Mansfield Notts NG21 9HN or telephone the above number. Open all year dawn to dusk. Visitor Centre - 1030am to 5.00pm Apr to Oct: 1030am to 4.30pm Nov to Mar. Free admission, although there may be a charge for some events, and there is a car parking charge at weekends and Bank Hols from Apr to Oct.

★ Sherwood Pines Forest Park
(Forest Enterprise) F 1000ha
O.S.S. 120 - SK 612 646
☎0623 822447

Access from B6030 Mansfield to Ollerton Road east of Old Clipstone. Refreshments, toilets, childrens play equipment, bike hire (weekends); car park £1. Pony trekking is available in the forest. Waymarked walks include picnic areas and wheelchair route. A 6 mile cycle trail includes an off-road mountain biking area. Sherwood Pines Forest Park is the largest forest open to the public in the east Midlands. Its size and variety make it attractive to many forms of wildlife, including fallow deer.

Thieves Wood
(Managed by Forest Enterprise) F 194ha
O.S.S. 120 - SK 541 558
☎0623 822447

OXFORDSHIRE

see map on p15

★ Blenheim Estates
(The Duke of Marlborough) **A** 840ha
O.S.S. 164 - SP 448 154
☎0993 811091

The main gate is on A44 about 1/4 mile SE of Woodstock. Educational tours by prior arrangement all through the year via Schools Liaison Officer in writing or by telephoning above number. There is a guide for children. Variety of woodland in varying stages of maturity looking at management problems, species, choice. Establishment, maintenance right through crop rotation. End uses of timber to be seen at the Estate Sawmill which is an important feature of educational visits, linking the growing tree with the produce we so often take for granted.

Cowleaze Wood
(Managed by Forestry Enterprise) **F** 29ha
O.S.S. 165 - SU 728 950
☎0296 625825

From A40 between Stokenchurch and Postcombe, take road heading SW to Christmas Common and Nettlebed. The sculpture trail is signed by brown tourist signs from A40. Facilities include car parking, forest trails, and sculpture trail. There is free and full access at all times. This small wood was planted with a mixture of conifers and broadleaves between 1957 and 1966. Management is aimed at producing a final crop of oak, with conifers removed during the rotation. In conjunction with the Oxfordshire sculpture project a "Sculpture Trail" has been set up. The number of sculptures will increase over time and, on occasions, the artists can be seen working on the site.

Foxholes
(Berks, Bucks and Oxon Naturalists Trust) **F** 64ha
O.S. Ref - SP 254 206
☎0296 433222

A424 from Burford to Stow-on-the-Wold. Take R and just before Bruern Abbey turn L along track past Cocksmoor Wood Car park on R after half a mile. A leaflet describing a wildlife walk around the reserve is available from the above phone number. No charge is made for access and the reserve is open all year. A BBONT nature reserve and an SSSI: all dogs must be kept on a lead. Adjoining woods are private: please keep to rights of way. Mainly a remnant of the ancient Wychwood Forest, soils and past management have created various habitats; wet ash - maple woodland, planted beech, hornbeam, larch, and mixed deciduous woodland, and open rides. In the ash - maple, early purple orchid and goldilocks buttercup appear in spring, with herb paris and common twablade in summer. The rides support uncommon mosses and the heath spotted orchid. The wood is also good for fungi.

Piddington Wood
(Woodland Trust) F 10.36ha
O.S.S. 165 - SP 628 163.
☎0476 74297

From Bicester take the A41 towards Aylesbury. Turn R onto the B4011 towards Oakley. After 3 miles Piddington Wood may be seen on the R and you may park along the verge. There is full and free access to the wood. National Tree Week events may take place in this wood during late Nov-Dec. Please phone the Woodland Trust for details in the autumn. Early maps show that Piddington is likely to have once been just outside the historic boundary of Bernwood Forest, but there is little doubt that it would have been managed as coppice woodland. Classic oak and ash standards are the main tree species with blackthorn as the dominant shrub. The wood is rich in ground flora such as primrose and yellow archangel. A variety of wildlife inhabits the wood, including muntjac and fallow deer, badger, woodcock and elusive black and brown hairstreak butterflies.

Shabbington Wood
(Managed by Forest Enterprise) F 287ha
O.S.S. 165 - SP 611 117
0296 625825

The wood is situated on minor road running from B4011 at Oakley, and B4027 at Stanton St John. Shabbington Wood is a forest nature reserve and SSSI. Facilities include car parking, picnic area and Bernwood butterfly trail.

Warburg Reserve
(Berks, Bucks and Oxon Naturalists Trust) F 103 ha
O.S.S. 175 - SU 720 880

Leave Henley NW on the A423 and fork R at the end of the Fair Mile onto the B480. Turn L just N of Middle Assendon and follow the twisty lane for two miles. Shortly after the lane becomes a track you reach the reserve and car park. There is a reserve centre and nature trail. No charge is made for access and the reserve is open all year. A BBONT nature reserve and an SSSI: dogs must be kept on a lead. A complex of woodland and grassland lying on chalk slopes in a winding valley. Over 450 species of higher plants have been recorded, as well as 850 species of fungi, 37 species of butterflies, 250 species of moths and 75 species of birds. Among the higher plants are 15 species of wild orchids and 50 plants usually only found in ancient woodland in the south of England. Management includes copping some of the woodland and grazing of chalk grassland.

Whitecross Green Wood
(Berks, Bucks and Oxon Naturalists Trust) F 62 ha
O.S.S. 164 - SP 603 145.
0296 433222

A43 north from Oxford. Turn right

to Islip. In Islip turn left to Merton
then first right. One mile after
Murcott turn right onto track into
the reserve. Go through two gates
into car park. A leaflet describing a
wildlife walk around the reserve is
available from the above phone
number. No charge is made for
access and the reserve is open all
year. A BBONT nature reserve and
a Site of Special Scientific Interest
(SSSI): dogs must be kept on a
lead. This is an ancient woodland
harbouring about 200 plant
species. Half the wood was felled
in the sixties by the Forestry
Commission and replanted with
conifers. This area is now being
returned to native woodland. The
remainder is blackthorn - hawthorn
thicket and overgrown hazel
coppice with oak and ash
standards. Some coppicing is done
to encourage wildflowers such as
bluebells, ramsons, and yellow
archangel which are seen between
April and June. The nightingale
nests here, with many butterflies
including black hair streak and
purple emperor.

SHROPSHIRE

see map on p17

Bury Ditches
(Managed by Forest Enterprise) F 276ha
O.S.S. 137 - SO 334 839
☎0584 874542

From Clunton, on the Craven Arms/Clunton road (B4368), take lane towards Brockton for 2½ miles (a brown tourist sign is sited on this junction). Car park on L. 3 waymarked walks passing through the magnificent Bury Ditches. Iron Age Hill Fort. Also cycle tracks. Contact Forest District Office on the above telephone number for brochure. Open all year dawn to dusk.

★ Edge Wood
(Anne Dyer) F 28ha
O.S.S. 137 - SO 479 876
☎0584 73293

From Craven Arms take Much Wenlock road for 3½ miles. At the bottom of the second dip turn L. Two miles on rise up a hill to the car park at the top where the wood crosses the road. Car parking for 10 cars, buses on the road verge only. Picnic tables available. Open all year. There is open access to the wood despite the brambles and there are bridleways. There is a self guided nature trail through the first part of the wood. Some areas need avoiding if trees are being felled. Guided walks can be arranged by contacting Anne Dyer at Westhope College, Craven Arms, Shropshire SY7 9JL. Telephone number above. Please allow one week's notice.

Charge nominal. Donations made to the Forestry Trust. This is an SSSI planted about 1880 on scrubland. The remains of hedges and ditches cross the wood. Part of the 20 mile long Wenlock Edge escarpment. There are badgers, polecats and long-tailed tits, Buzzards nest there now and then. This is an oak and ash woodland with a rich understorey. The wood includes other species such as conifers and beech. The plantation is presently suffering from various problems such as mice and spruce beetle. Ash, oak and hazel coppice with standards - 100 year old oaks with native scrub layer. This wood also has some rare plants.

Haughmond Hill
(Managed by Forest Enterprise) F 132 ha
O.S.S. 126 - SJ 546 148
0584 874542

3 miles out of Shrewsbury on B5062, turn R. at top of bank after Haughmond Abbey, car park on R. 2 waymarked walks and all ability trail. No charge. Open all year dawn to dusk.

Helmeth Wood: Church Stretton
(Woodland Trust) F 23.79 ha
O.S.S. 137 - SO 468 938
0476 74297

From the A49 take the B4371 signposted to Much Wenlock. Immediately turn L along the Watling Street North for about 300 yards and park in the vicinity of

Helmeth Road. Open at all times of the year. The paths to the wood, and within the wood, are usually muddy. Wellington boots or stout shoes are advised. National Tree Week events may take place in this wood during late Nov/Dec. Please phone the Woodland Trust for details in the autumn. Helmeth Wood is an ancient sessile oak woodland, which has been traditionally coppiced. You will see some very impressive stools, or stumps, some as much as nine feet across. In springtime, the woodland ground cover is especially colourful with bluebell, primrose and dog's mercury. In summer, the woodland is alive with the song of summer visitors such as willow warbler and chiff chaff as well as resident birds, which include wren and great tit. Buzzards have also been known to nest here.

Hopton Forest
(Managed by Forest Enterprise) F 338 ha
O.S.S. 137 - SO 355 783
☎0584 874542

8 miles SW of Craven Arms off B4367 at Hoptonheath, through Hopton Castle, turn L up forest road. Mountain bike trail - an innovative and exhilarating mountain bike course. Waterproof map showing numbered stations and contours is available from district office (£1.25). Walkers beware - specialist mountain bike area.

Longdon and Withybed
(E P Cadbury) F 80 ha
O.S.S. 138 - SO 761 774 (Car Park) SO 752 780 (Button Oak Inn)
☎0691 653400

Both grid refs are on B4194 Bewdley to Kinlet. Car park belongs to Forest Enterprise. Picnic area at Hawkbatch. Across road stile gives access to Withybed Wood. Footpaths and bridle paths only. No parking. Always open to walkers, never to cars and cycles. Dogs on leads only. Keep to footpaths. Many forest roads lead nowhere. A steep and dangerous stream valley should be avoided. Old coppice being converted to high oak forest by underplanting with conifers, Norway spruce, Scots pine,, Tsuga, abies grandis, and Douglas fir. Paths run on into SSSI where oak regeneration is being encouraged. This area let to English Nature , to whom enquiries should be referred. Fallow deer. Some wild service trees. - Norman E. Hickin's "Natural History of an English Forest" gives further information.

Mortimer Forest
(Managed by Forest Enterprise) F 950 ha
O.S.S. 138 - SO 474 732
☎0584 874542

High Vinnalls car park is 4 miles W. of Ludlow on Wigmore road. The district forest office is two miles from Ludlow along this same road. During office hours please call in for details. 4 waymarked walks, 1½ to 10 miles long, all ability trail, geological trail and educational trail. Open all year round dawn to dusk. Forest events programme with 35 annual events available from district forest office. This beautiful mixed woodland has four waymarked walks (one of which has a superb panoramic view of the surrounding countryside, an all ability trail which passes two attractive ponds, a geological trail which explores the Ludlovian rocks in the Silurian system, 24 page booklet available from district forest office and a self-guiding educational trail. An attractive and comprehensive information pack detailing woodland walks within 20 separate Forest Enterprise woods available from District Forest Office for £2.25 plus p+p.

Wenlock Edge
(National Trust) F 225 ha
O.S.S. 137 - SO 613 996, SO 584 976
☎0694 723068

Access to northern section of Wenlock Edge (Harley Bank) from N.T. car park situated ½ mile S of Much Wenlock on the B4371 - alternative car park at Blakeway Coppice 3 miles SW. of Much Wenlock adjoining the B4371. This mixed woodland limestone escarpment which lies within an AONB., runs from Ironbridge to Craven Arms and provides fine views over the surrounding countryside. It is famous for its geology, in particular its coral reef exposures. A rich limestone flora includes the wild service tree and several species of orchid.

SOMERSET

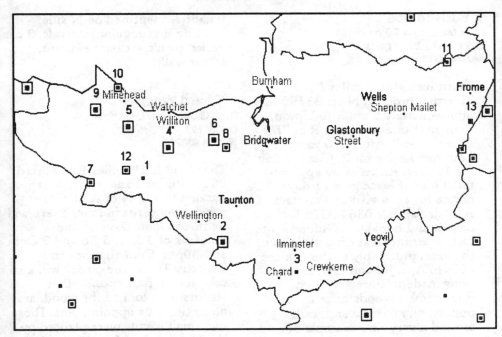

1 *Bittiscombe
2 Blackdowns
3 Chard Wood
4 *Coombe Sydenham
5 *Dunster Wood
6 Great Wood
7 *Hadborough Plantation
8 Hawkridge
9 Luccombe and Horner Plantations
10 *Moor Wood
11 Nap Wood, Amberdown
12 Wimbleball Lake Woods
13 *Witham Park Woods

★ Bittiscombe
(B H Malyon) A 89 ha
O.S.S. 181 - ST 011 293
☎0364 3316

From Bampton 7 miles N of
Tiverton, proceed N on B3190 for
approximately 5 miles to Upton,
then after one mile turn R at *"The
Lowtrow Inn"*. After 200 yards
Lowtrow Lodge on R. Car parking
for 10 cars. All visits by appointment only. Please give 21 days
notice for each visit and contact
Alistair Sandels 0364 3316 for
details and bookings. Guided visits
can be arranged at certain times of
the year, preferably in the months
of Feb, Apr, Jul and Oct. Donations made to Forestry Trust.
Bittiscombe Woods offer the
opportunity to view and walk
around a very fine example of a
multi purpose forestry estate, with
four trout lakes and ancient
semi-natural woodland. The
conifers were established between
1954 and 1971. Planted with a
mixture of Douglas fir and larch
which are highly productive. Small
areas of western hemlock, red
cedar, spruce, grand fir and
redwood can be found. Also beech,
poplar and ancient semi-natural
oak woodland. Deer, wildfowl and
birds of prey can be regularly seen.

Blackdowns
(Managed by Forest Enterprise) F 400 ha
O.S.S. 181/193 - ST 174 158
☎0392 - 832262

Exit M5 at junction 26. Head S At
top of hill approx. 3 miles turn L.

Facilities identified on N side
heading E at regular intervals. 3 car
parks, picnic areas, viewpoint,
forest walks.

Chard Wood
(Dr J D Jackson) L 17 ha
O.S.S. 193. - ST 345 092
☎0258 453262

The wood is 1½ miles E of Chard
on Avishayes Lane which runs
parallel to and N of A30. Car
parking on verge in lane. There will
be three Open Days on the
Sundays of 3 Apr, 3 Jul and 2 Oct
at 2.30pm. Contributions to
Forestry Trust. The owner will also
take school parties and other
visitors on a tour of the wood, at
other times by appointment. These
two small woods were planted by
the Lord of the Manor following
the enclosure of Chard common in
1918. The earthen boundary
embankments made at the time can
still be seen together with a few of
the original oak. After extensive
felling in both World Wars, most of
the wood has been replanted more
than once and now contains some
useful Scots pine, Douglas fir and
some beech and oak. The shallow
and poor soil causes the trees to be
subject to wind-throw. A stream
runs through Tudbeer towards
Chard Reservoir.

★ Combe Sydenham
(Theed Estates) RE 200ha
O.S.S. 181 - ST 074 364
☎0984 56284

From Taunton take the Minehead

road A358 to Bishops Lydeard, L onto B3224 (under railway bridge), follow brown signs to Combe Sydenham Country Park turning R at crossroads in 5 miles. Entrance in valley 1 mile on L. There is parking for 10 coaches and 350 cars. There are WCs on the site. Attractions include flyfishing for beginners, working watermill and bakery, fish farming, ancient trail of trees, Alice trail, tearoom serving lunches, restored Court Room, deer park, deserted hamlet and ornamental tree nursery. Combe Sydenham, the family home of Sir Francis Drake's second wife, has an extensive schools' programme. There are forest trails with different themes and information leaflets contribute to the enjoyment and understanding of the woodlands which are open from Easter to end Oct, Sun to Fri, 10am to 5pm and all Sundays in Nov. No booking is necessary for individual visits, 7 days notice is required for all group visits. Car parking is free. Visits are £4.00 for adults and £1.50 for children 5-16 years, children under 5 free. The woods are set in a deep valley rising from 300 to 1000 feet with viewing points over the Bristol Channel and taking in the whole of the Quantocks. The coniferous plantations have been planted over the last thirty years and are interspersed with ancient and amenity woodlands. The woods produce fine timber and are exceptional to walk in, recently recognized by a Forestry Authority Centre of Excellence Award.

Dunster Wood
(Crown Estate) RE 400 ha
O.S.S. 181 - SS 978 424
☎0634 821309

Head S from Dunster, taking a LH turn off the A396 towards Luxborough. After 1/2 mile bear R at fork and the car park is situated approximately 1/2 mile along the L-hand side and is signposted "Nutcombe Bottom". Facilities here include car parking, picnic areas and a children's play area. Special parking and picnic facilities are available for disabled visitors. Along the trails are various stops which have on-site interpretations - these refer to forest operations and archaeological evidence such as hill forts and enclosures. The tallest tree in England is also to be found.

Great Wood
(Managed by Forest Enterprise) F 600 ha
O.S. S. 181 - ST 175 375
☎0392 832262

From Taunton follow signs to Kingston St. Mary, pass through Kingston St. Mary, follow signs to Nether Stowey. 1 mile S of Nether Stowey turn L (sign Over Stowey), take next turning L Toilets (with disabled access), car parks, forest walks.

★Hadborough Plantation
(Somerset County Council/Exmoor National Park) F 18.5ha
O.S.S. 181 - SS 868 284
☎0398 23665

B3180 from Bampton following

signs to Wimbleball Water Park. Follow for about 4 miles. At top of climb road turns sharply R, Haddon Hill car park signed. Free car parking, toilets, picnic area, information boards. A circular walk is possible through the mixed plantation, turning right and back on oneself to return via the higher moorland track. Sitka spruce, western hemlock, Scots pine, Japanese larch and beech. Spectacular views across Exmoor moorland landscape as well as Wimblewell Dam and Lake. Red and Roe deer frequent the plantation as well as foxes, badgers, and several species of butterfly.

Hawkridge
(Stephen Penny) F 10.8 ha
O.S.S. 181/182. - ST 202 358

From Bridgwater (Junctions 23 and 24, M5) follow signs for Durleigh, then keep straight on past four forks to Hawkridge reservoir (about 5 miles). About 50m after the end of the car park is a gateway with stile. (OS Sheet 182) From Taunton (Junction 25, M5) follow signs to Kingston St. Mary. Follow main road through village and up Buncombe Hill (2 miles). At top of hill go straight (slightly L.) over at five cross roads. Keep straight on through Lower Aisholt until the west end of Hawkridge reservoir is reached. Turn R and the gateway with stile is 100m on R (OS Sheets 183 and 193. For this gateway park at reservoir car park. There is another gateway with stile on the

Aisholt road with parking for one or two cars outside the gate. (NG ST 201357) No access when forestry operations in progress. This attractive woodland is situated on the edge of the Quantock Hills, which is an area much frequented by the public. Hawkridge has a nice balance of semi-mature broadleaves and conifers, which were planted between 1963 and 1968. It is very rich in both flora and fauna, containing some rare plant species and also both red and roe deer are present. Within the woodland is an interesting old lime kiln, which is in reasonable condition, together with a number of quarries. These are fenced on the top edge but please take care.

Luccombe and Horner Plantations, Holnicot Estate
(National Trust) F 444 ha
O.S.S. 181- SS 903 440
☎0643 862452

2 miles S of Porlock in Exmoor National Park. Parking at Horner and Webber's Post. Education centre at PPiles Mill, Allerford woods, above Luccombe and Chapel Cross consist almost entirely of conifers planted in 1920s. They contrast with extensive natural oakwoods of Horner Wood to the W. Public welcome to walk on the rides and paths in these woods. Walks leaflet.

★ Moor Wood
(Somerset County Council/Exmoor National

Park) F 22ha
O.S.S. *181- SS 953 475*
☎0398 23665

Turn off Minehead High Street into Blenheim Road. Turn L just past "Plume of Feathers" pub (signed to North Hill), Follow road for 2 miles around tight bends. past church and uphill. The wood is located above a small campsite. Car park, picnic tables, woodland trail (available form Information Centres). The wood contains a great variety of tree species, both conifer and broadleaf, due to its past as an amenity estate woodland. It was severly damaged in the gales of January 1990, but has now been restocked with European larch, Scots pine and beech. This was for visual attractiveness and an early return from the conifers. A longer term crop is represented by the beech. Various establishment systems have been used to experiment and demonstrate restocking techniques. These include 2m deer fencing, 1m rabbit fencing, multi sized tree shelters and plastic mesh guards. The pros and cons of these techniques are demonstrated. Both roe and red deer frequent these woods and many woodland birds species are also well represented. Close proximity to the sea and large areas of coastal heath and farmland make this wood a varied and complex site.

Nap Wood, Ammerdown Park
(Lord Hylton) F 20.1 ha
O.S.S. *183. - ST 715 535*

☎0761 437382

Take A362 (Frome) road SE. from Radstock junction with A367 for 2½ miles. At junction A362/A366 (Terry Hill) enter wood through iron gate on S side of crossroads. Nature trail marked. Open at all times in daylight. Dogs on leads. Visitors to keep strictly to marked paths. No vehicles. Parking by entrance gate. No horses. Conifer and broad leaved woodlands at all stages of development from young plantations to mature stands. Full spectrum of indigenous flora.

Wimbleball Lake Woods
(South West Water Services Limited) F 39 ha
O.S. S. *181 - SS 970 310*

Follow signs from A396. to Wimbleball Lake. Car parking and WCs available on site. There is a charge for car parking in the main Cowlings car park, other smaller areas free. Open all year round. West Hill Wood consists of ancient oak coppice, full of wild flowers in the spring. Other woods are more modern but being converted to mainly broadleaf. Many wonderful views over Wimbleball Lake.

★ Witham Park Woods
(The Duke of Somerset) L 240 ha
O.S.S. *183. - ST 770 383*
☎0985 844317

From Maiden Bradley to Bruton for approximately 4 miles, at the

T-junction the car park is straight ahead. There is a charge of £1 for car parking or 50p to Forestry Trust. Open 29th May and 17th Jul from 12 noon to 5 p.m. Guided tours 2nd Oct at 12 noon and 2.30 p.m. Witham Park is part of the ancient Forest of Selwood straddling the Wiltshire/Somerset boundary. It is in the North Wessex Downs AONB near the chalk downs on a greensand scarp looking W over the clay of the Witham Vale. Long term woodland management has produced an attractive mixture of species and ages and areas of both native hardwoods and commercial exotic softwoods. Fallow, roe and occasional muntjac deer are present with a wide variety of bird species. The woodlands are managed to produce the timber you need and use, whilst contributing to the landscape and wildlife you enjoy

STAFFORDSHIRE

see map on p17

Big Wood
(Peter Giffard) R 100h ▪
O.S.S. 127 - SJ 864 068
☎0902 850768

From the N, M6 to Junction 12. From the S, M6 to Junction 10A and M54 to Junction 2. Take A449 (Wolverhampton to Stafford road). Turn off at double roundabout, through Coven to Brewood and follow signs to Chillington. Free parking in front of the house. This is not suitable for coaches. Coaches must always make a prior appointment. The charge for the house and grounds, which includes the woodlands, is £2 per person. The charge for the grounds only is £1 per person. Children are half price. The grounds, which include the woodlands, are open on all days when Chillington Hall is open to the public. In 1994 the opening days are Thursdays from May to Sept 14, Easter Sunday and Sundays prior to May Day and Spring Bank Holidays and all Sundays in Aug, 2.30 to 5.30 p.m. Parties of at least 15 can come at other times by prior arrangement; applications should be made in writing at least 4 weeks ahead. Visitors should park in front of the house and call at the house to obtain a pass. Big Wood forms part of Chillington Park which was enlarged and improved by 'Capability' Brown. Much of the woodlands is a site of Ancient Semi-Natural Woodland. All is comprised within the Chillington conservation area. The woods are managed commercially but with a view to enhancing Brown's Park and Brown's great lake of 85 acres. There is a signed walk around the lake for 4 miles which passes through the woods for most of its way. There are young trees as well as mature trees and an observant visitor may be able to spot 30 different species of trees.

Black Firs
(Staffordshire Wildlife Trust) F 3 ha
O.S.S. 127 - SJ 746 500
☎0897 508534

Off A531 Crewe-Newcastle road, at Balterley Heath. Park at Post Office Lane. Paths and interpretative signs. Open at all times. A wood which has developed on an old wetland site as a result of planting and natural regeneration. Still shows character of wetland habitat.

★ Cannock Forest
(Managed by Forest Enterprise) F 2,600 ha
O.S.S.127/128 - SK 019 171
☎0889 586593

Take the A51 through Rugeley. Turn into Hagley Road at the traffic lights between the two roundabouts signposted to Cannock Chase visitor centre. Follow road out of the town, in approximately 1_ miles turn L. into forest centre. Signposted. Car parking, deer museum, caravan site, orienteering, permit fishing, permit horse riding, education

175

facilities, wildlife hide, forest walks. Mountain bikers are requested to follow the mountain bike code and give way to pedestrians.

Dimmings Dale
(Managed by Forest Enterprise) F 260 ha
O.S.S. 119/128 - SK 063 432
☎0889 586593

From Cheadle take the B5417 to Oakamoor Village, turn R at the bottom of steep hill, before the bridge in the village. Take first L and follow narrow lane towards Alton. In 1½ miles car park is on L by the *Ramblers Retreat Café*. Forest walks, car park, café, all ability access along valley floor from car park. Please, no mountain bikes on the forest walk. Dimmings Dale in the Churnet valley has a rich industrial heritage with ore smelting and quarrying. In the 1800s the Earl of Shrewsbury laid out magnificent carriage drives leading from his country seat at what is now Alton Towers. The forest walk winds through ancient woodland, and crosses the Ranger SSSI, one of the last remaining ancient hill pastures in the area. Water flows quietly down the valley through a series of large fish ponds.

Hem Heath Wood
(Managed by Staffordshire Wildlife Trust) F 8 ha
O.S.S. 118 - SJ 885 412
☎0889 508534

On S side of A5035 between Trentham and Longton. This is on the southern fringe of Stoke-on-Trent. Nature trail, access for disabled, interpretive signs on site. Open at all times. This wood was planted about 150 years ago and includes 34 species of tree. Plants include moschatel, yellow pimpernel, common twayblade, broadleaved helleborine, marsh marigold and marsh cinquefoil. A wide variety of woodland birds use the wood, including sparrowhawks. There is a large pond which is being restored.

Himley Plantation
(Woodland Trust) F 23.87 ha
O.S.S. 139 - SO 870 914
☎0476 74297

Approaching from the E, leave the A449 Wolverhampton to Kidderminster road on to the B4176 to Bridgnorth. From the W, the B4176 is signposted to Dudley off the A454. Continue along the B4176 Bridgnorth road to Himley and turn off into Himley Lane, signposted to Halfpenny Green and Swindon. Immediately after passing under the railway bridge, turn R into the country park car park. Please note that the car park is closed overnight; the closing time is displayed at the entrance to the parking area. You will find the main access point to Himley Plantation is at the far end of the car park. The wood is open at all times of the year. National Tree Week events may take place in this wood during Nov/Dec. Please phone the Woodland Trust for details in the autumn. Some paths may be muddy so stout footwear is advisable particularly in the winter months. The main body of Himley Plantation is mixed high forest with oak and common lime as the main tree species. There is a variety of birds present in the wood such as tawny owl, barn owl and three species of woodpecker. Other birds in the wood are more difficult to observe, including hawfinch and bullfinch. There are some fine, tall alder trees in the wood and areas of thick willow scrub which remain wild, and largely undisturbed. Under these conditions sphagnum, the 'bog-moss', and many species of sedge can be found.

★ Jacksons Bank
(Duchy of Lancaster) A 35ha
O.S.S.128 - SK 139 233
☎0283 512244

The wood lies to the W of the A515 Lichfield to Ashbourne Road, approximately 4 miles N of Yoxall. Turn L at Newchurch. The wood is approximately 1/2 mile on the RH side. There is parking for 30 cars. There is a picnic area with hard path access, woodland trails and a horse trail. All group visits by appointment only. There are self-guided trails in the wood. For further details/appointments please contact C P Meynell, Messrs John German, 1 Lichfield Street, Burton on Trent, Staffordshire, DE14 3QZ or telephone above number. Jacksons Wood forms part of the ancient forest of Needwood and is within the National Forest boundary. Felled during the second World War, the wood was replanted between 1949-53 with a mixture of conifers and broadleaf and has further developed with natural regeneration, providing a changing character and colour throughout the year. There is a wide variety of ground flora, some of which is rare and particular to the Needwood Forest area in Staffordshire.

The Lower Avenue
(Peter Giffard)F 11 ha
O.S.S. 127 - SJ 898 076 or SJ 882 075
☎0902 850768

Take the A449 Wolverhampton to Stafford road. Turn off at double roundabout (O.S. 913063) and proceed towards Brewood. A small car park (not suitable for coaches) should be available in 1994 in Park Lane. Open all the year. A broadleaved wood in the making. The Lower Avenue is over a mile in length and runs from Brewood to Coven road (O.S. sheet 127 - 898076) to Park Lane (O.S. 882075). Originally a beech avenue which was part of the private approach to Chillington Hall. Most beeches have been removed and the whole Avenue has been planted (1955-1975) as an oak wood with some elm, sweet chestnut, beech and hornbeam. The driveway down the centre has been dedicated as a public right of way on foot. The Lower Avenue forms part of a designated Conservation Area. It crosses the Shropshire Union Canal by a fine ornamental bridge by Telford.

Moseymoor Wood

(Managed by Forest Enterprise) F 23 ha
O.S.S. 128/119 - SK 025 476
☎0889 586593

The wood can be entered on foot
by the footpath from Froghall
wharf, signposted from the A52 at
Froghall between Ashbourne and
Stoke-on-Trent.

Parrot's Drumble

(Managed by Staffordshire Wildlife Trust) F
12 ha
O.S. S. 118 - SJ 817 523
☎08897 534

Between A500 and Janage
Industrial Estate. Access is by
public footpath from layby on
eastbound carriageway of A500
between Alsager and Newcastle-
under Lyme turn-offs. Path. Open
at all times. A rich deciduous valley
woodland and stream, dominated
by oak, birch, alder and hazel.
Around the edge are a number of
mature beech and occasional
turkey oaks. Along the stream are
several hybrid poplars, thought to
have been planted in the early
1800s and a sizeable patch of
alder.

Somerford

(A.S. Monckton)A 40 ha
O.S.S. 127 - SJ 911 080
☎0902 850214

A449 N from M54. Meet in lorry
park of transport café on W side of
A449, 3 miles N of M54. All
transport café facilities. Open by
appointment only in Apr, May,
Aug. Afternoons preferred.

Coaches and/or school parties
welcome. No dogs. Only on days
owner is available. Private wood
with large variety of hardwoods
and conifers. Easy walking - 1-2
hours.

Stafford Plantation, Shugborough Park

(National Trust - managed by Staffordshire
County Council) F 49.7 ha
O.S.S. 127 - SJ 991 216
☎0889 881388

4 1/2 miles E of Stafford, on the
A513 Stafford/Lichfield road. The
meeting point is the farm car park
which may be approached via the
main entrance (well signposted) or,
if this is closed, via the exit to the
park, one mile to the E. Guided
walks available by prior arrangement. Schools and coach parties
welcome. Charges - variable for
guided walks. Open throughout the
year. It may be necessary to
restrict access to parts of the
woodland during forestry
operations, which take place in the
winter. An attractive mixed
woodland of oak, beech, sweet
chestnut and Scots pine, with
specimen trees, most of which were
planted between 1820 and 1833 by
Viscount Anson, later created Earl
of Lichfield. The woodland is
managed on continuous cover
principles. The Shugborough
estate, which is the seat of the
Earls of Lichfield, comprises 400
ha of parkland, woodland and
formal garden. The mansion
House, county museum and
working farm museum are to the
public. Details from the property.

SUFFOLK

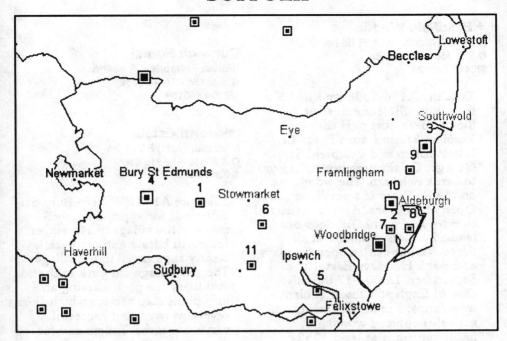

1 *Bradfield Woods
2 Chillesford Wood
3 Dunwich Forest
4 Ickworth Estate
5 Pinmill
6 Priestley Wood
7 *Rendlesham Forest
8 Sudbourne
9 Theberton Woods
10 Tunstall Forest
11 Wolves Wood

★ Bradfield Woods
(Suffolk Wildlife Trust) R 68 ha
O.S.S. 155 - TL 935 581
☎0449 737996

Take the A134 Sudbury Road S from Bury St. Edmunds. At Sicklesmere, just past the *Rushbrooke Arms*, turn L. for Lt. Whelnetham and Bradfield St. George. Go through both villages towards Felsham. The woods are on the R. There is a small car park. Open at all times. Access restricted to rides and paths. All dogs on leads. Leaflets available at all times. Visitor centre open Sundays and Bank Holidays Easter to end September, 13.00 - 17.00 only. One of England's finest ancient woodlands. Foremost example of actively coppiced woodland unbroken since at least 1252. Many ancient stools, masses of spring flowers, oxlip, wood anemone, herb paris. Migratory birds, invertebrates, fungi, small mammals. N.B. The fences are for deer exclusion! Educational visits welcome at all levels. Contact Asst. Warden. Occasional green wood work courses. Groups may arrange guided walks - £1.30 per head, £16 minimum. More detailed information sheets available on some subjects. From Apr 1 1994 Bradfield Wood will have National Nature Reserve status as designated by English Nature.

Chillesford Wood
(Forest Enterprise) F 62ha
O.S.S. 156 - TM 377 519
☎0394 450164

Dunwich Forest
(Forest Enterprise) F 484ha
O.S.S. 156 - TM 461 712
☎0394 450164

Ickworth Estate
(National Trust) F 241 ha
O.S.S. 155 - TL 815 616
☎0284 735480

Take the A143 SW from Bury St. Edmunds for approximately 3 miles to the village of Horringer. Ickworth Estate and car park is clearly signposted in the village. There is a large car park in the middle of the park offering an info-point map service which shows several waymarked routes of varying lengths. Toilets and tea room are available when the house is open. There is a deer enclosure near the main car park. The woodlands are open year round to the public. There is a charge of £1.50 adult, 50p children Apr to Nov or £2 per car at other times. No charge for walkers. These woods form a visual perimeter around the park and are predominantly hardwood. Some of the woods are ancient semi-naturall woodlands. Large areas - Lownde Wood - are oak standards with hazel coppice. In the associated park there are over 200 ancient oak pollards (2 oaks being over 700 years old). There is a wide range of fauna and flora associated with these woods.

Pinmill

(National Trust) F 26ha
O.S.S.*169 - TM 206 379*
☎0263 222669

Coastal wood near Chelmondiston on River Orwell. Free parking.

Priestley Wood
(Woodland Trust) F 23.47 ha
O.S.S *155. TM 080 530*
☎0476 74297

From Stowmarket follow the B1113 S to Needham Market. Turn R on to the B1078 to Barking. Priestley Wood is to the R of this road, just before the village of Barking. The wood is open at all times of the year. National Tree Week events may take place in this wood during late Nov/Dec. Please phone the Woodland Trust for details in the autumn. Priestley Wood is considered to be one of the finest woods in Suffolk for plant life. Ash and maple coppice poles spring from stools - occasionally gigantic and ancient - in a mixture with other species. Small-leaved lime, hornbeam and wild pear, considered the rarest of all native trees, are present in the wood. Nightingales frequent areas of dense coppice regrowth, while the secretive woodcock and many roe deer are also present in the wood.

★ Rendlesham Forest
(Forest Enterprise) F 1443ha
O.S.S.*169 - TM 353 484*
☎0394 450164

TAke A12 from Ipswich towards Lowestoft. After bypassing Woodbridge take A1152 through Melton and over a level crossing, then take B1084 to Orford After 3 miles turn right at sign for Forest District Office and facilities. Phoenix Trail car park is 1 mile on. Car park, toilets, disabled facilities, picnic areas, 4 waymarked trails with interpretation (of which 2 are surfaced for wheelchairs), cycle trail, privately run campsite. No charge but walks leaflet 50p and cycle leaflet 80p. Rendlesham Forest suffered catastrophic damage during the 1987 gale although attractive ares of mature forest remain and damaged areas have been replanted. The Phoenix Trail passes through areas of mature and young forest and information is available on how Forest Enterprise took the storm damage as an opportunity to create a more diverse forest than before with special management for woodlark and nightjar populations as well as the encouragement of other local heathland species on ride edges and in scallops. Also of significance is the conservation of the Tang Valley wetland area which has a series of large ponds with bridge and boardwalk access where necessary.

Sudbourne
(Forest Enterprise) F 78ha
O.S.S. *156 - TM 420 520*
☎0394 450164

Theberton Woods
(Forest Enterprise) F 32ha

O.S.S. *156 - TM 422 655*
☎0394 450164

Tunstall Forest
(Forest Enterprise) F 950ha
O.S.S. *156 - TM 381 560*
☎0394 450164

Wolves Wood
(Royal Society for the Protection of Birds) F
37 ha
O.S.S. *155 - TM 055 436*
☎0255 886043

The Reserve entrance is 1½ miles
E of Hadleigh on the A1071
Ipswich to Hadleigh road. Bold
entrance sign. Marked visitor path.
Seasonal information centre. Car
park. No charges but donations
appreciated. Open at all times.
Reserve leaflet available from
Warden (50p). Occasional guided
walks - details from Warden.
Lecture service. A very wet wood -
wellies often advisable. Not
suitable for wheelchair users at any
time. An extensive area of mixed
species coppice characterised by
the large number of ponds (46). A
diverse flora includes herb paris,
several species of orchids and a
wide range of tree and shrub
species. Nightingales abound in
spring along with willow warblers,
blackcaps and occasionally
hawfinches; casual woodcock can
be seen at dusk and dawn. The
ponds attract a range of dragonfly
species including the ruddy darter,
and Grass snakes are common.

SURREY

see map on p15

★ Alice Holt Forest
(Managed by Forest Enterprise) F 925ha
O.S.S.186 - SU 810 416
☎0420 23666

The forest centre is signposted from Bucks Horn Oak village, SW of Farnham (Not Alice Holt Lodge). Visitor centre, toilets, car parking, fishing by permit only. A regular events programme is produced. The forest centre is open Wed- Sun, 1000 - 1600 hours.

Ashtead Common
(Corporation of London) F 200ha
O.S.S. 187 - TQ 175 580
☎081 763 0464

Approaching Ashstead from Leatherhead on the A24, turn L down Woodfield Lane opposite the *Leg of Mutton and Cauliflower* pub. Continue down the lane for 800m, straight on at the mini roundabout, then over the level crossing and Ashstead Common lies in front of you. There are no facilities. There is fully open access to the wood with rights of way on foot and bridlepaths. Guided visits can be arranged by appointment, please contact Bob Warnock, Community Woodlands Officer, on the above number. First recorded history dates back to 1st century AD, the earliest evidence of human habitation being the remains of a Roman villa. Contains five major types of habitat: ancient pasture woodland, secondary woodland, bracken dominated areas, scrubland, and grassland. Designated as an SSSI in 1955. Pollarded oaks, birch, and aspen. The various habitats support many species of invertebrates together with a rich community of breeding birds, roe deer thriving in the woodland areas; purple emperors and purple hairstreaks are amongst the numerous species of butterflies and months.

Box Hill
(National Trust) FE 217ha
O.S.S. 184 - SU 179 513
☎0306 742809

A24 Dorking to Leatherhead. 1 1/2 miles N of Dorking follow signs to Box Hill at roundabout. Large car park with parking charge. There is a refreshment kiosk, National Trust Shop. The woodland is semi-natural beech, yew and box with some areas of open downland.

Hindhead
(National Trust) F 155ha
O.S.S. 186 - SU 892 357
☎0428 683207

There is a car park but there are no facilities. Full and free access. Telephone above number for further information.

Leith Hill
(National Trust) F 269.5ha
O.S.S. 187 - TQ 132 428
☎0306 742809

There is a car park. Full and free access. Telephone above number for further information.

★ Nower Wood

(Surrey Wildlife Trust) A 33 ha
O.S.S. 187 - TQ 193 546
☎0483- 488055

Off Junction 9 of M25, follow signs to A24. Join A24 S. Turn off 1st exit at "Beaverbrook" roundabout onto B2033. One mile along this road - entrance on L. Car park, field centre, WCs, nature trail. Refreshments on open days. Phone 0372 379509 for details of charges. Open to public 3rd Sunday Apr - Oct, 10 a.m. to 4 p.m. Otherwise by appointment for school groups, interest groups and clubs/ uniformed organisations. Nower Wood provides an excellent nationally-respected education facility for all ages - advance booking. No dogs. Nower Wood is 81 acres of mixed woodland, mainly broadleaved, with 40 different tree and shrub species. Over 70 species of birds have been seen in this ancient woodland, many of which breed on site. There are also areas of marshland, heath and chalk grassland, and several pools and ponds. The Surrey Wildlife Trust purchased Nower Wood in 1971 and gradually established it as an educational nature reserve.

Ranmore

(National Trust) F 266.4ha
O.S.S. 187 - TQ 142 504
☎0306 742809

There is a car park (parking charge). Free and full access. Telephone above number for further information.

★ Winterfold Forest

(J A McAllister) AE 125 ha
O.S.S. 186 - SU 965 435
☎0486 413474

From A254 Guildford toDorking road take A248 signposted Godalming. After ½ mile cross small bridge then L into New Road up hill over level crossing to Farley Green, then L at village green into Shophouse Lane, then 1 mile to forest sign. Parking for 25 cars and 2 coaches by arrangement. There are some WCs on site. Access for the disabled is particularly good. Motorised trips for the elderly can be arranged. Open at any time by booking in advance by phoning 0483 203474 or 071 499 6616. Details can be left on answer-phone if unattended. Densely planted working forest in the Surrey Hills (highest point of SE England). 23 different species of trees , Corsican pine, Douglas fir, cypress,lLarch, Japanese cedar etc. Wildlife includes deer, badger, fox, snakes. Many species of birds including birds of prey. Hopeful of reintroduction of red squirrel in near future. Heathland re-creation project in hand. Schools welcome.

Witley Common
(National Trust) F 152ha
O.S.S. 186 - SU 933 407
  0428 683207

7 miles SW of Guildford between
the Portsmouth (A3) and
Haslemere (A286) roads. Free
public access. There is a large car
park, an Information Centre, and
nature trails. Mixed age Scots pine
and some areas of open heathland.

SUSSEX - EAST

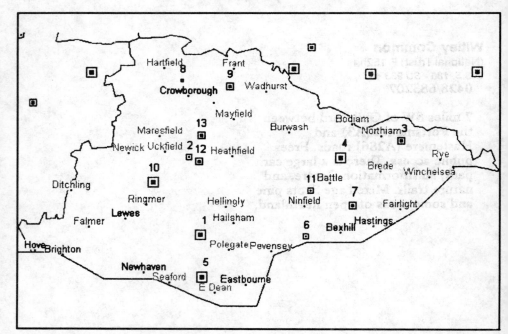

1 Abbotts Wood
2 Blackdown Wood
3 Flatropers Wood
4 Footland Wood
5 *Friston Forest
6 Gillham Wood
7 Marline Wood
8 *Morris's Wood
9 Nap Wood
10 Plashett Wood
11 Powdermill Wood
12 Selwyn's Wood
13 *Wilderness Wood

Abbots Wood
(Forest Enterprise) F 356ha
O.S.S. 199 - TQ 556 074
☎0528- 211044

Take the A22 S from the Boship roundabout. Turn R onto minor road after approximately 2 miles, then take the next L. The car park is on the L 400 yds beyond *The Oak* public house. Facilities include car park, toilets, way-marked walks. Free access.

Blackdown Wood
(D E Gunner) F 3ha
O.S.S. 199 - TQ 538 202
☎0435 862016

3/4 mile from Blackboys village on road to Waldron village. Park on verge by Countryside Commission board. There are no facilities. Entrance is free but guided walks are £2 per head, by appointment. Open from 0800 hours to sunset, daily. Permissive footpaths and bridleways in wood, with open access to adjoining fields managed under countryside stewardship scheme. Rotational cutting of chestnut coppice with oak and Scots pine standards. 7 year old amenity planting, with all indigenous species. Excellent display of bluebells in May. Attractive walk by the stream.

Flatropers Wood
(Sussex Wildlife Trust) F 35ha
O.S.S. 199/189 -TQ 861 231
☎0273 492630

Nearest town is Rye. There is good access throughout along a system of paths and rides linking with the entrance on Bixley Lane, which joins the A268 on a sharp bend just W of Beckley. This beautiful reserve is an example of typical E Sussex woodland which has been used to produce various sorts of timber in the past. In many parts the mass of young birch has been cut and regenerates profusely on the light, sandy soils of this area. In other places, sweet chestnut has been cut as coppice, and there are small plantations of beech and pine, growing up over a ground layer full of bracken and wood ants' nests. Throughout the reserve standard oaks provide a continuity of woodland cover. Cutting across the reserve is an open heathy ride formed when electricity lines were put in. Here, heather grows alongside birch, bracken and gorse, and a small pond supports hundreds of palmate newts. The open, sunny conditions along the woodland tracks and paths are the ideal habitat for many invertebrates such as the pearl bordered fritillary and the beetle. The fast growing birch in this wood has always been cut to give a timber crop and we are continuing this management and taking the opportunity whilst an area is clear, to plant in more oak. We are also maintaining the rides by controlling bracken and birch to encourage the spread of heather.

Footland Wood
(Forest Enterprise) F 167ha

O.S.S.199 - TQ 764 204
☎0580 211044

From the A21 take the B2089 S of John's Cross. The car park can be found on the R some 600 yards distant. There is free access and the wood is open permanently.

★ Friston Forest
(Forest Enterprise) F 858ha
O.S.S. 199 - TQ 519 001
☎0580 21104

Take the A259 W from Eastbourne. On reaching the Seven Sisters Country Park at Exceat, take the minor road to Litlington on the R. The car park is on the R 100 yards beyond the R turn to Westdean village. There are two car parks, one with toilets. There is free access and the forest is permanently open. Friston Forest is situated on the South Downs between Eastbourne and Seaford. The woodlands are predominantly beech and were planted mostly between the two world wars. There are waymarked walks from both car parks which are situated on opposite sides of the forest and the extensive network enables the more adventurous walker to venture further afield. There are several sites of botanical interest where typical chalk downland plant communities may be found and there is a National Nature Reserve managed by English Nature on the northern edge of the forest.

Gillham Wood
(Sussex Wildlife Trust) F 3.2ha
O.S.S. 199 - TQ 718 069
☎0273 492630

The nearest town is Bexhill-on-Sea. Access to the woodland is from the lay-by on the N side of Withyham Road, Cooden. The Cooden and Little Common areas of what is now Bexhill-on-Sea were once farmland and Gillham Wood is a remnant of those times. Surprisingly intact though surrounded by housing, it has been little altered over the years and consists mainly of oak with a thick shrub layer and bramble beneath. Most of the oak is of similar age and size, indicating that the wood was probably felled about 50 years ago and allowed to redevelop naturally. It may have been used for tanbark or charcoal in the past.

Marline Wood
(Sussex Wildlife Trust) F 40ha
O.S.S.199 - TQ 783 123
☎0273 492630

Nearest town is Hastings. Visitors should park in Napier Road and cross to the footpath signed by the Queensway - Marline Wood is open at all times along the footpaths. Just W of Hastings lies the Marline Valley whose woodlands extend down across the rocky sandstone ghyll which holds the stream itself. The steep sides, outcrops and humid conditions of the ghyll lend it a character more like that of a western oakwood than a Sussex valley. It supports a great number of mosses and ferns in its damp crevices, some of which are relics from theAtlantic period of about 7000 years ago. Storm damage has left many trees uprooted and strewn along the valley floor. On the gentler slopes above, large oaks stand over a coppice worked for centuries and composed largely of hornbeam, a common coppice tree only in the SE. Its very hard timber was probably used for charcoal. Mixed with it are the more traditional coppice species such as ash, sweet chestnut and hazel. Between the woods and the road are a series of hay meadows and pastures which have never been ploughed up or fertilised. These fields are full of flowers and insects in the summer, and the numerous hawthorn bushes provide food and shelter for breeding and migrating birds.

★ Morris's Wood
(Muriel and George Fry) A 37ha
O.S.S. 188 - TQ 506 332
☎0892 653047

Take Groombridge Road from Crowborough Cross. After 1.25 miles take drive on L marked "Highfields". Access is necessarily by prior appointment because main entry crosses private garden of house. Some car parking is available. Morris's Wood is ancient woodland in two south-west valleys on the border of Ashdown Forest. Management is on active silvicultural principles with broadleaf and conifer species. Care is taken to avoid disturbance to wildlife. The forestry work is confined to the

main species but there are many specimen trees and at least one of each will be found in the Shakespeare Memorial Garden. There is a wide variety of wildflowers, fungi, butterflies and birds and a nature trail of about 2 1/2 miles.

Nap Wood
(National Trust managed by Sussex Wildlife Trust) F 44.6ha
O.S.S 188 - TQ 583 327
☎0273 492630

Nearest town Crowborough. Access to the woodland trail is from a small pull-in on the eastern side of the A267 between Mark C ross and Frant. Nap Wood is a beautiful example of the oak woodlands found on the sandstone areas of the High Weald of E Sussex and is very different from those on the clays further W. The oak, whilst the dominant tree in the wood, gives way to areas of chestnut, coppice and clumps of pine planted in certain areas. In many parts of the reserve the oaks have grown up as wide spreading standard trees, but near the entrance they have been cut and worked as coppice. This coppice oak was usually used for tanbark or charcoal and is more typical of the W of Britain than of the SE. Streams have cut steep valleys in the sandstone to form moist habitats for mosses, liverworts and ferns more commonly found in Wales, Cumbria and Scotland. In the higher parts of the wood the spring cover of bluebells becomes overtopped by bracken in summer.

It is the profusion of bracken and birch that betrays the acidic nature of the soil below. The October 1987 gale blew many smaller trees down on the southern side of the wood, and the light and space created will be filled by the natural growth of seedling trees already present.

Plashett Wood
(I V Askew Charitable Trust) A 150ha
O.S.S. 198 - TQ 460 163
☎0825 750750

The wood is alongside the A26 half way between Lewes and Uckfield. There is parking for 20 cars/2 or 3 coaches. Access is by appointment only and with the forester to act as a guide. It is necessary to charge the forester's time for this. A predominantly broadleaved woodland managed for timber production, nature conservation and shooting. An educational programme is being developed. Plashett Wood is the largest block of broadleaved woodland under one management plan in E Sussex. The wood is managed as a working woodland and has a resident charcoal producer as well as various other value adding activities.

Powdermill Wood
(Sussex Wildlife Trust) F 1.8ha
O.S.S. 199 - TQ 735 144
☎0273 492630

Nearest town is Battle. A circular nature trail winds through the whole of Powdermill Wood and passes across the reserve. The trail starts at the car park on the B2095, Battle-Catsfield Road. Much of this area of woodland was probably once cut as coppice for charcoal, an ingredient of gunpowder and the name "Powdermill Wood" was quite common in the Weald. Battle was reputed by Daniel Defoe to produce "the finest gunpowder in England, and probably the best in Europe". Surrounded by commercially worked chestnut coppice is a wet valley bottom filled with alder, a tree which thrives in waterlogged conditions. The multi-stemmed growth is regeneration from coppicing about 30 years ago, and grows over greater tussock sedge, wood anemone, marsh marigold and the tiny, but distinctive, opposite-leaved golden saxifrage. These and other plants on the reserve are typical of marshy stream valleys in woodland. Many species of insect live amongst the sedge tussocks.

Selwyns Wood
(Sussex Wildlife Trust) F 11.3HA
O.S.S. 199 - TQ 552 206
☎0263 492630

Nearest town is Heathfield. There is a small car park on the track to Selwyns Wood house from which a network of paths run round the woodland. The woodlands of Sussex were extensively worked to produce timber, firewood and charcoal throughout Medieval times and up to the present century. Selwyns Wood shows signs of this throughout its history of management. The areas near the entrance consist mainly of sweet chestnut, a tree introduced to Britain in Roman times, which has been repeatedly cut as coppice. The extremely durable timber is now used for fence posts. The central area was clear-felled of mature pine, fir and larch. It has been planted with oak and associated native species. The eastern side of the woodland is predominantly birch over bracken. Most of the trees are young and have probably grown up in the last 40 years after previous felling. Heather survives in some open areas, thriving on the combination of light and an acidic soil, and there are numerous wood ant nests. To the west there is more variety, with large Scots pine in some places; beech, oak and chestnut in others. Amongst the holly, rowan and birch which grow beneath the main canopy are myriad of sycamore seedlings. This highly invasive tree, not native to Britain, will need to be controlled if it is not to dominate.

★ **Wilderness Wood**
(C & A Yarrow) RCE 24ha
O.S.S. 199 - TQ 536 240
☎0825 830509

On A272 in Hadlow Down village, which is 5 miles NE of Uckfield. There is parking for 40 cars and 2 coaches. The whole wood is open to explore; woodland trails and exibition in timber barn give an insight into growing and using wood, and woodland wildlife. Guided walks, children's activities and "hands on" demonstrations available for schools and other booked groups. Picnic areas, barbecues for hire, adventure playground, teas, souvenirs, WCs. Barn. WCs and yard area are accessible to the disabled. Open access to the wood (10 am to dusk). Further guided visits can be arranged by appointment (one weeks notice). Admission: Adults £1.30, OAPS £1, children 70p (reduced rates Nov-Feb); Groups of 15 + people, £1.13, 90p, 63p; Guided walks/demonstrations (including admission): £2.40, £2.10, £1.75. Minimum £22 per group. School rates: Children 70p; one free adults per 10 children; extras £1.17. Guided walks/ demonstrations £17 per group in addition to admission charge. Sweet chestnut coppice, beech and conifer plantations, Christmas tree plantation. Wide range of native and introduced trees; abundant bluebells - springtime bluebell walk - wood anemones, foxgloves, autumn fungi. Wood products on sale from firewood to rustic furniture. Dig-your-own Christmas trees. Centre of Excellence award for access and education. Duke of Cornwall's award for forestry and conservation.

SUSSEX - WEST

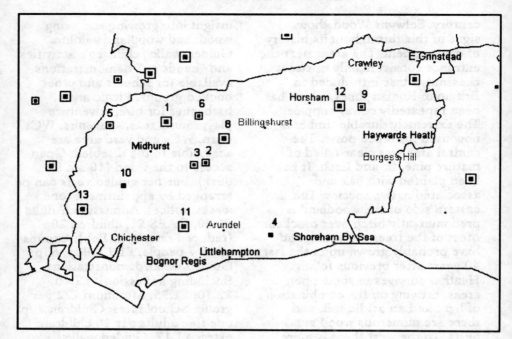

1 Blackdown Wood
2 Burton Pond Woodlands
3 Burton Rough
4 Clapham Woods
5 Durnford Wood
6 Ebernoe Common Nature Reserve
7 Gravetye
8 The Mens Nature Reserve
9 Nymans
10 *Rabbit Warren
11 Slindon Wood
12 St Leonard's Forest
13 *Stansted Forest

Blackdown
(National Trust) F 303ha
O.S.S 186 - SU 920 308
☎0428 683207

No facilities Full and free access. Telephone the above number for further information.

Burton Pond Woodlands
(Sussex Wildlife Trust) F 27.1 ha
O.S.S.197/198 - SU 978 181
☎0273 492630

Woodlands enclosing areas of bog and heath, and surrounding a large mill pond. Nearest town - Petworth. There is a small car park just below the old mill, from which both sides of the reserve are within easy reach. For details of disabled access contact SWT. The reserve consists of four areas of woodland known as Newpiece Wood, Welch's and Crouch Common and the Warren. Though much altered in the past, they all derive from the oak and birch woodlands typical of the sandstone parts of the Weald. The acidic nature of the soil creates many heathy areas where trees were cleared in the past and a walk through Newpiece Wood reveals clearings of heather and purple moor- grass, whilst Welch's Common includes the aptly named Black Hole - a bog now partly covered by alder and willow. These wetter areas support the white-flowered bogbean, marsh cinquefoil, and our native cranberry - all species more usually associated with the north and west of Britain. In the drier woodlands, the birch which is now so common was quite scarce in comparison with trees such as oak and lime which formerly predominated. Felling of the latter species over recent centuries has allowed the pioneering birch to spread into the large open areas created instead of being largely confined to glades. The pond is a good place to see a variety of wildfowl, including the coot, moorhen and great crested g rebe, and is fringed by areas of reed and alder with the rare cowbane. It is extensively fished. Our work aims to keep the heathy glades and bog open by removing alder and willow, and to replace blocks of birch with a more natural mix of broad-leaved trees, including a high proportion of oak. Has SSSI status. Part of Local Nature Reserve designated by West Sussex County Council, who own the Mill Pond.

Burton Rough
(Miss P. E. Merriman) F 22 ha
O.S.S. 197- SU 968 186
☎0234 750927

Take the A285 from Petworth, then the first L after crossing the river. Entrance to the wood is on the left after 300 yards. Open any time. Mixed conifer plantations, chestnut coppice and a small area of southern beech (Nothofagus).

Clapham Woods
(J F Somerset) A 145 ha
O.S.S. 197/198 - TQ 105 059
☎0903 264686

Off A27 Arundel to Worthing road. The drive to Holt Farm House is on the N side of the road opposite Castle Goring to the W and the *Coach and Horses* public house to the E. Open by appointment in Apr/May. Primroses and bluebells in the hazel with oak standard trees. No coppicing or cutting has been allowed by the local authority since March, 1989 when a blanket tree preservation order was served on the whole wood.

Durford Wood

(National Trust) F 25ha
O.S.S 197 - SU 790 260
☎0243 814554

There is a car park. Free and full access. Telephone above number for further information.

Ebernoe Common Nature Reserve

(Sussex Wildlife Trust) F 71.7 ha
O.S.S. 197/186 - SU 976 278
☎0273 492630

Nearest town - Petworth. Ancient woodland with glades, pools and archaeological remains. The reserve is open at all times, but the complex network of tracks and rides is confusing and can lend the woodland an enchanted air. Take care not to get lost - we advise you strongly to stick to paths! The ack to the church car park leads from the minor road between Ebernoe and the A283. This reserve has probably been wooded since the last ice age and has been used for hundreds of years by the commoners to graze livestock under its huge oak and beech trees. The system of `wood pasture', still found in the New Forest, ceased in this century and this has resulted in an explosion of holly scrub under the trees. Other indicators of the Common's history are the grassy glades and rides, the furnace pond used by the wealden iron industry from the 16th century, and the brick kiln, probably dating from the early 18th century, which used local clay and firewood until the 1930s. The diverse habitats and age of Ebernoe Common give rise to a great variety of wildlife, including over 300 species of plants, 100 of mosses and 400 of fungi; many of the latter flourishing on dead and dying timber. Every part is different: with wild service trees in one place and wild daffodils in another, nightingales and scarce butterflies breeding in the thickets, frogs and toads in the ponds, and with roe deer and the elusive woodcock in the dense forest. Threatened with imminent destruction about fifteen years ago, the Trust launched an emergency appeal and purchased the woodland. Pond clearance, and the removal of bracken and holly from glades and rides, are annual tasks on the reserve. The woodland areas are deliberately left to continue a natural cycle of growth and decay, the October 1987 storm being one of the more dramatic and irregular parts of this process. Status: SSSI owned by the Trust. Registered Common.

Gravetye
(Forest Enterprise) F 316 ha
O.S.S. 187 - TQ 360 347
☎0580 211044

From Turner's Hill take the B2028 SE for approximately 1 mile. Turn L towards Sharp thorne and L again into Vowells Lane. The car park is on the R 500 yards beyond the entrance to Gravetye Manor. Car Park. Open permanently.

The Mens Nature Reserve
(Sussex Wildlife Trust) F 155.1ha
O.S.S.197/198 - TQ 023 237
☎0273 492630

Nearest town - Petworth. The reserve is crossed by a network of paths and rides which can be confusing, so take a compass! Access is easiest from the car park on the minor road to Hawkhurst Court from the A272. We have a continuing problem with horse riders using footpaths which get very muddy indeed. Licensed bridle routes in addition to bridleway. The Trust's largest reserve, the name is derived from the Anglo-Saxon word `ge-maennes' meaning `common' and this ancient woodland is, indeed, common land. To look into its component woodlands is to look into history; some contain old tracks and banks, others `assarts', areas of land illicitly cleared in medieval times and still open today. There are sections where the oak and beech trees are tall and narrow- crowned, indicating dense forest conditions for hundreds of years, whilst in others there are wide spreading giants which must have grown in much more open conditions, such as the massive-trunked Idehurst Oak over three hundred years old. The woodland varies in composition as well as structure. On the Bedham escarpment to the south the canopy is of beech with a sparse understorey of holly; elsewhere there is more oak with such unusual species as the wild service tree. Shrubs include midland hawthorn, rowan and spindle. The great diversity is a product of the immense age of the wood and the variety of soil types beneath it. As there are relatively few open areas in The Mens, it does not have the large numbers of plants, birds and butterflies associated with glades. Its secret specialities are those of the underlying cycle of growth and decay; there is an immense variety of insects and fungi reliant on rotting timber - so often removed from woods but here in abundance. The Mens is unusual in southern England as in recent times it has not been used as wood pasture nor exploited for timber, but due to lack of recent management is reverting to the nature of "wildwood". We therefore leave it as it is, and consider an event such as the October, 1987 gale as a natural part of the development. We restrict management to maintaining paths and edges. Status: SSSI largely owned by the Trust. Registered Common.

Nymans
(National Trust) F 76ha
O.S.S. 184 - SU 264 295
☎0444 400321

On the B2114 at Handcross just off the London to Brighton (M23/A23)road. There is a large car park. Full and free access and newly created waymarked walk. Mature broadleaved woodland with areas of younger planted woodland.

★ Rabbit Warren
(Trustees of The Edward James Foundation) A 130 ha
O.S.S. 197 - Ref. SU 846 148
☎0243 811205

From Chichester take the A286 in a northerly direction to West Dean. Turn L opposite *The Selsey Arms* public house and continue until the marked meeting point is reached on the R (about one mile). There is parking for 12 cars and 1 coach. There are no WCs on site. Guided walk on 3 Jul, 1994. Other guided walks can be arranged by appointment. For all visits, please book two weeks in advance. Please contact I J Odin on above number. Donations to the Forestry Trust. This woodland is planted on the site of a mediaeval rabbit warren, hence its name, and is on the dip of the South Downs comprising shallow soils over chalk. The original plantations were severely damaged in the storms of 1987 and 1990 so a large area has been replanted with various species of

trees, including Norway spruce, Douglas fir and Japanese larch, since these dates. The remainder of the area has varying age crops, the oldest being 1940s plantings of beech, and also an area of chestnut coppice. Both roe and fallow deer are present in large numbers and nightjars regularly nest in the new plantations. The wide ride through the centre of the area produces a good variety of plant and invertebrate life.

Slindon Woods
(National Trust) F 329.1ha
O.S.S. 197 Ref - SU 952 073 and 960 077
☎0243 814554

There are car parks. Full and free access. Telephone above number for further information.

St Leonard's Forest
(Forest Enterprise) F 242 ha
O.S.S. 187/198 TQ 207 298
☎0580 211044

From Horsham take the A281 to Mannings Heath. Take the minor road running from Mannings Heath. Turn L at the T-junction (just over ½ mile) and the car park can be found on the R some 400 yards distant. Car park, Waymarked walk. Open permanently.

★ Stansted Forest
(Stansted Park Foundation) R 400 ha
O.S.S.197 - SU 753 105
☎0705 412265

From Rowland's Castle SE for 1.5 miles, then L and L again. Stansted Forest is 1 mile N on L, whilst the house is on R. Car parking for 35 cars. Some WCs on site. Other facilities include a shop, picnic area, children's play area and disabled paths. Shop, tea room and WC are open when the house is open (Sun, Mon and Tue from May to Sept) with additional opening at Easter. There are rights of way on foot through the wood and bridleways through parts. Please contact Head Forester on above number for details and give one month's notice for group visits. The woodlands are open throughout the year with some restrictions during the shooting season. Please give one month's notice of a visit by a large group. A large area of multipurpose woodland incorporating wildlife habitats and landscape features. Many large, ancient, environmentally important trees and over 200 species of flowering plants recorded. The main avenue over 1.5 miles long was one of the longest beech avenues in England, now much reduced by disease and storms.

TYNE & WEAR

see map on p13

★ Chopwell Woodland Park
(Forest Enterprise) F 375ha
O.S. S. 88 - NZ 139 589
☎0669 20569

From the A1 just south of River
Tyne take A694 to Rowlands Gill,
then turn R on the B6315 for 11/2
miles. Woodland walks, mountain
bikes, horse riding, orienteering.
Mixed broadleaf/conifer woodland
with views over the River Derwent.

Gibside
(National Trust) R 148.77 ha
O.S.S. 88 - NZ 172 583
☎0207 542255

Situated 6 miles SW of Gateshead.
A694 to Rowland's Gill, then
B6314 towards Burnopfield. Car
park, picnic area, tea-gift shop and
WCs. Limited wheelchair access.
The woodland is open to the public
during the open season for Gibside
Chapel and grounds - Easter to the
end of October. Gibside has been
described as "one of the grandest
idylls of the 18th century", the
landscape and associated buildings
are a rare survival of the transi-
tional period in landscape design
incorporating both formal and
informal elements. In 1950 the
majority of the parkland was leased
to the Forestry Commission by the
then owners. Extensive planting
was carried out; however, most of
the original vistas were left as
woodland rides. Snipes Dene Wood
is an SSSI. There are footpaths in
Snipes Dene Wood and along the
River Derwent.

Spen Banks
(Forest Enterprise) L 64ha
O.S.S. 88 - NZ 145 595
0669 20569

see map on p17

★ Claywood

(Mrs and Mrs Slatem) F 14ha
O.S.S. 139 - SP 237 725
☎0926 484673

4 miles N of Warwick and just off the A4177. The nearby Honily Court Hotel is a local landmark. Claywood lies on the opposite side of the road 1/2 mile from the hotel. Car parking for 6 cars. 1 WC, teas, picnic areas and a woodland produce shop. There is fully open access to the wood. Guided visits can be arranged by contacting Mr or Mrs Slatem on the above telephone number. Please allow 7 days notice. Donations received. Originally an old oak wood and part of the Forest of Arden., formerly known as "Clattylands". Claywood was replanted in the early 60s with mainly conifers. It has now matured into a secluded woodland of different varieties, including regenerated oak and birch. Claywood neatly combines woodland of interest for all, including its own tim,ber conversion for wood products, fencing, furniture, and compost. The site has 2 clay pit diggings from earlier brick making activities, much overgrown, with plans for cleaning to introduce water habitats into the woodland theme - ideal for children to see the varieties growing in different stages and their practical uses and yet a woodland atmosphere to enjoy.

Hartshill Hayes and St. Lawrence's Wood

(Warwickshire County Council) F 50 ha
O.S.S. 140 - SP 317 944
☎0827 872660

B4114 from Nuneaton to Chapel End, turn R to Hartshill and then L (signposted) on Oldbury Lane, or B4111 Atherstone towards Nuneaton, R to Hartshill and R (signposted) on Oldbury Lane. Visitor Centre, car park, toilets, shop-café, interpretive exhibition, playground, paths, picnic tables, self guided trails, events, rangers. Charges - car park 70p. Open every day except Christmas Day - closed at dusk. Reputed to be a remnant of the former Forest of Arden, much of the wood was replanted at the end of the 18th century with oak and lime. The lime was coppiced and used by Atherstone hatmakers for the hat blocks on which felt hats were moulded. Most of the hardwoods were cropped in 1981 and replaced by conifers. The County Council's long term aim is to return the woodland to an ancient semi-natural state.

Hay Wood

(Managed by Forest Enterprise) R 105 ha
O.S.S. 139 - SP 205 713
☎0889 586593

From M42, Junction 5 follow A41 towards Warwick, in 5 miles wood is signposted to the R, at Baddesley Clinton. Car park, picnic area.

Oversley Wood

(Managed by Forest Enterprise) R 94 ha
O.S.S. 150 - SP 111 568
0889 586593

From Stratford upon Avon take the
A422 to Alcester. In 4½ miles turn
R, signposted Oversley Green, in
100 yards turn L up track and
drive under new road bridge, forest
gate on R. Forest trail and
Arboretum. A gate key is available
for school parties from Warwick
museum. Very rich display of
woodland flowers during the
Spring.

Thornhill

(The Marquess of Hertford) F 23 ha
O.S.S. 150 - SP 055 565
☎0789 726455

Thornhill is just off the A422 from
Worcester to Stratford on Avon, 2
miles W of Alcester. Open May 1st
- August 31st. The wood includes
the following stands: 1.Ash and
sycamore from which larch and
spruce (nurse crop) have been
removed, showing how silly it is to
plant pure hardwoods. 2. Oak and
Norway spruce aged about 25
years. 3. Lodgepole pine, not very
successful. 4. Old oak ready to be
felled. 5. Corsican pine, planted
1992.

WEST MIDLANDS

see map on p17

Saltwells Wood
(Dudley Metropolitan Borough Council) F
40 ha
O.S.S. 139 - SO 933 868
☎0384 261572

2 miles S of Dudley. Follow signs
to Merry Hill Centre: S along
A4036 (Pedmore Road); L at
island into Coppice Lane; follow
signs to *Saltwells Inn* Car Park.
Public car park at meeting point,
visitors' centre in wood, WCs.
Information leaflets and maps,
displays. Visitor centre open
0800-1630 hours. Remainder of
wood and reserve (180 ha) open
access. Guided walks require
pre-booking. Dogs welcome - must
be on lead (in SSSI only - Doultons
Claypit). Saltwells Wood is the
oldest-established part of the
reserve, originally part of Pensnett
Chase. The large trees are mainly
oak, sycamore and beech. Over
50,000 other native hardwoods
have been planted since 1981
within the fenced sections and as
underplanting below the mature
trees. Typical woodland birds
occur, such as nuthatch, great-
spotted woodpecker, jay, blackcap
and willow warbler. Surprising by
their presence, given the nearby
urban area, are willow tit, wood
warbler, lesser-spotted and green
woodpecker and pied flycatcher on
migration. Mammals include field
vole, common and pygmy shrew,
woodmouse, weasel, hedgehog and
several species of bat. Foxes are
common. In May the floor of the
wood is a carpet of bluebells. There
were brine baths near the site of
the *Saltwells Inn*, using the brackish
water which came up in the early
mine workings. Saltwells Spa
enjoyed its greatest popularity in
Victorian times.

WILTSHIRE

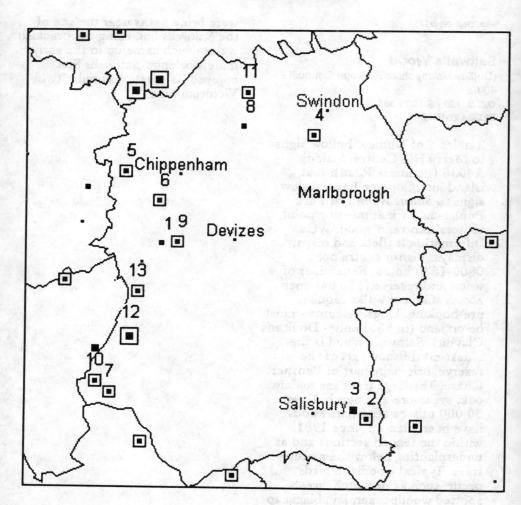

1 Biss Wood
2 Blackmoor Copse
3 *Clarendon Park Estate
4 Clouts Wood
5 Colerne Park & Monks Wood
6 Corsham Court Arboretum
7 *Great Combe

8 Great Wood, Grittenham
9 Green Lane Wood
10 *Jack's Castle
11 Ravensroost Wood
12 *Swancombe Wood
13 *The Woodland Park

Biss Wood
(Gilbert W. Green) **A** 22 ha
O.S.S. 173 - ST 881 567
☎0380 830369

On the W side of the A350 between Westbury and Semington. Car park at entrance opposite Castle Lodge, West Ashton. (½ mile northwards from West Ashton Village in direction of Semington.) Car park for 10 cars. Open by appointment between Mar and Oct. Ancient pedunculate oak, ash, hazel. maple coppice. Regrown from major felling in 1930-33, active management since 1985. 200 vascular plant species. Numerous bird species, roe deer, 32 butterfly species including white admiral and silver- washed fritillary. 180 fungus species recorded since 1986.

Blackmoor Copse
(Wiltshire Wildlife Trust) **F** 31ha
O.S.S. 184 - SU 233 288
☎0380 725670

Six miles E of Salisbury between A30 and A36. On W side of minor road from Winterslow to East Grimstead Entrance at junction with Ben Lane, the road to Farley. Limited parking on wide road verges. Open at all times. The Copse is one of the Wiltshire Trust's loveliest ancient woodlands. Mainly oak and birch with hazel coppice, it is particularly noted for its butterflies, including the silver-washed fritillary, white admiral and purple emperor. The variety of vegetation results in a rich and varied wildlife. In spring primroses, bluebells and violets abound, whilst in the autumn the paths are bright with berries of the hawthorn, wild rose and honey-suckle. King Charles Pond supports sedges, rushes and wetland flowers and the mossy stumps of ancient oaks provide an ideal habitat for a host of invertebrates.

★ Clarendon Park Estate
(A. W. M. Christie-Miller) **A** 400ha
O.S.S 184 - SU 198 306
☎0722 710233

Take the A30 E of Salisbury. After 2½ miles turn R to Pitton. In Pitton village turn R at crossroads by bus shelter and follow the road to gate and Lodge. Parking for 10 cars and 2-3 coaches. No WCs on site. [Open - to be discussed] Donations to Forestry Trust. Formerly a royal forest, this woodland includes the site of Clarendon Palace, a favourite haunt of medieval Kings. The woodland is a mixture of conifer and broadleaf and includes large areas of ancient and semi-natural woodland. Oak and ash predomi-nate along with Douglas fir and larch. There are a large number of woodland birds and other fauna, including roe deer.

Clouts Wood
(Wiltshire Wildlife Trust) **F** 13ha
O.S.S. 173 - SU 136 801
☎0380 725670

On A4361 Swindon to Avebury road, 1 mile SW of Wroughton. 2 nearby laybys for parking. Open at all times. Clouts Wood is an outstanding area of ancient ash woodland. Within a mosaic of trees, shrubs and plants may be found the spiked Star of Bethlehem (unusual so far east) and the nettle-leaved bell flower. Decaying wych elms provide habitat for a variety of birds and insects, including woodpeckers, nuthatches and tits. Several mammals inhabit the wood including badgers, foxes and roe deer. In the valley bottom the moist soil supports a variety of wetland plants such as horse tail, goat willow and hemp agrimony.

Colerne Park And Monks Wood
(Woodland Trust) F 48.3ha
O.S.S. 173 - ST 838 734
☎0476 74297

Situated close to junction 17 on the M4, between the A4 main Bath to Chippenham road and the A420 Bristol to Chippenham road. The wood is reached from a no through road, leading off the narrow lane between Slaughterford and Thickwood. Open at all times. National Trust events may take place in this wood during late Nov/ Dec. Please phone the Woodland Trust on above number for details in the autumn. Colerne Park and Monks Wood are situated near the Fosse Way in the County of Wiltshire and fall into the Cotswold Area of Outstanding Natural Beauty. The most attractive features of the woods are the glades and swathes cut through the

trees. In the summer, when the meadow flowers are blooming, you will see a great number of butterflies attracted to these open spaces. Also there are a number of different types of bird to be found, including green and great spotted woodpeckers and marsh tits.

Corsham Court Arboretum
(The Rt. Hon. A. J. Baron Methuen) R 10.5 ha
O.S.S. 173 - ST 874 705
☎0249 712214

4 miles W of Chippenham. Signposted from The Cross Leys Inn on the A4 Bath Road. Free parking. Historic house on site open to the public. Charges - Adults £2.00, OAPs £1.50, Children £1.00, Group rates for 20 or more. Open daily from 2-4.30 p.m. except Mondays and Fridays. From Good Friday to Sept 30 open until 6 pm. including Fridays and Bank Holiday Mondays. Closed Dec. Groups by appointment. Go to cash desk in house for tickets. Abundance of daffodils and cowslips when in season. Many rare and exotic species in newly planted arboretum. Mature specimen trees in Capability Brown landscape including oriental plane and magnificent copper beech.

★ Great Combe
(H. C. Hoare Esq.) FE 40 ha
O.S.S..183 - ST 748 353
☎0747 840824
Turn off the A303 W of Mere,

signposted for Stourhead, on the B3092. Take the 4th turning L, after 2 miles, follow signs for Alfred's Tower. After about 2 miles the parking area will be seen on the L, before the road descends a steep hill. There is parking for up to 40 cars. Open 365 days per year. There are rights of way on the foot and bridleways through the woodland. Guided tours by arrangement - please phone Jeremy Hoare on above number. Great Combe is an attractive, steep sided valley, sheltered from the prevailing wind. Its nature trail meanders through a variety of mixed scenery, where around every bend something new meets the eye. Conservation and wild life opportunities are good with something of interest throughout the year.

Great Wood, Grittenham

(Mr. N. L. Stewart) A 75 ha
O.S.S.173 - SU 018 816
✉Meon Lea, Droxford,Southampton SO3 1PA

Wootton Bassett-Lynham main road nr M4 junction 16; turn into Trow Lane and travel N for some half mile across main railway line. Ancient semi-natural woodland since 1970 restored to include conifer plantations. Size 185 acres. Predominant hardwood species is oak; conifer are Norway spruce with Douglas fir (new and old) and also larch. One acre newly planted with selected ornamental trees. Large excavated pond encourages amphibians. Fine display of bluebells and primroses in spring.

Green Lane Wood

(WiltshireWildlifeTrust) F 25 ha
O.S.S. 173 - ST 886 576
☎0380 725670

Beside W side of A350 between Semington and Westbury. Car park for about 8 cars but no coaches. Open at all reasonable times. Ancient pedunculate oak wood with areas of ash, alder, maple and hazel coppice. Mostly regrown from major felling 1930- 33. 160 vascular plant species. Roe deer and muntjac. 31 butterfly species including white admiral and silver-washed fritillary. Electricity pylon line swathe forms a distinctive open habitat, especially valuable for butterflies.

★ Jack's Castle

(H. C. Hoare Esq.) F 22 ha
O.S.S. 183. ST 748 353
☎0747 840824

Turn off the A303 west of Mere, signposted for Stourhead, on the B3092. Take the 4th turning on the L, after about 2 miles, following signs for Alfred's Tower. After about 2 miles the parking area will be found on the L, before the road descends a steep hill. There is parking for up to 40 cars. Open 365 days per year. There are guided tours by arrangement - please phone Jeremy Hoare on above number. Jack's Castle is steeped in history. The beech clumps quite possibly replaced earlier landscape features, and even the current ones are about 200 years old. The edge of the ridge on a fine day provides spectacular views of Somerset from the Quantocks to the Mendips.

Ravensroost Wood

(Wiltshire Wildlife Trust) F 39ha
O.S.S.173 - SU 024 877
☎0380 725670

W of Swindon, approximately 1 1/2 miles S of Minety and 2 1/2 miles N of Brinkworth. Main car park at S of wood. Open at all times. Once part of the Royal Forest of Braydon, the wood consists predominantly of matured oak over a hazel-dominated coppice layer. An SSSI, the area is rich in bird and animal life, characteristic of ancient woodlands. Among the rarer species are the wild service tree, small leaved lime and midland thorn. Much of the coppiced area supports a wide variety of butterflies including the silver-washed fritillary. Several ponds provide another important habitat and dragonflies are common.

★ Swancombe Wood

(The Marquess of Bath) Fc 160ha
O.S.183 - ST 828 423
☎0985 213507

From Warminster take the A362 to Frome. At the Longleat round-about turn L towards Horningham and drive about 1 mile. Nockatt car park is situated on the L. Car parking for cars, surfaced path to Shear Water lake. Open through-out the year. Please use parking provided at Nockatt Car Park on the Horningsham/Warminster road. Educational visits, for which a charge will be made, can be

arranged by contacting John McHardy on the above number. The part of the wood named Nockatt dates back over 400 years but other areas were planted from the 1820s on what was previously heath land. After the second world war, the emphasis was on commercial softwood management, but more recently a change in emphasis to amenity and conservation values has become effective. Natural regeneration of species is encouraged which include Noble fir, Douglas fir, western red cedar, coastal redwood, oak, birch, Wild azalea, sycamore, hornbeam etc. The timber from the wood is marketed to provide saw logs for construction, veneers for furniture, with low grade timber being used on the estate itself. The wood has a wide range of plant and animal life. At Shear Water lake there are water activities, sailing and coarse fishing, and a small restaurant and café.

★ The Woodland Park

(A. G. Phillips, OBE, CC.) R 48ha
O.S.S. 183 - ST 840 525
☎0373 822238

Signposted from A361 and A36 roads - brown tourist board signs indicate location from Yarnbrook, Southwick and North Bradley. There is car parking for 100 cars and 10 coaches. There are 3 WCs on site. Other facilities include: shop, caravan and camping sites, picnic area, adventure playground, disabled groups assisted, tearoom, showers for camping site and an audio visual theatre in the museum. Open all year. There is fully open access to the wood. Group visits arranged by appointment only. Please contact Mrs. S. Capon (0373 822238). All the year round admission charge: £2.00 and children £1.00. Accompanied children under 14 free. Other events include: supper evenings with guided walks, Dawn chorus walks with continental breakfast in May, all by appointment only. Special events for children include bunny trails, adventure trails and educational activity trails for schools. Ancient woodland, five groups of owners since 1066. 86 species of trees and shrubs, a lake created in 1960, Museum built in 1970. Shop and tearoom, camping and caravanning facilities, coarse fishing, schools, party visits, supper evenings, special guided walks arranged, wide range of flora and fauna, adventure playground and railway. Garden furniture and sale of forest products. Wide range of bird life. Butterflies include white admiral. 48 types of lichen and moss recorded and a very good specimen of wild service tree. Woodlands felled over in late 50s early 60s and now restored.

YORKSHIRE - NORTH

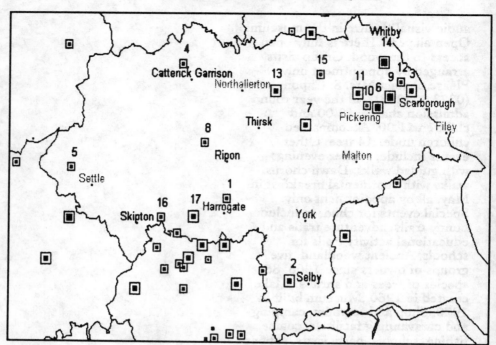

1 Bilton Beck
2 Bishopswood
3 Broxa Forest
4 Calfhall Round Howe & Billybank Woods
5 *Clapdale
6 *Dalby Forest
7 *Duncombe Park
8 Hackfall Wood
9 Langdale Forest

10 Levisham Wood
11 Newtondale
12 Scar and Castlebeck Woods
13 Silton Forest
14 Sneaton Forest
15 Sonley, Sikehill and Hall Woods
16 Strid Wood
17 Swinsty Reservoir

Bilton Beck and Rudding Bottom Wood

(Woodland Trust) F 18ha
O.S.S.104 - SE 315 584
☎0476 74297

From the A59, in Bilton turn either along Bilton Lane or Woodfield Road. There are no facilities but there is some parking near railway bridge. National Tree Week events may take place in this wood during late Nov-Dec. Please phone Woodland Trust for details in the autumn. This woodland lies along the southern bank of the beautiful River Nidd, eastwards from the impressive, now disused, Nidd Viaduct. Oak, ash and alder are the main tree species with hazel and rowan forming the shrub layer. The wood is home to a large number of plants and animals, including celandine, bluebell, wood sorrel, pink purslane, townhall clock, fungi, roe deer, mink and fox. The combination of river and woodland provides plenty of insect food and roosting sites for several species of bat; the dipper, grey wagtail and kingfisher.

Bishopswood

(Managed by Forest Enterprise) F 330ha
O.S.S. 105 - SE 561 333
☎0751 72771

Broxa Forest

(Forest Enterprise) F 733ha
O.S.S. 94/101 - SE 965 945
☎0751 72771

Calfhall Round Howe and Billybank Woods

(National Trust) F 38ha
O.S.S. 92 - NZ 153 005
☎0904 702021

Between Richmond and Hudswell just S of A6108. Access on foot, 1/2 mile upsteam from Richmond bridge. Local Authority car park off the A6108 just W of Richmond. Ancient semi-natural woodland on the S side of the River Swale to the W of the ancient town of Rich- mond. Rich and mature calcareous woodland. Part of the property is an SSSI.

★ Clapdale

(Dr J A Farrer) R 20ha
O.S.S. 98 - SD 749 692
✉Ingleborough Estate, Clapham, via Lancaster, N Yorks LA2 8DR

A65 Skipton to Kendal road between Settle and Ingleton. Dales car park in the village. An information centre in the village. There is a hard surface for walking and wheel chairs. Part of Estate/ Nature trail on way to cave. The wood is open during daylight hours, and charges are Adults 20p, Children 10p (liable to small increase). Student studies by arrangement. Woodlands consist of mature beech; lake scenery and an area of rhododendrons. Geological fault, new planting, developing woodland views of improving silviculture.

★ Dalby Forest

(Forest Enterprise) Fc 3000ha
O.S.S. 100 - SE 857 874

☎0751 472771

Eastwards on A170 from Pickering, turn N on the Whitby Road at Thornton le Dale and follow brown signs to Dalby Forest Drive. Turn R about 2 miles from Thornton into Forest Drive. Visitor centre, forest drive, WCs, picnic places, waymarked walks, cycle trails. Parking: £2.50 cars, £12.50 minibuses, £25 coaches. Open all year, 7.30am - 8.30pm. Group visits and coaches by appointment only. Guided visits are available at £10 per hour. Dalby Forest is an attractive mixed age conifer woodland. The drive allows motorists to go into the heart of the forest and provides picnic places with waymarked walks to enable exploration on foot. For the energetic visitor there are waymarked cycle routes and a permanent orienteering course, maps of which can be purchased at the visitor centre, which also has souvenirs and leaflets on the Deepdale Habitat Trail starting at the Bickley Forest Garden. The different habitats of the beautiful Deepdale valley are interpreted by a series of information boards.

★ Duncombe Park

(The Rt Hon Lord Feversham) R 165ha
O.S.S.100 - SE 603 833
☎0439 70213

Duncombe Park is in Helmsley off A170 Thirsk/Scarborough Road. Entrance 3 mins from Market Square.. Facilities include a restaurant, WCs, shop and car park. Admission charges is £2.75 (Garden and Park) £1 (Park only). The Park is open from Apr to Oct but there could be restricted access due to special events. Telephone above number for details (24 hours). On the site of a medieval Deer Park and landscaped in the 18th century Duncombe Park contains multipurpose deciduous and coniferous woodlands. The wooded dale rides form a natural landscape of river, grazing land and forest. The "green garden" at the Mansion House contains the tallest lime and one of the tallest oak trees in England. The undisturbed hardwood ecosystem hosts a wealth of insect, herbaceous and birdlife with rare species identified and is designated a National Nature Reserve. There are no public rights of way but entry charge gives access to woodland paths, visitor facilities and the garden (when open).

Hackfall Wood

(Woodland Trust) F 45.32
O.S.S. 99 - SE 234 773
☎0476 74297

From Ripon Market Square, head W on the B6265 (signposted Hackley Bridge). After about 500 yards take the RH fork to Grewelthorpe. Follow this road through the village and on towards Masham for about 1/2 mile. Park in the car park and follow the signs to the wood. There are no facilities. There is full and free access. National Tree Week events may take place in this wood during late

Nov-Dec. Please phone the Woodland Trust for details in the autumn. Hackfall Wood remains wet even in the hottest summers. Boots or wellingtons are recomended. This ancient woodland, at least 350 years old, forms a remarkable landscape feature on the NW facing side of a 100 m deep gorge cut via the River Ure. The wood provides a diversity of habitats for a range of wildlife, including wood warbler, nuthatch and kingfisher. Tree species such as oak, ash and spindle can be found in the wood. The ground flora is also characteristic of old established woodland with dog's mercury, primrose,bluebell and wild garlic. If you move quietly, you may catch a glimpse of roe deer.

Langdale Forest
(Forest Enterprise) F 4256ha
O.S.S. 94/101 SE 927 926
☎0751 72771

Levisham Wood
(North York Moors National Park) F 63.9ha
O.S.S. 94/100 - SE 826 897
☎0439 70657

Take A169 N from Pickering to Whitby. Turn L to Lockton and Levisham after 5 miles. Drive through Lockton to Levisham. At top of Levisham village turn L by church and follow back lane until it becomes track. Park at end where Green Lane begins. Do not obstruct gateway to adjoining

agricultural land. There is full and free access at all times. Levisham Woods are all ancient semi-natural woodland and included within the Newtondale SSSI. Previous ownership by the Forestry Commission resulted in extensive felling of broadleaves and conifer planting. Long term objectives included reverting the woods to native broadleaved species. Steep slopes are a management constraint but give exceptional views into Newtondale. The woods adjoin a series of unimproved pastures which together with the woods contain an extensive range of flora and fauna.

Newtondale
(Forest Enterprise) F 500ha
O.S.S. SE - 824 938
☎0751 72771

North York Moors railway to Newtondale Halt. By road: turn W off A169 at Lockton and drive through Levisham to Newtondale Forest Drive or E of the Stape to Egton Bridge road at Mawley Cross. Forest drive, picnic places and walks. Parking 50p, no coaches. Special arrangement for school parties and educational groups. Within the dramatic scenery of Newton Dale, mainly conifer woodland well into the second rotation. Superb views of a mixed forest and moorland landscape. Explore the woods by means of the waymarked walks from Newtondale Halt or along one of the many public rights of way which intersect the wood. A rich and varied wildlife population.

Scar and Castlebeck Woods
(Woodland Trust) F 32.61ha
O.S.S. 94/100 - SE 947 971
☎0476 74297

On the main A171 Scarborough to Whitby Road, take the road running S to Harwood Dale. Access to the woods is at two points, 1 mile and 1 1/2 mile along this road on the A171 junction. For the latter entrance follow the bridleway just before Chapel Farm. This leads into the southern part of the property. Cars can be parked on the roadside verge opposite the bridleway. Please DO NOT park in the farmyard. There are no facilities and there is free and full access all year. National Tree Week events may take place in this wood during late Nov-Dec. Please phone the Woodland Trust for details in the autumn. Paths within the woods can be quite muddy and stout footwear is advisable. Caution should be taken if the stream is crossed at the northern end as the stepping stones can be very slippery. Scar and Castlebeck Woods lie in a deep, secluded valley in the North York Moors National Park. Alder and rowan line the stream edge with oak, ash and elm also present. The wood has a rich and interesting fauna and flora. On the valley side a wealth of mosses and liverworts, known as bryophytes, flourish in the damp atmosphere. Wood club rush, broad buckler fern, and wavy hair grass grow in abundance. Of special interest is the brimstone butterfly; in Scar and Castlebeck woods it has reached the most NE point of its range in England.

Silton Forest
(Forest Enterprise) F 465ha
O.S.S. 100 - SE 469 943
☎0751 72771

Sneaton Forest
(Forest Enterprise) F 1209ha
O.S.S. 94 - NZ 888 036
☎0751 472771

B1416 from Rushwarp and turn S at Red Gate junction down minor road to Falling Foss car park. Waymarked walk, picnic places, car parks. School parties by appointment. The old woodland around Falling Foss is most attractive, mature broadleaf giving way in the south to young conifer plantations established mostly in the late 1960s on open moor. Much work has been done in the young plantations to ameliorate edges and diversify habitats. Waymarked walks from both the Falling Foss car park and the Maybeck car park (893024) enable the visitor to explore the forest on foot.

Sonley, Sikehill and Hall Woods; Farndale woodlands
(National Trust) R 13ha
O.S.S. 94/100 - SE 654 994
☎0904 702021

Access is by foot from minor public highways running N from Church Houses. Mixed woodlands in Upper Farndale famed for its wild daffodils, in the North York Moors

National Park. Bought in 1991 jointly by the Council for National Parks, the Ramblers' Association, and the Council for Protection of Rural England and Open Spaces Society, with help from the Countryside Commission. Presented to the National Trust to commemorate the life of Francis Ritchie, who campaigned all his life, in a voluntary capacity, for the designation and protection of National Parks.

Strid Wood: (Bolton Abbey)
(Trustees of the Chatsworth Settlement) F 46ha
O.S.S. 104 - SE 077 533
☎0756 710533

4 miles E of Skipton take the B6160 N from the A59 Skipton-Harrogate Road. In 1 mile turn down private drive to the Cavendish Pavilion car park. Car parking for 1500 cars and 50 coaches (note height restriction of 10'9"). Other facilities include: restaurant, snack and ice cream facilities at the Cavendish Pavilion, shop and nature trail, interpretation area, 3D colour slide presentation of estate work for organised groups. There is fully open access to the woodland trails and there are rights of way through the wood on foot. The woods are open every day of the year, from 9am until 5pm. Guided tours for groups can be arranged, please contact Mrs Barbara Allen, Estate Office, Bolton Abbey, Skipton, BD23 6EX on above telephone number. These start at 10am and 2pm. The cost of guided tours :

Adults £1.50, Children 75p. Please give 7 days notice for group bookings. Two electric vehicles are available for less able visitors, free of charge. The Strid, straddling the River Wharfe has long been a place of legend and beauty. An SSSI the abundance and variety of species is a result of the management of the ancient woodland by selective felling and regeneration, retaining a continuous canopy with a diversity of species. Records show 62 nesting species of birds, 98 species of mosses, 97 of fungi, 80 lichens, 49 molluscs, 42 liverworts and an abundance of vascular plants. Visitors have been welcomed to the Strid since the early 19th century when a series of views, summer-houses and trails were created by the 6th Duke. These now form the basis of the present nature trails.

Swinsty Reservoir
(Yorkshire Water) F 200ha
O.S.S. 104 - SE 197 538
☎0532-312576

From the A59 Harrogate/Skipton road, take the turning to Otley at Blubberhouses. Once on that road take the side road marked "Timble" down to Swinsty and Fewston. Facilities include car park, WCs, picnic area, footpaths. Fishing is also available but there is a charge for this facility. The wood is open all year. Woodland walks with a wide variety of wildlife - especially on the water. The woods surround Swinsty Reservoir, providing superb views along the Washam Valley.

YORKSHIRE - SOUTH

see map on p13

★ Cawthorne Park

(Cawthorne Park Woodlands) A 105ha
O.S.S.110 - SE 283 102
☎0226 295197

At Junction 38 M1 towards
Barnsley, first R at bottom of hill to
'T' junction. Turn right at High
Hoyland Road. Wood on L at top
of ridge, second gate. There is
parking for 10 cars and 1 coach but
no other facilities. Guided visits
can be arranged by appointment.
Please book 2 weeks in advance.
Charges: car parking £1. Visits:
adults £2, children 50p. Group
rates by negotiation. Donations
made to the Forestry Trust. For
ALL visits please contact Len
Batty on the above number. The
wood is a replanted ancient
woodland being part of the original
Bretton Hall Estate, replanted in
the late 50's with a selection of
hard and soft woods. Within the
stream valley that runs down the
centre of the wood is evidence of
ancient ironstone workings. There
is some hearsay that this iron was
used to make cannon balls used
against the Spanish Armada. There
is also a series of ponds holding a
selection of aquatic wildlife. The
woodland is being managed on a
select thin regime with underplanting of hardwoods. The mains
species on site are hybrid larch and
Corsican pine with a good
proportion of mixed hardwoods.

Ecclesall Woods

(Sheffield City Council) F 130ha
O.S.S. 110- SK 309 820
☎0742 500500

Approximately 4 miles from City
Centre - A625 - turn off onto Limb
Lane or alternatively A621
opposite Abbeydale Industrial
Hamlet (well signed) - O.S.Ref -
SK 326820. Across busy main
road. There is no crossing point.
Car parking and picnic area at
Limb Lane meeting point. No
WCs. Free access all year round.
There is an extensive footpath/
bridleway network. Please keep to
the paths as much as possible and
avoid entering bird sanctuary. An
ancient woodland though much
modified has passed through
various stages from 'wildwood' to
wood pasture/park to coppice
woodland to the present high
forest. Has rich industrial history.
Contains commemorative
tombstone of wood collier
(charcoal burner) dated 1786. A
bird sanctuary was established over
part of the wood in 1929. Has rich
flora and fauna with over 200
recorded plant species and nearly
60 bryophytes. Leaflet available.
Also comprehensive booklet by
Sorby Natural History It lies next
to interesting Abbeydale Industrial
Hamlet. Scheduled to become local
nature reserve.

Langsett Reservoir

(Yorkshire Water) F 150.5 ha
O.S. S. 110 - SE 212 005

The car park is off the A616

Stockbridge by-pass which links the M1 with the Manchester road (A628). Car park, picnic area, footpaths, information centre (summer only), WCs, café, pub. Open all year. The wood is mainly coniferous and surrounds Langsett Reservoir. There are spectacular views over the reservoir and onto the moors of the Peak District, especially attractive in September when the heather is in flower.

Roe Wood

(Sheffield City Council) F 13.5 ha
O.S. S.110 - SK 358 904
☎0742 787863

Entrance is by junction of Norwood Road and Herries Road, Sheffield S5, opposite Northern General Hospital. Open all hours. Great Roe is a broadleaf wood, mainly beech and oak. Indicators of its ancient origins include dog's mercury and yellow archangel. In autumn numerous types of fungus abound, with jew's ear and destroying angel. The wood is managed on traditional lines by Sheffield City Wildlife Trust using, for instance, coppicing and heavy horses. It has a unique tree sculpture and a picnic site, carved by a local sculptor from felled beech trees. Little Roe is, by contrast, partly the remains of a formal garden with introduced species and an old orchard, and partly woodland with a fine beech avenue and ,in spring, a carpet of bluebells growing in the soft grass called yorkshire fog.

Wharncliffe Woods

(Forest Enterprise) F 456ha
O.S.S. 110 - SK 325 950
☎0623 822447

Wyming Brook

(Sheffield City Council) F 50ha
O.S.S. 110 - SK 275 865
☎0742 500500

A57 Manchester Road - turn off by old waterworks house (O.S.Ref -SK 276869) and travel across access road to Rivelin Dam. Alternatively access can be obtained from Redmires Road (O.S. Ref - SK 269858) where there is a small car park. There are no other facilities other than footpath network. Free and full access all year round. Stout footwear required if taking stream-side path. Please keep to paths as much as possible. A very attr active mixed woodland mainly of native broadleaves and conifers, notably Corsican pine and spruces. Valuable wildlife site. Good views obtainable from higher areas; rises to 300m. Adjoins Water Authority woodland and reservoir. Scheduled to become local nature reserve.

YORKSHIRE - WEST

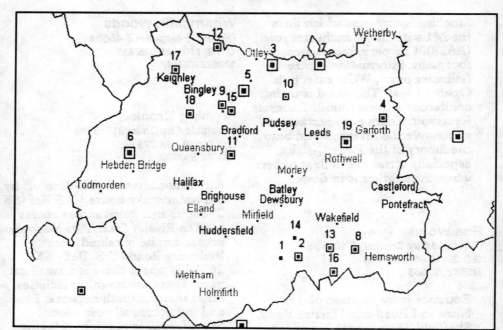

1 Bank Wood
2 Bella Vista
3 *Chevin Forest Park
4 Coburn Hill Wood
5 Esholt Woods
6 Hardcastle Crags
7 *Harewood
8 Haw Park Wood
9 Hirst Wood
10 Ireland Wood

11 Judy Wood
12 Middleton Wood
13 Newmillerdam Country Park
14 North Wood
15 Northcliffe Wood
16 Notton Wood
17 Park Wood
18 St Ives Wood
19 Temple Newsham Estate

Bank Wood
(Job Earnshaw & Bros. Ltd) A 35 ha
O.S.S. 110 - SE 268 139
☎0924 830099

Junction 38 M1. Take A637
towards Huddersfield. Turn L at
West Bretton roundabout and
follow A636 for half mile, then turn
R. Follow track down to wood.
Some public footpaths, all other
access by appointment. Bank
Wood is an ancient woodland site
although opencast coalmining has
affected some areas. Relics of
bellpits from 18th Century
ironstone mining are to be found in
the wood. The wide rides support a
range of butterfly species. Tree
cover is predominantly sycamore,
larch and Scots pine, with some
ash and occasional beech.

Bella Vista
(Job Earnshaw & Bros. Ltd) R 16 ha
O.S.S. 110 - SE 277 142
☎0924 830099

Junction 38 M1. Take A637
towards Huddersfield. Turn L
along A636 at West Bretton
roundabout. Car park is approximately 200 yards on the L hand
side. There are rights of way on
foot through the woods. Please
keep to footpaths. No dogs allowed
away from official footpaths.
Information sheet available. Bella
Vista plantations were probably
planted for visual and sporting
purposes by the owners of Bretton
Hall in the 19th century. They are
bisected by the remains of a
mediaeval road and the relic of a
17th century brickworks can be
found in the west of the woodland.
Tree cover is predominantly
sycamore and Japanese larch with
some oak and beech.

★ Chevin Forest Park
(Leeds City Council) F 283 ha
O.S.S. 104 - SE 216 444
☎0532 586655

The Park is signposted from Otley
town centre. Car parking for 200
cars and 3 coaches. There is a
Visitor Centre and a café. There
are rights of way, bridleways and
self guided trails through the park.
All group visits are by appointment
only and require 30 days notice;
please contact Mr. Terry Cree on
0943 465023. This park of
woodlands and crags was
designated a Local Nature Reserve
in 1989. It is home to a wide range
of flora and fauna; of particular
interest are green hairstreak
butterflies and bog asphodel, roe
deer and woodcock. The woodlands are made up of many tree
species, both native and exotic,
including beech, oak, sweet
chestnut, hemlock and Corsican
pine. The park is criss-crossed by
paths and bridleways, and offers
fine views across the Wharfe valley.
The site can be explored using the
permanent orienteering course of
self guided trails. School visits are
catered for with the field s
e offering an opportunity for indoor
study of the natural environment.

Coburn Hill Wood
(Leeds City Council) F 20 ha
O.S.S 105 - SE 450 360
0532 586655

From Garforth take the A642, after going under the A1 turn R into the B1217. After ½ mile turn R into Lotherton Hall Estate. Coburn Hill Woods are reached by a footpath which runs off to the S of the estate. Car parking for 100 cars and 4 coaches. There are WCs, including WCs for the disabled, a shop, a picnic area, a café, a bird garden, a hall and chapel. There is open access to the woods, rights of way and bridleways. There are also self guided trails. For group visits please allow 2 weeks' notice. Contact the Ranger Service on 0532 813068. Coburn Hill Wood is one of a number of woodlands running N to S between Lotherton Hall estate and the Fairburn Ings nature reserve. It lies on a bed of magnesium limestone to the E of Leeds. Many plants and animals which are not seen in other parts of Leeds thrive in the wood. The wood was purchased by Leeds City Council in the 1980s. It formerly belonged to the Forestry Commission.

Esholt Woods
(Bradford Metropolitan District Council) F 120 ha
O.S.S. 104 - SE 182 404
☎0274 754826

From Shipley, take the A6038 and follow the signs for Esholt. Car park is on the L just before the village. There is car parking for 12 cars and 4 coaches. There is open access and bridleways through the wood. Guided visits can be arranged; please contact Richard Dunton on above telephone number. A number of small conifer plantations and deciduous woods locally known as Esholt Woods, surrounding the village of Esholt, of 'Emmerdale Farm' fame. Some of the woods in the bottom of the valley are owned by Yorkshire Water, with restricted access for operational reasons.

Hardcastle Crags
(National Trust) F 125 ha
O.S. S. 103 - SD 988 295
☎0422 844518

1 1/2 miles NW of Beden Bridge. Parking at entrance, coaches by arrangement only. Guided walks -please contact the Warden on 0422 844518. Braille guide available. Information caravan (seasonal weekends). Woodland, NW of Hebden Bridge, comprises two steep wooded valleys, each with a stream running through it. The woodland is pre- dominantly broadleaved, with areas of conifer. Rock outcrops and millponds are attractive features. Riverside walks beside Hebden Water take you through deciduous woodland and past a disused 19th century cotton mill. The main path is accessible by wheelchair users.

★ Harewood
(Viscount Lascelles) F 400ha
O.S.S.104 - SE 313 346
☎0532 886331

Harewood is on the A61 between Leeds and Harrogate. There is free parking for 500 cars and 30 coaches. Shops, picnic areas, adventure playground, restaurant, coffee shop, education centre and conference facilities. There are public footpaths through some of the main woodland areas. Guided party visits can be arranged by appointment between 13 Mar to 31 Oct 1994, Mon to Fri, 1000 - 1400 hours. Weekends and evenings by special arrangement. Please book 2 weeks in advance for all guided visits. Charges for guided visits: adults £2.75, children £1. For ALL guided visits please contact Mr E Cruickshank on the above number.

Haw Park Wood
(Wakefield Metropolitan District Council) F 65 ha
O.S. S. 110/111 - SE 375 154
☎0924 296203

Follow brown tourist signs to Anglers country park from either A61 Wakefield/Barnsley road or A638 Wakefield/Doncaster road. Car park at Anglers country park, Haw Park wood ¼ mile. Visitor Centre, car park at Anglers Country Park. Open every day. Haw Park Wood is an ancient replanted woodland formerly owned by the Forestry Commission. The northern part of the wood was part of the eminent naturalist Charles Walton's estate. Pleasant walks and a bridleway go through the wood. It is predominantly coniferous but the long-term aim is for it to become mixed deciduous. Management is to enhance, diversify and improve the woodland for people and wildlife.

Hirst Wood
(Bradford Metropolitan District Council) F 15 ha
O.S.S. 104 - SE 140 380
☎0274 754826

Follow the A650 to Saltaire. At the roundabout, take the third L, carry on over the railway bridge to the car park on the L. There is car parking for 30 cars, with a picnic area next to the car park. There is full access to the wood. Guided visits can be arranged by appointment, please contact Richard Dunton on above number. Hirst Wood is an SSSI due to the presence of a glacial bog. It is bounded by the river Aire and the Leeds-Liverpool canal, next to the historic village of Saltaire. A mature broadleaf woodland with some notable beech trees. A woodland walk is signposted and waymarked within the wood.

Ireland Wood
(Woodland Trust) F 4 ha
O.S.S. 104 - SE 255 392
☎0476 74297

From Leeds take the A660 signposted to Otley through

Headingley to the main round-about (Leeds ring road). Continue on the A660 and take the first main turning L, signposted to Cookridge. Along this road turn L to Cookridge Hospital. The woods are about 500 yards along this road opposite the hospital. Ample roadside parking. National Tree Week events may take place in this wood during late November-December. Please phone the Woodland Trust for details in the autumn. This remnant of long established woodland is situated within a heavily developed residential area and is well used by local people. It is an attractive wood containing oak growing from old coppice stools, along with birch, wild cherry, rowan, beech, holly and sycamore. Robin and thrush are just two of the many common bird species living in this wood.

Judy Woods

(Bradford Metropolitan District Council) F
40 ha
O.S.S. 104 - SE 160 301
☎0274 754826

3 miles from Bradford on the A641, turn R towards Norwood Green, park on the road 200m after the bend. Car parking for 20 cars. Disabled access into the woods on surfaced paths and picnic areas are also provided. There is open access to the wood. Guided visits can be arranged by appointment, please contact Richard Dunton on 0274 754826. A number of small broadleaf woods

known locally as Judy Woods. There has been small scale mineral extraction in the past. Mainly mature beech, planted to supply bobbins for the local textile industries. A woodland walk is signposted and waymarked within the wood.

Middleton Wood

(Bradford Metropolitan District Council) F
51 ha
O.S. S. 104 - SE 110 480
☎0274 754826

From the centre of Ilkley, travel down Brooke Street over the bridge. Take the next R. The entrance is a quarter of a mile on the L. Car parking for 15 cars. There is open access to the wood. Guided visits can be arranged by appointment. Please contact Richard Dunton on above number. An ancient deciduous woodland as noted before Doomsday. It is of outstanding landscape value with views over Ilkley Moor and the Wharfe Valley. It is particularly noted for its wildlife and an abundance of bluebells in the spring. A woodland walk is signposted and waymarked within the wood.

Newmillerdam Country Park

(Wakefield Metropolitan District Council)F
95 ha
O.S. S 110/111 - SE 331 157
☎0924 296203

4 miles from Wakefield on the A61 Barnsley/Wakefield road. Pay and display car park, pubs, café etc. in Newmillerdam village. Open every

day. An historical landscape with woodland and lakeside walks. The lakeside walk is suitable for wheelchairs. Marked bridleway and a permanent orienteering course in the wood. There is good wildlife interest at all times. The conifers were planted for the mining industry and are now marketed for saw-logs, fencing etc. The wood is managed to improve, diversify and enhance its character.

North Wood

(Job Earnshaw & Bros. Ltd) A 35 ha
O.S.S. 110/111 - SE 277 153
☎0924 830099

From junction 38 on M1, follow the A637 towards Huddersfield. Turn R down the B6117 and R again. All access by appointment except for public rights of way. North Wood is an ancient woodland site. There is some evidence of late 19th century coal mining and the remains of a mineral railway. Badgers are occasionally found in the woods and jays and woodcock both breed. A wide range of tree species occurs - sycamore, oak, Scots pine and larch predominate. Ash, rowan and beech are also present.

Northcliffe Wood

(Bradford Metropolitan District Council) F
17.5 ha
O.S.S. 104 - SE 150 370
☎0274 754826

Take the A650 from Bradford to Shipley, after 2.5 miles turn L into Cliffe Wood Avenue. Car parking for 20 cars. Other facilities include a picnic area, children's play area and model railway. There is open access to the wood. Guided visits can be arranged by appointment, please contact Richard Dunton on above number. A broadleaf woodland with oak as the dominant species. Bounded by playing fields and a golf course with views over the historic village of Saltaire, Salts Mill, and Baildon and Ilkley Moor. There is evidence of small scale mining and charcoal burning pits. A woodland walk is signposted and waymarked within the wood.

Notton Woods

(Wakefield Metropolitan District Council) F
48 ha
O.S.S. 110 - SE 338 123
☎0924 296203

6 miles from Wakefield on the A61 Wakefield/Barnsley road. Turn L into Keeper Lane (minor road). Parking ½ mile on R as road turns L. Follow track at side of field to wood. Open every day. Notton is an ancient replanted woodland which has been replanted predominantly with conifers. The long-term aim is to convert it back to a mixed deciduous woodland.

Park Wood

(Bradford Metropolitan District Council) F
14 ha
O.S.S. 104 - SE 064 420
☎0274 754826

Situated quarter of a mile from the centre of Keighley and above the Worth Valley Steam Railway. Car parking for 10 cars. Other facilities include picnic area and a children's play area. There is open access to the wood. Guided visits can be arranged by appointment. Please contact Richard Dunton on above number. A mature broadleaf wood with an old cobbled path running through it. The wood is an important landscape feature with good views along the Aire Valley to the Dales.

St Ives Estate
(Bradford Metropolitan District Council) F 65 ha
O.S.S. 104 - SE 090 390
☎0274 754826

Take the B6429 Harden road. From Bingley, the entrance is on the R at the top of the hill. Car parking for 80 cars and 2 coaches. Other facilities include various picnic areas, ornamental gardens, children's play area, disabled access to parts of woods, 3 self guided nature trails, golf course and fishing pond. There is open access with bridleways through the wood, and self guided trails. Guided visits can be arranged by appointment, please contact Richard Dunton on above number. A woodland estate dating back to the 13th century, when it was given to the monks of Riveaulx Abbey. The woodland is mixed with some recent conifer plantations. There is evidence of an entrenchment from the English Civil War and other notable features. A large oak from the estate was used in the recent building of the south transept of York Minster.

Temple Newsam Estate
(Leeds City Council) F 485 ha
O.S.S. 104 - SE 358 323
☎0532 586655

Follow the A64 York road out of Leeds, then take the A63 Selby road signposted. Nearest locations are Halton and Crossgates. Car parking for 1,000 cars and 20 coaches. There are toilets, including disabled. Other facilities include a souvenir shop, tea rooms, adventure play ground, Tudor-Jacobean mansion, ornamental gardens, lakes and good disabled access around the park, Home Farm Museum and Rare Breed Centre. There is fully open access to the woods via rights of way and bridleways. There are also self guided trails. Guided visits can be arranged by contacting M Akers on 0532 645535. Please give 2 weeks notice. Temple Newsam is a 485 hectare country park with a recorded history as a private estate of 1,000 years. The woodland is of mainly semi-natural appearance although planted with new plantations. Much of it dates from the 18th century when the estate was landscaped by Capability Brown. All the main timber species are represented in clearly defined stands - oak, beech, sycamore etc. The old hazel coppice is currently being brought back into rotation.

WALES

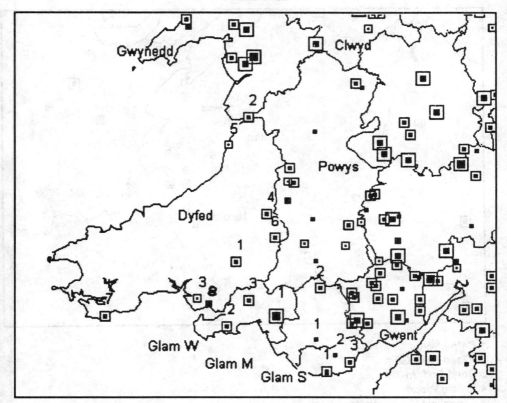

See separate map for
Clwyd p224
Gwent p235
Gwynedd p243
Powys p248

DYFED (p229)
1 Castle Woods Nayture Reserve
2 Coed Penrhyn-Mawr
3 Coed Rhyal
4 Dinas
5 Parc Natur Penglais
6 Poor Man's Wood
7. Stackpole Estate Woodlands
8. Stradey Estate Woodlands

GLAMORGAN MID (p232)
1. *Llanharan Wood
2. Taf Fechan

GLAMORGAN SOUTH (p233)
1 Cliff Wood
2 Coedarhydglyn
3 Cogan Wood

GLAMORGAN WEST (p234)
1 *Afan Forest Park
2 Bishopston Valley
3 Cwm Clydach

CLWYD

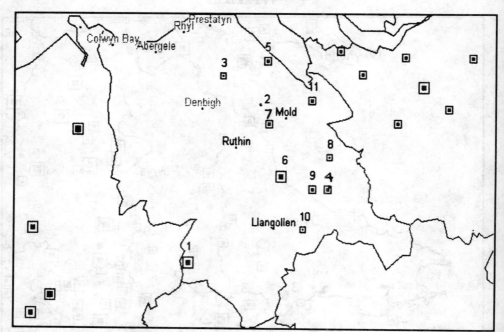

1 Cefn Llwyd
2 *Coed Nant Gain
3 Coed Sodom
4 Erddig Wood
5 Greenfield Valley Heritage Park
6 Llandegla
7 Loggerheads Country Park
8 Nant-y-Gaer Woods
9 Plas Power Woods
10 Tan-y-Cut Woods
11 Wepre Country Park

Cefn Llwyd
(Shotton Paper Co Ltd) R 439.4ha
O.S.S.125- SH 997 343
☎0974 3688

4 miles SE of Bala on the B4391 Bala to Llangynog road. Car parking for 6 vehicles. Open all year. Guided tour Sat 9 Jul 1994, 1pm for 3 hours. Please contact P.R. Morgan 6 weeks in advance. A conifer forest planted between 1952 and 1991 as part of a larger woodland estate. Comprises open moor and woodland with great diversity of habitats supporting raptors, black and red grouse, and red squirrels. The forest is managed on a small coupe felling system which will provide a diverse age structure at the end of the restructuring period. Group strip and selection systems are being practised. The views of the forest and moor are impressive with paths leading to the Berwyn mountain. There are also spectacular views down the Dee valley.

★ Coed Nant Gain
(Iliff Simey) A 8.05ha
O.S.S. 116 - SJ 186 651
☎0352 741039

4.5 miles out of Mold. Take Pantymyn road, then Cilcain road down steep hill, over narrow bridge, park on road side. Limited space. Gate at end of parking space. Donations collected for the Woodland Trust and Tree Aid. Appointments can be made anytime. Please telephone as above. Guided tours for schools, societies and individuals interested in ancient woodlands. Narrow glacial valley woodland between river limestone escarpment and open moorland. Rich habitat diversity. Natural regeneration of trees to restore the ancient woodland under Woodland Grant Scheme for timber, intensive production of wildlife, and as practical demonstration of harmony in the countryside. Ancient woodland flora, wide variety of birds, fungi, bryophytes, lichen, etc. Spring flowers peak late April/early May. Rural history evident in past management and use and of agricultural encroachment over hundreds of years (see Journal of Royal Forestry Society, April 1993).

Coed Sodom
(Mr & Mrs J D Binnian) F 8ha
O.S.S. 116 - SJ 097 723

From Denbigh take A541 towards Mold. 4 miles on turn L in Bodfari to Tremeirchion on B5429. 1 mile N of Bodari turn R up steep hill; first L, straight over cross road and continue to meeting point. Limited car park only. Donations to the Forestry Trust £2. Please acknowledge donations are from visiting Coed Sodom. Open any time, with Forestry Trust booklet. Coed Sodom is alongside Offa's Dyke Path, with views to the sea and to the hills of the vale of Clwyd. The woodland was bought from the Forestry Commission in 1985 and a winding track leads down through the well thinned sitka spruce and Douglas fir to a lower lane. Young plants and bushes have colonised the ride margins to produce attractive glades. There is a vigorous badger sett; buzzards are present and the russet bark of Californian redwoods can be seen at the lower edge among fine Douglas fir stems.

Erddig Wood
(National Trust) F 72ha
O.S.S. 117 - SJ 330 485
☎0690 710636

On the outskirts of Wrexham; take the A534 from A483 or Wrexham town centre, and follow signs to Erddig house. Car parking at Erddig house where the facilities at the house include WC, shop and tearoom. Erddig Wood comprises several woodlands in Erddig Park, predominantly broadleaved of high landscape value. Some fine mature oak and beech. Most of the woodland is classified ancient semi-natural. Points of interest include the historic Erddig house gardens and park, and Watts Dyke with associated earthworks..There is an extensive network of parkland and woodland paths.

Greenfield Valley Heritage Park
(Delyn Borough Council) F 20ha
O.S.S. 116 - SJ 195 775
☎0352 714172

Free parking is available off the B5121 Greenfield - Holywell road. Toilets, cafe, exhibitions, picnic area, play area, woodland trail, museum. Public park. Visitor centre open 10am - 5pm 1 Apr - 31 Oct. Ranger service all year round. During the 18th century the valley was a hive of industrial activity, its factories producing copper goods, spinning cotton and a wire works. Once industrial activities ceased trees and shrubs colonised the valley. The characteristic and dominant tree species are oak on dry acid slopes and ash in the damper valley bottom. There is an extremely attractive area of mature beech woodland and much scrub has been colonised by sycamore. 5 reservoirs set in the woodland atract much wildlife.

Llandegla
(Shotton Paper Co Ltd) R 653.2ha
O.S.S. 117 - SJ 228 521
☎0974 3688

7 miles W of Wrexham, the forest lies to the S of the A525, and 11/2 miles E of the village of Llandegla. Access is off the unclassified "Old Chester Road". Limited car parking. Open all year. Guided tour on Sat 3 Sept 1994, 1pm for 3 hours. Please contact P R Morgan 6 weeks in advance. Please keep to the paths to avoid disturbance to nesting birds. Dogs to be kept on leads April - June. A predominantly conifer forest planted in early 1970s. Formerly a grouse moor and adjacent to Llantysillio Mountain and Minera SSSI. The forest is at thinning stage and the intention is to convert this even age plantation into a perpetual forest.

A number of footpaths and bridleways have been cleared and improved. The Offas Dyke long distance path runs through the forest.

Loggerheads Country Park
(Clwyd County Council) F 35ha
O.S. S116/117 - SJ 198 626
☎0352 702303

Adjacent to A494(T). 3 miles W of Mold. Main car park on R - see brown direction signs. Car park 50p (All day) main car park closes 9pm, cafe, information centre, WCs, disabled access, nature trails. An area of mixed woodland with limestone cliffs from which there are superb views westwards to the Clwydian Hills. Evidence of early mining gives added interest. A nature trail and an industrial trail are laid out. Delightful all the year round but especially in spring (wild flowers) and autumn (colours). River Alyn flows through the site giving added interest, especially where the river disappears into swallow holes.

Nant-y-Gaer Woods
(Wrexham Maelor Borough Council) F 4ha
O.S.S. 117 - SJ 335 557
☎0978 292046

Take New Llay Road out of Wrexham B5425, into Llay village, take 2nd R down Nant-y-Gaer Road, continue for 1/4 mile. Limited parking alongside houses and walk down valley, turn L into woods. There are no facilities and access is free and full all year round. The wood is a small steep sided river valley adjacent to the village of Llay. The valley is dominated by mature oak, sycamore and ash and is easily accessible along surfaced footpaths. The woodland is situated half a mile from Alyn Waters Country Park and can form part of a walk in the Alyn Valley.

Plas Power Wood
(Woodland Trust) F 33.75ha
O.S.S. 117 - SJ 297 495
☎0476 74297

Take the A525 out of Wrexham towards Ruthin. On entering Coedpoeth turn L onto a minor road towards Nant Mill. Park in the public car park and picnic area at Nant Mill, just before crossing the River Clywedog. National Tree Week events may take place in this wood during late Nov-Dec. Please phone the Woodland Trust for details in the autumn.. Plas Power Wood is of considerable historical interest, as a well-preserved section of Offa's Dyke runs through the middle of the wood. Offa's Dyke dates from the 8th century and is a scheduled Ancient Monument. Plas Power is a large mixed woodland with mature ash, oak and alder, which have been underplanted with western hemlock and other exotic species. It is a valuable wood in terms of wildlife habitat, due to the variety of woodland, streams and rock face habitats to be found there.

227

Tan-y-Cut Woods

(Wrexham Maelor Borough Council) F
2.7ha
O.S.S. 117 - SJ 278 411
☎0978 822780

Take B5606 through Newbridge, at junction turn R along A5 towards Llangollen. Take 2nd sharp R (before cafe) and follow unmade track alongside canal. Park in the small lay-by, walk underneath canal bridge and follow lane until wood is reached on L. Free and full access all year. The wood is a mature, mixed, deciduous woodland sloping down towards the River Dee on the opposite bank of the river from Ty Mawr Country Park. The Wood is approached via a trackway adjacent to Llangollen canal. A boardwalk and footpath have been created around the woodland which is boggy in places with a calcerous stream running across the site. Good displays of spring flowers.

Wepre Country Park

(Alyn & Deeside District Council) F 66ha
O.S.S. 117 - SJ 295 685
☎0244 814931

From A55, exit to Mold, turn L at traffic lights in Northop follow brown tourist signs once in Connah's Quay. Signposted off A548 in Connah's Quay. Facilities include a car park, WCs, visitor centre, Events Programme - ring above number for details. Free and full access all year round. 160 acre semi-natural ancient woodland running from Connah's Quay to Ewloe Castle, a 13th century Welsh castle. Mixed woodland with good native flora. Well surfaced footpath network and nature trail. A Visitor Centre is on the site of Wepre Hall and there is a small garden and arboretum dating from 1880. The Ranger Service run a wide ranging series of events and activities. School visits are encouraged. Please contact for more details for groups. Guided visits can be arranged.

DYFED

see map on p 223

Castle Woods Nature Reserve
(Dyfed Wildlife Trust) F 28ha
O.S.S. 159 - SN 622 222
0437 765 462

The southern outskirts of Llandeilo
Town off the A483 by the River
Tywi bridge. Facilities include a
visitor centre (disabled access),
open Easter - October, weekends/
Bank Holidays, no toilets.
Programme of guided walks and
"watches". An ancient semi-natural
woodland, the reserve is probably
the most important in south Wales
for its invertebrate and lichen
communities. The woods surround
the old Dynevor Castle - home to
the former Princes of Deheubarth -
and overlook flood meadows and
oxbow lakes. The flora, which is
rich with fine old trees, extensive
bluebells and even the parasitic
toothwort, supports a diverse fauna
of mammals such as badgers and
fallow deer, and a wide variety of
woodland birds, including all
species of British woodpecker.
There are also the overwintering
wildfowl and numerous butterflies
and dragonflies.

Coed Penrhyn - Mawr
(RSPB) R 12ha
O.S.S. 135 - SN 683 964
0654 781265

6 miles S of Machynlleth on A487.
12 miles N of Aberystwyth on
A487. (Ynys-Hir Reserve).
Facilities include a visitor centre,
information, displays, paths,
observation hides. Entrance £3 non
members of RSPB (children 50p)
RSPB members free. Open every
day 0900 hours to dusk. The
reserve area is 1000 acres. In
spring the woods are carpeted with
bluebells and wood anemones.
Speckled wood and greenveined
white butterflies are common here
and you can see holly blue
butterflies in most years, especially
in Cae'r Berllan Wood. The oak
woodlands, a mid-Wales speciality,
have a rich community of breeding
birds in spring including buzzards,
pied-flycatchers, wood warblers,
redstarts and lesser-spotted
woodpeckers. See if you can spot
elusive purple hairstreak butterflies
fluttering around the top of oak
trees in July and August.

Coed Rhyal
(British Coal Opencast) F 5.6ha
O.S.S. 159 - SN 432 028
0267 222933

From Carmarthen, take A484 S,
through Kidwelly, and on towards
Pembrey. Just before Pembrey take
L turn onto B4317 for 1 mile. turn
R at bus stop, along track, past
farm and woodland is on RH.
Limited parking in layby (to be
signposted). Permissive paths
approx. 1 mile long. No charges.
Open all year. Groups by
arrangement. Visitors requested to
stay on paths for safety reasons
-old drift mines and bell pit which
are fenced but caution advised.
Dogs strictly on leads. Badgers
often dig up paths - again care
advised of holes, which may turn
ankles! An oak/hazel woodland on
a steep slope above coalmeasures.

Abundant spring flora, especially bluebells. Active badgers and dormice. Excellent views across Pembrey peninsula.

Dinas
(RSPB)F 45ha
O.S.S.146 - SN 788 471
c/o Troedrhiwgelynen,
Rhandirmwyn, Llandovery, SA20
OPN

Follow signs for Llyn Brianne and RSPB Dinas from A483 in Llandovery. There is a car park which is free to RSPB members, £1 per car for non-members. Open all day all year round. Part of the path round wood is very rocky and unsuitable for infirm. See signs in car park for details. The Dinas is an ancient semi-natural oak wood of high conservation interest. About half the wood has a long history of management; the remainder has been left undisturbed. The wood is an SSSI. Birds like buzzards, peregrines and ravens are frequently seen and in summer the wood is famous for its populations of pied flycatchers, wood warblers and redstarts. It is probably best known, though, as a site to see the very rare red kite.

Parc Natur Penglais
(Cyngor Dosbarth Ceredigion) F
8ha
O.S.S. 135 - SN 590 822
0970 634314

The wood is located in the NE fringe of the town of Aberystwyth; main entrance on the corner of Penglais and North Road. Facilities include picnic areas, information and self guided trail leaflet. Access is free, all the year round, but there will be a small charge for schools education pack. School and college field study visits welcome. Please contact the project officer on the above telephone number to arrange times. The woods form part of Parc Natur Penglais which, together with 4ha of disused quarry are managed by local people and the District Council for nature conservation, public access and recreation. Trees on the quarry edge of the woods have been affected by the strong sea winds and exposed conditions. Sessile oak, sweet chestnut, ash, wild cherry, sycamore, beech, and hazel are some of the tree species to be found. There is an extensive display of bluebells and wildlife includes badger, buzzard, blackcap, jay and pied flycatcher.

Poor Mans' Wood
(Llandovery Town Council) F
16.8ha
O.S.S.146 - SN 779 344
0267 222933

Take A40 Brecon road from Llandovery 1/2 mile from town is a sharp L turn along a track, opposite caravan park. Follow footpath 1/2 mile to reserve entrance. Parking in town, unless by special arrangement with Carmarthenshire reserves officer. There is a circular permissive path. - no horses. Free access open all year. Leaflet to be published in spring 1994. Apply c/o Llandovery

Tourist Office. Dogs strictly on leads. (vulnerable setts). Typical Welsh upland oak wood - steep slopes with bilberry. Attractive circular walk, mainly level walking, approx. 1 hour duration within reserve. Wild service trees, active badgers, tawny owls, pied flycatchers, buzzards.

Stackpole Estate Woodlands
(National Trust) R 61ha
O.S.S. 158 - SR 980 965
0646 661359

A477 to Pembroke then B4319 S to Stackpole - the wood is just W of village. Permissive horse trail. Varied mixed woodland with extensive network of trails. Boardwalk through wet woodland section. The woods occupy the valleys in the catchment of the eastern arm of the Bosherston Lakes and are of high nature conservation interest.

Stradey Estate Woodlands
(D C Mansel Lewis) A 140ha
O.S.S. 159 - SN 492 014
0554 773059

Stradey Castle is on the B4308 just NW of town of Llanelli. Visit by arrangement only to societies or recognised forestry bodies. £2 per head to cover cost of donation to the Forestry Trust. Post war replanting of softwoods, Japanese larch, Douglas fir, sitka spruce, Thuja, Tsuga and some Sequoia sempervirens - about 250 acres. Old hardwood amenity woodlands recently suffering damage in the 1991 gales and progressively being underplanted and overstocked with similar species with amenity in mind. Essentially an "old fashioned" estate woodland of character which still retains some interesting old trees - about 100 acres..

GLAMORGAN - MID

see map on p223

★ Llanharan Wood

(Managed by Sovereign Woodlands) **A**
40ha
O.S.S. 170 - ST 016 830
✉Office 6, 96 Monnow Street, Monmouth,
Gwent NP5 3EQ

From Jn 34 of M4 take the A4119
N. After 2 miles turn L at
roundabout at Talbot Green onto A
473. The wood is some 2 miles
on, on the R. There are no
facilities and all visits are by
appointment only. Please write to
Sovereign Woodlands at the above
address. Educational / Schools
visits particularly welcome.
Llanharan is a productive wood,
predominantly coniferous with the
main species being Japanese larch,
but there is a belt of ancient
semi-natural woodland within it
where sessile oak, holly and yew
are amongst the main native
species that have been retained.

Taf Fechan

(Glamorgan Wildlife Trust) **F** 42ha
o.s.s. 160 - SO 035 085
☎0656 724100

In the Taf Fechan valley between
Old River Bridge at Cefn Coed y
Cymru and the river bridge at
Pontsam, about 2.5kms N of
Merthyr Tydfil. There is a car park
and picnic site. Taf Fechan is
ancient limestone broadleaf
woodland consisting of mainly ash,
alder, beech, birch and grey willow.

Tawny owl, buzzards, great spotted
woodpeckers and dippers are
frequently present and the flora
includes wild thyme, rough hawkbit
and mouse ear hawkweed.

GLAMORGAN - SOUTH

see map on p223

Cliff Wood

(Vale of Glamorgan Borough Council) F
13.4 ha
O.S.S. 170 - ST 087 660
☎0446 733589

1 mile W of Barry, access from
Park road, Barry. Car parking for
500 cars and 10 coaches, WCs,
disabled facilities, café, adventure
playground, pitch and putt golf
course. Car parking charge on
Sundays and Bank Holidays. Open
all year round. There is full access
to walkers with self guided trails.
Guided visits may be arranged with
prior bookings with the warden.
School parties accommodated.
Cliff Wood is an ancient woodland
site and an SSSI with dominant
oak, ash and yew. It has corre-
sponding rich shrub and floral
layers. Notable is purple gromwell.
Home to a wide variety of
mammals and birds including
badgers, foxes, weasels, sparrowhawks, tawny owl and woodcock.
Contained within the wood is the
remains of a 14th century corn mill
and water course and 17th century
cottages and footpath.

Coedarhydyglyn

(Sir Cennydd Traherne KG) A 15.5 ha
O.S.S. 171 - ST 110 750
☎0446 760321
☎

A48 from Culverhouse Cross
Roundabout on the W side of
Cardiff. Take Cowbridge/ Port
Talbot road. About half a mile up
the hill small turning to R. marked
by white stones, then to Lodge.
Open by appointment only. Early
19th century landscaped wood
planted in 1810 as a feature in the
building of the present house
completed in 1820. Pinetum and
cypress garden planted 1944 and
1947. Larch plantations planted
1940 and 1953. Chestnut with
some beech planted 1987.

Cogan Wood (within Cosmeston Lakes Country Park)

(Vale of Glamorgan Borough Council) F 20
ha
O.S.S.171 - ST 178 693
☎0222 701678

5 miles S of Cardiff, Cosmeston
Lakes country park can be reached
via the B4267 from Penarth to
Sully. Visitor centre, café, gift shop,
toilets, facilities for disabled, car
parking, adventure playground and
reconstructed mediaeval village.
Open all year. Access for walkers
only. Designated an SSSI in the
early 1980s, Cogan Wood is a
mixed broadleaf, wood, predominantly mature hawthorn but with
ash, poplar, field maple and birch.
Of interest is an ancient parish
boundary. An area of English elm
cleared in the early 1980s was
replanted with indigenous species.
The wood helps to support
badgers, foxes, little and barn owl
and is home to pipistrelle and
noctule bats, green and great
spotted woodpeckers.

GLAMORGAN - WEST

see map on p223

★ Afan Forest Park

(Forest Enterprise) F 3250ha
O.S.S. 170 - SS 822 951
☎0639 710221

Follow signs from M4 (exit 40), 6 miles N of Port Talbot along A4107 to Cymer. Facilities include Visitor Centre, waymarked walks, cycle trails, adventure play areas, orienteering course, barbeque sites, facilities for the disabled, cafe and miners museum for which there is a small charge, historic farm trail and long distance Coed Morgannwg way (2 miles), Forest Garden and Mountain Bike trail, cycle hire centre. Full and free access to the Visitor Centre and Forest Park all year round - 1030am to 6pm in summer and 1030am to 5pm in winter. For prearranged educational group visits please write to the Forest District Manager, Morgannwg District Resolven, Neath W Glam SA11 4DR. Remnant native woodlands on the Afan valley floor give rise to larch, pine and spruce planted in the 1930s and 1950s, which sweep over the plateaux, masking numerous scars left in the wake of a thriving industrial heritage which lasted late into the 1960s. The Forest Park is the focal point and flag-ship of the community based Valley's Forest Initiative and is a well supported educational resource centre.

Bishopston Valley

(National Trust) R 42ha
O.S.S. 159 - SS 575 894
☎0792 390636

6 miles SW of Swansea via A4067 and B4436. Not suitable for disabled. This deeply incised and sheltered valley has one of the best and most extensive areas of ancient woodland on the Gower peninsula. The underlying geology is carboniferous limestone, and here it displays features such as swallow holes, potholes, dry valleys, collapsed caverns and limestone screes. Apart from ancient woodland, this valley has excellent variety of habitat, with wet meadows, herb-rich limestone grassland, bracken scrub and a stream which is above ground in part of valley. The area is rich in archaeological remains, especially those of the limestone industry.

Cwm Clydach

(Lt. Col. A. D. Holland and RSPB) R 91 ha
O.S.S. 159 - SN 684 026
☎0792 842927

Four miles N of Junction 45 of M4, through the village of Clydach, at *New Inn* in Craig cefn parc. Parking, toilets and food at *New Inn*. Access at all times along public footpaths and RSPB trails. Please keep to marked paths at all times. Nesting buzzard, sparrowhawk and raven are common. Nestboxes are used by pied flycatcher, redstart and tits, while wood warbler, all three species of woodpecker, nuthatch, tree-creeper and tawny owl also breed. Dipper and grey wagtail frequent the river and tree pipit and wheatear the higher ground. Snipe, woodcock, redpoll and siskin are frequent in winter. 28 species of butterfly are present, including purple hairstreak and silver-washed fritillary.

GWENT

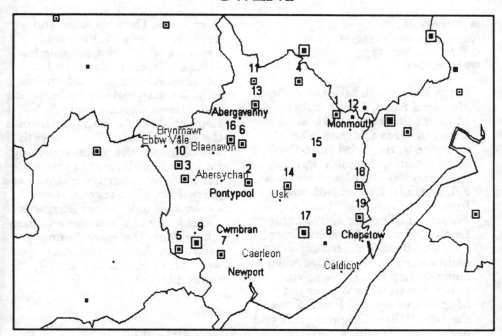

1 *Buckholt
2 Coed Bryntovey
3 Coedcae Cendle
4 Craig Farm Wood
5 Craig Goch
6 Craig Syddi
7 Craig y Wenallt Wood
8 *Cwm
9 Cwmcarn Forest Drive
10 Cwm Merddog

11 Great Triley Wood
12 *Newton Court Estate
13 Pant Skirrid Wood
14 *Parkwood
15 *Penyclawdd
16 The Punchbowl
17 Wentwood
18 Whitestone
19 Wyndcliff

★ Buckholt

(Venture Properties Ltd) FD 84ha
O.S. 162 - SO 500 168
☎0497 820242

From Monmouth take the A466, Hereford Road, 1 mile from Monmouth turn L at Mansons Cross towards Oldshop. The entrance to the wood is on the R approximately 1.5miles. Parking for 5 cars. Rights of way and self guided trails. Leaflet with map from the Manager, Fountain Forestry Ltd on the above number. Donations to the Forestry Trust. This woodland is splendidly set amid rolling Border countryside, commanding fine views to all points but notably W over the Monnow valley and E and S over the Wye Valley. Originally oak and beech coppice with standards, European larch was first intro-duced around 1860 and following a substantial felling during World War two higher yielding conifers were used in the restocking. The main objects of management have been the commercial production of timber. The current mix of broadleaves with conifers makes for a diverse woodland landscape, rich in fauna and ground flora.

Coed Bryntovey

(R Hanbury-Tenison) FD 25ha
O.S.S. 171 - SO 317 022
☎0495 762921

A 4042 (T) Newport/Abergavenny. Exit to New Inn at roundabout S of Pontypool. First R in village and follow Jerusalem Lane for 2 miles.

Turn L into Cwmhir Road and keep on to the end. Park well beyond cottage. Not suitable for coaches. Open 1 March to 1 October. Access to wood on foot only. Keep to marked paths, which constitute a circular route. Replanted with ash and larch since the second World War. Below the line of pylons the ground was dug for brick clay during the war and has since been partly replanted and partly allowed to regenerate naturally. Look out for Buzzards and if lucky you may see a visiting fallow deer. There are damp patches in the wood in rainy weather, so gum boots are recommended.

Coedcae Cendle

(John and Susan Russell) F 11ha
O.S.161 - SO 188 058

On the A4046 2.5 miles S from Ebbwvale you enter the village of Cwm. At the police station you turn L. Park car on the hill, follow footpath sign to woods. There are no facilities. Caoedcae Cendle is an attractive little wood overlook-ing the village of Cwm. The wood was planted in 1971 with spruce and pine. There are nice areas of beech and oaks throughout the woods including a rich variety of wildlife and plants. There are interesting paths through the woods with seats and picnic tables. There are stiles leading to the mountain side. To the N is the Cwm Merddog nature reserve.

Craig Farm Wood

(Miss P E Merriman) F 46ha

O.S.S.161 - SO 410 224

From Abergavenny B4521 to Cross Ash then N on the minor county road. The woodland is mainly conifer planted in 1963 by the Forestry Commission. The plateau area is dominated by Sitka spruce with lodgepole pine, Norway spruce and Japanese larch at the southern end. There is an impressive view point looking W - it is worth the walk to see this. Fallow deer are regularly seen within the wood or heard crashing into the undergrowth.

Craig Goch

(Islwyn Borough Council) F 16ha

O.S.S.171 - ST 187 911

☎0495 200113

At junction 28 M4, take A467 then A4048 to Cwmfelinfach. Follow signs to Ynys Hymel. Ignore turning area and go to Wishing Stone picnic site car park. Alternatively, park at Ynys Hymel countryside centre and walk. It is a pleasant walk through farmland with superb views. Access is free and facilities include tea room, WCs etc at countryside centre. A remnant of the ancient woodland which once covered south Wales, Craig Goch is currently proposed for designation as a local nature reserve. It had been badly managed before acquisition, with bracken infestation and little regeneration. An active management programme is ensuring its survival. Forty species of birds breed in Craig

Goch, including the redstart, which has been taken as the symbol of Ynys Hymel countryside centre. There are signs of old charcoal hearths. The woodland contains some very old trees and consists of mainly beech and oak with some birch, ash, rowan and holly. Public access is being improved with the help of conservation volunteers and there is some on-site interpretation. The nearby countryside centre runs a programme of courses and events related to woodland management, willow craft and hedge laying.

Craig Syddi

(Monmouth Woodland Trust) F 28.5ha

O.S.S. 161 - SO 295 108

☎0600 772904

From A4042, near Abergavenny, take the B4269. Turn L after 1/4 mile into the "No Through Road". Go up the hill and over the canal. The woodland is on the L. Marked footpaths and an explanatory leaflet available. Caution is necessary when forestry operations are in progress. Signs will be erected. A leaflet guide and description of the woodland and its management is available from above telephone number or the Tourist Information Centre in Abergavenny. Craig Syddi is situated above Abergavenny. The woodland comprises well grown conifers planted in the early sixties including Douglas fir, western hemlock, larch and spruce. This primarily commercial woodland demonstrates how productive forestry can enhance the landscape and be of value to the local community. There are spectacular views over the Usk valley and a wide range of birds. Look for the old hardwoods which were retained when the woodland was replanted.

Craig y Wenallt Wood
(Woodland Trust) F 6ha
O.S.S 171 - ST 265 909
☎0476 74297

From the M4 take the B4591 towards Risca. Turn R onto the road leading to Risca comprehensive school. Just past the school turn R onto a narrow lane. At the T-junction turn L, then take the R fork. This track leads up to the wood. There is no parking; do not park on the track leading to Craig y Wenallt. National Tree Week events may take place in this wood in late Nov-early Dec 1994. Please phone the Woodland Trust in the autumn for details. Craig y Wenallt is a hillside wood on the outskirts of Risca above the Ebbw River. It contains some fine trees and there is an attractive display of bluebells in the spring. This woodland is a prominent feature in the landscape and is composed mainly of beech and birch with mature oak coppice and scrub, gorse and broom. There is a small area of open land within the wood which has been planted with native trees and shrubs.

★ Cwm
(Richard Micklethwait) A 10ha
O.S.S.171 - ST 460 928

☎0633 400 213

Leave M4 immediately N of Severn Bridge, 1 mile N turn W on A48 after about 5 miles turn N to Llanvair Discoed, Wentwood and Usk, then take 2nd R and immediately L to Penhein. (Drive 1 mile long). Open by appointment only and charges by agreement. Parties will meet at Penhein for tour of sites of interest on farm trailer(s). Semi-natural ancient woodland (SSSI) being managed to vary canopy which was uniform. Also sites of land in various stages of regeneration. Land last cultivated in 1918. Land grazed until 20 years ago. Land last grazed in 1954. Part of wood from which stock was excluded in about 1985.

Cwmcarn Forest Drive
(Forest Enterprise) F 345ha
O.S.S. 171 ST 220 930
☎0633 400205

Follow signs from M4 (exit 40)There is fully open access to the woods with rights of way on foot and bridleways throughout. There are self guided trails, please apply to the visitor centre for details. Donations made to the Forestry Trust. There is parking available for cars and coaches. The forest drive (a guide is available for 60p) is open from Easter to Oct, 11am to 7pm. There are picnic areas, barbecue sites, childrens play area, and a path for the disabled. Cwmcarn is part of Ebbw Forest which dates back beyond the 13th century. The valleys of south Wales had most of the tree cover removed for charcoal making and agricultural use. The industrial revolution hit the area, especially coal mining and the approach to the forest drive runs over the old colliery. The 7 mile long forest drive provides a rare opportunity for the less able to get deep into a working forest with spectacular views over the Bristol Channel. There is a diversity of tree species and age structure together with associated flora and fauna.

Cwm Merddog

(Gwent Wildlife Trust) R 22ha
O.S.S. 161 - S0 187 062
☎0600 715501

On the A4046, and 2.5 miles S from Ebbw Vale, there is a one-way system in Cwm; come out of this on the N side and turn R by a corner shop; 0.3 miles up this road there is a car park just SW of Cwm cemetery. From the car park walk northwards across a flat grass playing area and along a path to the entrance of the reserve. There is car parking for 8 cars. There are no WCs on the site. Nearest shops are in Cwm. There are rights of way on foot throughout the wood. Guided visits can be arranged by appointment, please contact Mr J Winder on the above number. The reserve is the most westerly, and forms part of the highest natural beech woodland in the British Isles. The splendid greater tussock sedge is work looking out for as is the broad leaved helleborine and the heath spotted orchid. An old

dragline is present that used to take coal from the surrounding hills. Nature has reclaimed the old coal tip with mosses and lichens, young hawthorns and other young trees are establishing themselves and a natural woodland is developing. Beech and alder dominate most of the woodlands but there is an area of young mixed woodland where anthills can be found suggesting that this area was once pasture. The green woodpecker, pied flycatcher and the redstart nest in the woodland.

Great Triley Wood

(Woodland Trust) F 6ha
O.S.S. 161 - S0 338 233
☎0476 74297

The wood lies just between the main Abergavenny to Hereford Road, the A465 and the railway line just inside the National Park boundary. Parking is in the lay-by on the Abergavenny side of the site. National Tree Week events may take place in this wood in late Nov early Dec. Please phone the Woodland Trust in the autumn for details. As the woodland is wet and boggy in places, visitors are advised to walk with care. The woodland lies on the marshy banks of the river Gavenny, just inside the Brecon Beacons National Park. It is a most attractive area of woodland containing many fine oaks and ash trees. The marshy area of wood supports some very large alder and willow. The ground flora is varied and rich and among the more interesting plants is the unusual flower, herb paris.

conifers.

★ Newton Court Estate
(Charles Griffin and Major Ralph Griffin) A
40ha
O.S.S. 162 - SO 522 144
☎0600 712992

From Monmouth take the A40 N.
Turn L for Newton Court half a
mile after the Dixton roundabout.
There is one right of way through
the wood. All visits by appointment
only. Please contact Mr C F
Griffin on the above telephone
number. Donations made to the
Forestry Trust. The woods have
been in possession of the family for
over 200 years and are made up of
several smaller woods. <u>Orles Wood</u>
species include: ash, cherry, thuja,
plane, small leafed lime, grand fir,
hornbeam and birch. <u>Sitting Bull
and Many Guns</u> species include:
sequoias, thuja, red oak and
chestnut. <u>Great Wood</u> species
include: European larch, beech,
tsuga, Douglas fir, oak, Norway
spruce and Corsican pine.

Pant Skirrid Wood
(National Trust) R 14ha
O.S.S. 161 - SO 329 164
☎0874 625515

The car park below Pant Skirrid
wood is situated on the B4521
(Old Hereford Road) leading out of
Abergavenny. There is one public
path and an extensive network of
woodland rides which are
permissive paths. All are waymarked. Mixed hardwoods and

★ Parkwood
(J H L Humphreys) Fc 36ha
O.S.S. 171 - SO 389 027
☎0291 672563

From Usk take the old Raglan
road, fork L signed Gwehelog and
the lay-by is on the L one mile up
the road after sharp bend. There
are no facilities but there is parking
at the lay-by on old Usk/Raglan
road. Walk 300 yards up stone
track to information shed and start
of walk, except on open days when
the gate will be open and parking
will be up in the wood. There is a
marked circular walk of approx 40
mins; and permitted access for
walkers on paths and tracks within
the wood. Guided visits can be
arranged by appointment from Apr
to the end of Oct. Please contact
owner on the above telephone
number 3 weeks in advance. Rates
by negotiation. Donations made to
the Forestry Trust. Park Wood was
only scrubland prior to 1936 and
was planted by the present owner's
father. A special feature of the
wood is the way it has been laid
out in comme
morative rides lined with hardwood
species. There is an abundance of
wildlife including foxes, buzzards,
herons and ravens. The woods are
at their best in the spring with
wood anemones, then bluebells.
Larch, Douglas fir, western
hemlock, sweet chestnut, oak and
red oak are mongst the main
species grown and marketed. There
is a particularly fine grove of

redwoods planted in 1949 given as a wedding plantation by Richard St Barbe Baker (The founder of Men of the Trees).

★ Penyclawdd
(S A J P Bosanquet) A 24ha
O.S.S. 161 - SO 440 080
☎0600 83238

Midway between Monmouth and Raglan - turn S off old A40 at Blue Door Corner. The wood is at top of the Graig Lees hill (map essential). There is parking for 10 cars. There is a right of way on foot through the wood. The owner would be particularly happy to arrange group visits and separate school visits, for which 6 weeks notice is required. Details from Mr Bosanquet on the above number. Cost of guided visits: Adults £2, children £1: no charge for schools. Donations to the Forestry Trust. An ex-Forestry Commission wood with about two thirds conifers - Norway spruce, hemlock, Douglas fir and larch - and one third mixed age hardwoods - oak ash, beech and birch. The conifers have just been thinned now being about 30 years old. Many wildflowers and butterflies in the rides. A very interesting amalgam of woodland species in a small area.

The Punchbowl
(Woodland Trust) F 36ha
O.S.S. 161 - SO 284 115
☎0476 74297

From A4042 leave at Llanellen onto the B4269 to Llanfoist. Take the lane to the L 1.1/4 miles along this road. Follow the lane steeply upwards for 1 1/2 miles take the R fork in the road and then proceed a further mile until the roadside rest area of the Brecon Beacons National Park is reached. Parking is available. National Tree Week events may take place in this wood in late Nov - early Dec 1994. Please phone Woodland Trust for details in the autumn. Visitors are advised to keep close to the public footpaths within this wood, as much of the site above the lake is steep or sheer. The Punchbowl is the largest of several hollows set in the side of Mount Blorenge. Undoubtedly the most striking trees are the huge ancient beeches some up to six foot in diameter, most of which have been pollarded in the past. Ash, hazel, oak and field maple are the other predominant tree species. The wood supports a variety of plant life including wood sorrel, wood avens and enchanters nightshade. The buzzard, green woodpecker and tawny owl, along with the noctule bat, are just some of the birds and mammals that frequent this site.

Wentwood
(Forest Enterprise) F 279ha
O.S.S. 171 - ST 421 949
☎0633 400205

5 miles W of Chepstow on A48, R turn signed Llanvair Discoed, Wentwood Usk 4 miles. Car and coach park at very top of hill. There are some WCs on site, including

facilties for the disabled. There are picnic and barbecue sites, childrens play area and a trim trail. There is fully open access to the wood with bridleways and rights of way on foot throughout the wood. A facts book is available at £1, covered barbecues cost £5. Donations made to the Forestry Trust. In the early days Wentwood belonged to the native Welsh princes and was much larger growing mainly oak and beech with many local people depending on the forest. There were local laws and justice dispensed at Foresters Oaks. Sheep stealing carried the death penalty with the last hanging at Foresters Oaks in 1829. The oak and beech were heavily cut with little left when the Forest Enterprise acquired part of the forest on lease in 1941. Wentwood is a popular walking area with good recreational facilities. Trails pass through the stands of larch, Norway spruce, Douglas fir and beech with a variety of wildlife.

Whitestone
(Forest Enterprise) F 98ha
O.S.S. 171 - SO 523 028
☎0633 400205

On the A466 in Tintern village take the road which runs by the side of the Wye Valley Hotel signed Catbrook for some 2 miles. Car park opposite road junction. WCs on site along with facilities for the disabled. Picnic areas, barbecues, a childrens play area and less abled trail. Full open access to the wood with rights of way and bridlepaths

throughout. Self guided trails available. Please contact above for further details. A guide to walks in Tintern Woods is available for 60p. Donations to the Forestry Trust. Whitestone Wood is where the productive coniferous woods of the plateau meet the ancient woodland of the Wye Valley AONB. The Tall Trees walk runs through magnificent Douglas fir and Norway spruce to the Jubilee Grove which celebrated the diamond jubilee of the Forestry Commission. The Grove planted in 1979 includes oak, cherry, sweet chestnut and beech. There are lovely views over the Wye Valley which are accessible to wheelchair users with a strong pusher! Very varied flora and fauna with many different species of butterfly and a variety of fungi. Birds abound with some rare species present.

Wyndcliff
(Forest Enterprise) F 95ha
O.S.S. 162 - ST 524 972
☎0633 400205

Chepstow A466 N towards Monmouth. Fork left N of St Arvans to Wyndcliff. There is car parking and a picnic site. Fully open access to the woods with rights of way and self-guided trails. Walks in Tintern Woods guide 60p, contact above. Donations to the Forestry Trust. Wyndcliff is part of the remnant primeval forest of the Wye valley which has been worked by man for thousands of years. Forest Enterprise own and manage this woodland to a plan agreed with the Countryside Council for Wales,

GWYNEDD

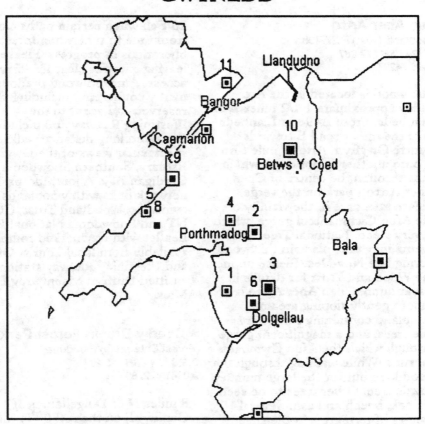

1 Coed Aber Artro
2 *Coed Llyn y Garnedd
3 *Coed y Brenin Forest Park
4 Coed Cae Fali
5 Coed Elernion
6 *Cwm Mynach
7 Glan Faenol
8 *Glasfryn Forestry Estate
9 Glynllifon
10 *Gwydyr Forest Park
11 Henllys Hall

Coed Aber Artro
(Woodland Trust) F 27.43ha
O.S.124 - SH 597 267
☎0476 74297

The wood is located in the Artr valley approximate 1 1/2 miles E of Llanbedr. From A496 in Llanbedr take the minor road E towards Pentre Gwyfryn. After 1 mile turn R onto another minor road, which runs through the centre of Coed Aber Artro - park on the verge. Please take care in the vicinity of the Afon Cwmnantcol gorge, which is very steep. National Tree Week events may take place in this wood during late Nov-Dec. Please phone the Woodland Trust for details in the autumn. Coed Aber Artro is a superb gently sloping area of woodland containing some very fine trees, and a magnificent gorge through which the Afon Cwmnantcol runs. While walking through the wood look out for the large monkey puzzle tree. Other trees to be seen are oak, beech and ash. Several species of fern grow in the sheer sided gorge with bluebell, wavy hair grass, bilberry and cow-wheat making up the ground flora.

★ Coed Llyn y Garnedd
(Managed by Tilhill Economic Forestry Ltd) Fd 200ha
O.S.S. 124 - SH 646 415
☎606783 206

From Porthmadog take A487 (T) towards Dolgellau. At Oakley Arms pub Maentwrog turn L to Rhyd. Entrance is 200m on L after passing under railway bridge. Full and free access at all times except 28 Feb when certain paths closed from time to time when forest operations in progress. Please park leaving gateway clear for lorry access, A mixed wood predominantly conifer and including two reservoirs adjacent to the Ffestiniog Railway and including short and long distance walks with spectacular views of the Dwyryd Estuary, Southern Snowdonia and Cardigan Bay. A joint footpath network links with woodlands owned by Woodland Trust, CCW, NT and Snowdonia National Park. Leaflet with waymarked route available from local Tourist Office and Ffestiniog Railway station entitled Duffryn Maentwrog Llyn Mair.

★ Coed y Brenin Forest Park
(Forest Enterprise) F 6300ha
O.S.S.124 - SH 715 277
☎0341 422289

8 miles N of Dolgellau, near Ganllwyd, on the A470 (T) road and well signposted. Facilities include, visitor centre with exhibitions, shop and cafe, WCs, facilities for the disabled, waymarked walks, mountain bike trails, adventure play area, orienteering course, picnic sites, Forest Nature Reserve, Forest Garden and mining trails (gold and copper), sign writing workshop and wildlife observation hide. Car parking - Pay and display 50p for 2 hours, £1 all day, annual permit £5. Please ring above number for opening times. For prearranged educational group visits please write to the Forest District Manager, Dolgellau Forest

District, Government Buildings, Arran Road, Dolgellau, Gwynedd LL40 1LW. The forest was formerly part of the Nannau estate, founded by Cadwgan, Prince of Powys, in 1100 AD. It has some of the most varied and beautiful landscapes in the southern part of Snowdonia National Park. An extraordinary diversity of rock and soil has enabled the forester to introduce a wide variety of tree species which are enriched by some of the original cover of semi-natural oak woodland. Richly varied plant, animal and bird communities have become established.

Coed Cae Fali

(National Trust) F 58ha
O.S.S. 124 - SH 629 407
☎0690 710636

Midway between Penrhyndeudraeth and Maentwrog. Adjacent and N of the A487. Parking in lay-by for 20 cars and woodland interpretation. No WCs. There are public and permitted paths which are open freely all year. Part of the extensively wooded Maentwrog valley in Snowdonia. Former Forestry Commission predominantly sessile oak woodland with conifer plantations; Norway spruce and Scots pine. Hardwoods being gradually reinstated by group felling with natural regeneration. Rich in typical western oakwood flora and fauna, particularly mosses and liverworts.

Coed Elernion

(Woodland Trust) F 20.27ha
O.S.S. 123 - SH 378 462

☎0476 74297

Turn off the main A499 Pwllheli to Caernarfon road onto the more southerly of the two minor roads leading to Trefor. The entrance is 200m from this junction on the LH side. This is a good example of a wet oak-ash woodland. In the wetter areas look out for bogbean and heath-spotted orchid. On the drier soils sessile oak is the main tree species, with a shrub storey of hazel below it. A spring visit to the wood is especially recommended, when the whole wood is a sea of bluebells; later honeysuckle covers the ground. A good variety of woodland birds can be spotted in this wood. Of further interest are choughs, which are rare members of the crow family.

★ Cwm Mynach

(C J Mygind and R G A Youard) F 450ha
O.S.S. 124 - SH 683 219
☎06783 206

From Dolgellau head for Barmouth along N side of estuary. Head N opposite toll bridge up steep single track road to end of tarmac. There is parking for 5 cars but no other facilities. Open all the time. Cym Mynach, although primarily a commercial conifer plantation contains significant areas of oakwood and upland heather, supported by Special Management Grant. Its views S to Cader Idris and W towards the Rhinogs make its location particularly attractive. It also features a lake, visited by migrating swans in winter; and numerous ex mine workings, in particular a 100 year old tramway to now disused manganese mine. Birdlife on the estate is monitored by the RSPB who also carry out conservation work (contact RSPB warden, Reg Thorpe, on 0341 250650).

Glan Faenol
(National Trust) F 55ha
O.S. 114 - SH 530 695
☎0690 710636

Access is via Parc Menai between Bangor and Felinheli/Port Dinorwic on A487. There is parking for 10 vehicles with visitor information. Nearby Plas Newydd house (2 miles) has WC, shop and tearoom, house open 31 Mar to 31 Oct, selected days. There are permitted paths leading from car park; they are freely open all year. Divided into eight woodland blocks, part of the formerly extensive and landscaped Vaynol Park, adjacent to the Menai Straits. Woods are a mixture of softwood and hardwood, some on ancient woodland sites where conifer is being converted back to hard-woods. Some impressive young plantations of sycamore. Network of woodland and parkland paths with fine views of Plas Newydd and Llyn peninsula.

★ Glasfryn Forestry Estate
(R C Williams-Ellis)A 250ha
O.S.S. 123 - SH 391 431
☎0758 750 623
Find Fencing Centre on the A499 (Caenarfon/Pwllheli) road 1/4 mile S of Llanaelhaern 5 miles N of Pwllheli. Facilities include a toilet. parking area, 5 miles Class 30 tonne forest roads. Charges are £10 per hour - any number of visitors. Appointment with owner - Mon to Fri. The only fully economical post war forest holding in Wales. It started with 2 hectares planted in 1926 which came into production in 1948. By 1972 195 hectares had been planted but taxation changes in 1974 totally halted progress reducing staff from 15 to 1. The Fencing Centre was opened in 1989. A further 80 hectares which had recently been felled were bought in 1992. Llyn Glasfryn, within the estate, is an SSSI, but the forest as a whole supports a far richer wildlife community than it did before. Glasfryn produces timber, mainly sitka spruce, averaging 20 tonnes per hectare per year, and now once more employs a workforce of 14 on sub-standard agricultural land, despite the further constraint of being inside an Environmentally Sensitive Area.

Glynllifon
(The Principal, Coleg Meirion Dwyfor) F 300ha
O.S.S 115 - SH 452 550
☎0286 830261

From Caernarfon, follow signs to Pwllheli, Glynllifon is approxi-mately 7 miles from Caernarfon and is clearly signed. There is car parking for some 50 cars and 6 coaches. Charge of 50p per car. Other facilities include the provision of WCs, a shop, country park, countryside museum, craft workshops, play area and a cycleway. The park is open from dawn to dusk and during these times there is fully open access, to the park only. Group visits to the forest by appointment only. Please contact the Associate Principal on the above number, giving one months notice for group visits. Group rates will be negotiable. Glynllifon has been an Agricultural College since 1952, offering courses in Agriculture, Forestry, Conservation and Horse Management. The site is shared with a country park which provides public access to part of the estate. Woodland interest is varied, from amenity and landscape to timber production.

★ Gwydyr Forest Park
(Forest Enterprise) F 7250ha
O.S.S. 115/116 - SH 795 566
☎0492 640578

Centre of Betws y Coed on the A5 (T) road. Facilities include Pay and Display at all car parks. Visitor Centre "Y Stablau", exhibition and shop, waymarked walks including one for the visually disadvantaged and another for the ambient disabled, mountain bike routes, picnic sites, wayfaring courses, fishing and forest coach tours, mining archeological trail. Open all year round 1000am to 5.45pm (summer): 1000am to 5.00pm (winter). For prearranged educational group visits, please write to the Forest District Manager, Gwydyr Uchaf, Llanrwst, Gwynedd, LL26 OPN. Gwydyr Forest Park ranges across the hills on Snowdownia's eastern flank. High wooded ramparts rise steeply from the level pastures of the Conwy valley. Salmon abounding in the healthy vital rivers, enfolded by the forest are a tribute to woodland and landscape management and conservation methods used since the Forestry Commis-

sion began its work here in 1921. A legacy of old engine houses, waste tips and reservoirs are charactersitic features of the forest landscape today. They bear witness to three centuries of mineral exploitation, developed by Sir John Wynn of Gwydyr Castle as long ago as the early 17th century.

Henllys Hall
(Country Moment Hotels) F 10ha
O.S.S. 114/115 - SH 600 776
☎0248 810412

In the centre of Beaumaris turn L on B5109 towards Pentraeth. After 300 yards turn R (sign to Henllys Hall Hotel). After 1/2 mile take second L (again signposted) and park at the back of hotel. There is parking for 50 cars, WCs, refreshments, meals, rooms, picnic area. There is no charge and the wood is open 1 hour after sunrise to 1 hour before sunset all year. The walks are not suitable for disabled. An ancient woodland, it was part of the estate of the Sheriff of Beaumaris Castle; the family lived there for over 400 years. The woodland is varied, dominated by sycamore, but there are many other species present including some very large beech and lime avenue. The spring flora is partcularly interesting with carpets of wild daffodils, bluebells and wild garlic. There is a 1 1/2 mile waymarked walk which forms a circular path through the woodland with fine views across the Menai Strait to Snowdownia. The woodland has not been managed for over 20 years but is entering into a programme of management for amenity, conservation and timber production.

POWYS

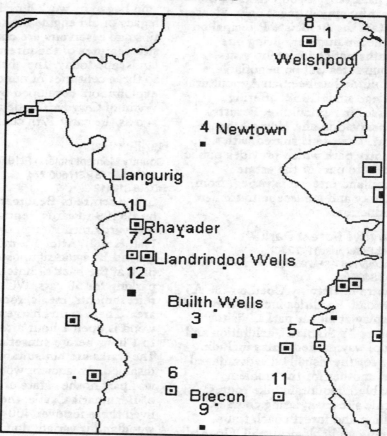

1 *Ackers Grove
2 Allt Ddu/Cwm yr Esgob/Bedw Caemelyn
3 *Cefnllysgwynne Estate
4 *Craigfryn Caeau-Bach Wood
5 Cilcenni Dingle Wood
6 Coed Dyrysiog
7 Cnwch Wood
8 Gaer Fawr Wood
9 *Held Wood
10 Pengarreg Wood
11 Pwll y Wrach
12 *Trallwm Forest

★ Ackers Grove

(Royal Forestry Society of England, Wales and Northern Ireland) L 12ha

O.S.S. 126 - SJ 225 075

✉The (RFS)Warden, Tan y Bryn, Wellington Road, Llandrindod Wells, Powys LD1 5NG

Meet at car park adjoining Spar shop in Welshpool where there are WCs - there are no facilities at Ackers Grove. Charge for entrance; Adults £2, school children £1. Open four Sundays - 3 Apr, 3 Jul, 2 Oct and 4 Dec 1994. A private collection of fine specimen conifers in the Naylor Pinetum, and the adjacent Charles Ackers Redwood Grove, the oldest and largest stand of coast redwoods in Britain. Because of the private ownership and the delicate nature of the habitat, the property is not normally open to the public. Please respect this.

Allt Ddu/Cwm yr Esgob/Bedw Caemelyn

(RSPB) R 40ha

O.S.S. 147 - SN 936 652

Off B4518, from town of Rhayader, at Elan village. Nearest rail station at Llandrindod Wells (14 miles) where there are bus and taxi services. The woodland is located on the hill slopes behind the village. There are no facilities. There is full and free access all year. An oak woodland with some ancient trees over 350 years old. Very quiet for wildlife during winter months but from mid Apr to early Jun the woodland supports large numbers of birds - of special interest are pied flycatchers, redstarts, wood warblers, tree pipits and woodpeckers. May be viewed from minor road and public footpath.

★ Cefnllysgwynne Estate

(C R Woosnam CBE) A 64ha

O.S.S.147 - SO 001 501

☎0982 552237 or 0982 553248

Cefnllysgwynne is to the W of Builth Wells. A location plan will be sent to those making appointments to visit. There is parking for 2 or 3 cars and a picnic site. No other facilities. Donations to the Forestry Trust. Visits on 14 May, 12 Jun, 10 Jul, 10 Oct are by arrangement with at least 1 months notice. No smoking. Groups of 5 to 10 preferred. Guided tours by the owner between 10am and 4pm. Local school visits are particularly welcome The woods represent one third of the estate, the rest being permanent pasture. It lies on the S side of the River Irfon, a tributary of the Wye, 500-1000 feet above sea level.The bulk of the woodland has been planted and managed by the owner since 1947, mainly conifers which will reach maturity over the next 15 to 20 years. The wood demonstrates how wildlife and landscape can be well served by good silvicultural management. Coupled with a small scale pheasant shoot and the development over the next few years of a network of footpaths and bridleways, both public and permissive, the woods illustrate the many benefits that forestry offers.

★ Craigfryn Caeau-Bach Wood, part of Dinam Woods
(Rt Hon Lord Davies) AC 54ha
O.S.S. *136* - SO 031 891
   0591 2309

A470 7 miles W of Newton and 6 miles E of Llanidloes, across river Severn at the "Davies" statue in Llandinam village, turn L - old railway line for one mile to meeting point at the wood. Guided visits can be arranged by contacting Mr Kahars on the above number. Donations made to the Forestry Trust. The wood consists of 15 hectares of broadleaved oak, ash, beech and others, mainly 50 to 120 years old, and 39 hectares of conifers, larch, Douglas fir and others, mainly 7 to over 30 years old. The site is partially old woodland and previously rough grazing on the River Severn valley side, rising steeply from 500 ft to 1000 ft, with a SE aspect. The objects of management are timber production, landscaping and conservation of wildlife. The silvicultural practice is directed towards a perpetual uneven aged mixed group forest.

Cilcenni Dingle Wood
(Woodland Trust) F 14.16ha
O.S.S. *161* - SO 175 414
   0476 74297

Just off the A438 Hereford to Glasbury road, not far from Hay-on-Wye on the Welsh-English border. From Glasbury, travel 1/2 mile beyond the turning to Maesyronen Chapel and look for a no-through road on the LH side.

Turn on to this minor road and park on the verge running parallel to the A438. There are no facilities. There is full and free access at all times of the year. National Tree Week events take place during Nov-Dec. Please phone the Woodland Trust for details in the Autumn. Cilcenni Dingle is a secluded valley woodland, lying along the steep slopes of a tributary of the River Wye. Mature oak and ash trees now dominate the wood and plant lovers can expect to find an excellent range of herbaceous plants, including the locally uncommon herb paris, slender st john's wort and soft shield fern. Many birds such as pied flycatcher, woodpecker, tree creeper and nuthatch inhabit the woodland, encouraged by the wealth of varied habitats.

Coed Dyrysiog
(Brecknock Wildlife Trust) F 7ha
O.S.S.*160* - SN 980 310
   0874 625708

From Brecon take the A40 W towards Sennybridge. After just over 3 miles turn N on minor road to Aberbran. At "T" junction turn R to Aberyscir/Cradoc after 500m take 1st L to Llanfihangel Nant Bran. Woodland is on L after just under 1 mile. There are no facilities but there is a footpath. Free and full access at all times of the year. A mixed broadleaved woodland developed on steeply sloping old red sandstone. One of the few afforested commons in Brecknock, the wood is ungrazed and has a diverse ground flora. The drier

banks support mainly oak of mixed ages, whilst ash is most common in wetter flushed areas. The rich shrub layer includes honeysuckle, hawthorn, field maple and guelder rose. A very
variable ground flora ranges from bilberry to common cow-wheat to sanicle, wild strawberry and marsh marigold.

Cnwch Wood
(Dwr Cymru Welsh Water) F 4.8ha
O.S.S. 147 - SN 931 648
☎0597 810449

Take the B4518 out of Rhayader in the direction of the Elan Valley - follow the signs for the Elan Valley visitor centre - approximately 3 1/2 miles. There is a nature trail with interpretative panels and leaflet but no other facilities. There is free and full access all the year. Please observe the country code and treat the area and other visitors with consideration.
A mainly sessile oak woodland situated below the Elan Valley reservoir complex. Wide variety of bird species present. The wood has recently been fenced to exclude sheep with a view to encouraging natural regeneration. The woodland is designated as an SSSI.

Gaer Fawr Wood
(Woodland Trust) F 30.35ha
O.S.S 126 - SJ 219 125
☎0476 74297

Take the minor road off the B4392 at Sarn Bridge on the northern edge of the village of Guilsfield. Climb the hill for about 1/2 mile to the quarry car park. There are no facilities. Free and full access at all times of the year. Stout footwear is advisable especially in winter. Gaer Fawr Wood is a striking landscape feature, overlooking the Severn valley. The wood covers most of the hilltop and is a Scheduled Ancient Monument. The variety of trees and shrubs especially those with scented flowers, nuts and berries such as rowan, hazel and wild cherry provide food for many insects and birds. Among the birds you can see are nuthatch and spotted flycatcher. Also buzzards are often seen and, if you are quiet, you may see a tawny owl.

★ Held Wood, part of Ffrwdgrech Woods
(Major W D D Evans) Ac 24ha
O.S.S 160 - SO 029 273
☎0591 2309

From A40 at W end of Brecon town turn S along Ffrwdgrech road opposite Drovers Arms. Meet at Ffwdgrech House - enter at lodge on L. Guided visits can be arranged by contacting Mr Kalnars on the above telephone number, or write 6 weeks in advance to, Ffrwdgrech House, Brecon Powys, LD3 8LB. There are picnic facilities and 4 acres of gardens and lawn. Woodland cover for about 200 years. Altitude 620 to 920 feet. All on old red sandstone. 40% compulsory clear fell First War and 60% Second War. Replanted in small compartments of various species now managed as a perpetual forest, multi storey in parts. Full exposure to SW winds.

Ravens and hawks nested annually in old Scots pine for at least 100 years. Very wide variety of small birds in spring and summer. Carpets of bluebells in some areas. Main tree species: Douglas fir, Japanese larch, Corsican pine, red cedar, ash, beech, oak. Marked increase in butterflies in recent years.

Penygarreg Wood
(Dwr Cymru Welsh Water) F 11ha
O.S.S. 147 - SN 915 674
☎0597 810449

Take the B4518 out of Rhayader in the direction of the Elan Valley - continue for approximately 6 miles. The wood is situated below Penygarreg Dam and adjacent to the guest house known as the "Flickering Lamp". There are no facilities but there are waymarked and leafletted walks. Free and full access all the year round. A mixed broadleaved woodland which is being positively managed to favour the broadleaved species and during late 1993, the wood will be fenced to exclude stock and encourage natural regeneration. The wood abounds in birdlife.

Pwll y Wrach
(Brecknock Wildlife Trust) F 8.5ha
O.S.S. 161 - SO 165 328
☎0874 625708

From Brecon take the A470 and A438 to Bronllys (12km) and then the A479 to Talgarth (2kms). Pass through Talgarth taking the minor road signposted to the Mid Wales hospital. The car park is 500 metres past the hospital. Wheelchair route, car park, interpretation panels, leaflet from Trust office. A fine broadleaved woodland of considerable botanical interest. The upper leached parts of the valley side support sessile oak over acid-loving species such as heather. Ash / elm woodland has developed lower down the valley side. The rich ground flora includes dogwood, spindle, herb paris and toothwort. In Jul 1991 the Pwll y Wrach geology trail was opened in this reserve which explores and explains the environment of 400 million years ago.

★ Trallwm Forest
(George Johnson) L 175ha
O.S.S. 146/147 - SN 881 543
☎05913 229

Turn off the A483 between Builth Wells and Llanwrtyd Wells at Beulah, signposted Abergwesyn - Trallwm is 3 1/2 miles on R. There is parking for 20 + cars but no other facilities. The wood is open on advertised days or by appointment. There is a variety of conifer crops, producing quality timber as well as providing a home for many species of bird, mammal, insect and reptile along edges of roads, rides, lake and farmland. We also have accommodation for up to 40 guests in s/c stone and slate cottages.

THE FORESTRY TRUST FOR CONSERVATION AND EDUCATION

Producing this handbook is part of the work of the Forestry Trust. We are a registered charity whose purpose is "to advance the education of the public (including those engaged in forestry and silviculture) by the creation of wider public appreciation of the role and importance of productive forestry, the promotion of a greater public understanding of silviculture and forestry management, and the demonstration that productive forestry is compatible with the conservation of wildlife and enhancement of the landscape."

The intention to establish the Trust was first announced by His Royal Highness The Prince of Wales following his Presidency of the Royal Forestry Society of England, Wales and Northern Ireland, our founding organisation. The Trust was formally established on 1st September 1988 at the Englefield Estate, near Reading.

We aim to promote formal and informal education and enjoyment through the generosity of woodland owners who make their woods available for study and exploration, and through the provision of supporting educational materials and services. There is a particular emphasis on young people and the provision of educational materials for use both in forest and classroom. The Trust offers a service that gives schools, organised groups and individual visitors a rewarding and enjoyable insight into the role of woods and forests in the working countryside and, through an appreciation of the need for management if all the potential benefits are to be fully realised.

The Trust has been invited by the Countryside Commission, the Countryside Council for Wales and the Forestry Authority to produce this annual handbook of woodlands and forests where a welcome is assured. The project is grant aided over three years but matched funding and more is needed if the full potential of the scheme is to be realised. By the end of 1995 it is hoped that the publication will be self financing. Thereafter, as with the National Gardens Scheme, the intention is to donate profits to other charities. The focus of the Trust's support will be on specific charities that manage forests on a sustainable basis in the developing world. Rather than telling them how they should manage their own forests, whilst ignoring our own, we wish to demonstrate how wise management of a renewable resource can bring both environmental and economic benefits in this country and abroad.

The woodlands listed in this book vary greatly. Not all produce timber. Some may be entirely unmanaged and left to nature. Part of the fascination of woodland visiting is to experience just how wide the variety is, from a nature reserve or small amenity wood to a large timber-producing forest. The Trust encourages woodland managers to exploit every opportunity to combine conservation with timber production and recreation to create a truly multi-purpose forest.

EDUCATION

WOODS OFFERING EDUCATIONAL OPPORTUNITIES

The following woods specifically welcome educational visits to study both timber production and wildlife conservation. This does not mean that those that are not listed below do not provide this educational welcome and support, merely that we have only been able to confirm those below as Study Woods (woods that have the growing of timber as a priority of management, a commitment to wildlife conservation and which welcome educational visits). It should be noted that educational visits can be arranged to most Forest Enterprise woods but only those with educational facilities or staff on site are listed here. If there is no Study Wood close to your location first check the visiting arrangements and description of the nearest wood. If they cannot help ring the number given for the nearest Forest Enterprise wood. Those woods not normally open to the public are shown with a # - this indicates that you are likely to have sole use / attention on your visit. Some woods may have self guided trails - check individual entries - but a preliminary visit is still recommended if best use is to be made of this facility. Reference later in this section to 'Link Woods' is to all intents and purposes synonymous with 'Study Woods' (a Link Wood has more specific criteria on the structure and productivity of the wood, the wildlife measures implemented and the educational commitment but the distinction between Link and Study Woods is not being made for 1994).

Avon - #Rocks East.
Beds - Maulden Wood, #Park Wood.
Berks - Ashley Hill, #Bearwood, Fencewood, Roundoak Piece, Rushall Woods, Swinley & Bagshot Forest, #Ufton Park.
Bucks - Bottom Wood, Cockshoots, Hockeridge & Pancake Woods, Howe Park Wood, Pavis Wood, Wendover Woodland Park.
Cambs - #Perry Woods.
Cheshire - Delamere Forest Park, Little Budworth Country Park, Marbury Country Park.
Cornwall - Cardinham Woods, Horse Wood, #Trelowarren.
Cumbria - #Beacon Wood, Brundholme, Grizedale Forest Park, Mirehouse & Catstocks Woods, Whinlatter Forest Park.
Derbyshire - Stand Wood.
Devon - Bovey Donn, Cookworthy, #Eastcottdown Plantation, #Gatherley North, #Gatherley South, #Harpford, #Heath Wood, #Heathercombe, #Hillersdon, Holne Woods(2), #Huntshaw, #Kedworthy, #Kennerleigh, Kiddens Wood, Knotts & Parsonage, Lukesland, #Pool Down, #Quicke Estate, #Riding Parks & Lawelldown, Shute Hill, #Stoke(1), Tavistock Woodlands, #Townleigh, #West Bowerland, #Whitehills Plantation.
Dorset - #Belstone, Warren & Chaffins Copse, Hooke Park, Moors Valley Forest, #Slepe Wood, Wareham Forest.
Durham - Hamsterley Forest.
Essex - Hockley Woods, Norsey Wood, Stour Wood.

Glos - Beechenhust, #Broomhill, #Miserden, #Newent, Owlpen, #Queens Wood.
Greater London - Fryent Country Park.
Hants & IoW - #Ashridge, The New Forest, Phrympth Wood, Queen Elizabeth Country Park.
Hereford & Worcester - Garnons Hill, #Kiln Ground, Langdale Wood & the Lills, Monnington Wood, #Wolfwood, Whitfield Woods, Wyre Forest.
Herts - Broxbourne & Bencroft, Bullens Green, Tring Park, Wall Hall Estate.
Kent - Bushy Wood (Bore Place), Blean Woods, Hemsted Forest, Tudeley Woods.
Leics - #Red Lodge Wood, #Staunton Harold.
Lincs - Bourne Wood, Chambers Farm, #Stenigot.
Norfolk - Sandringham, Thetford Forest, #Warren, #Weasenham.
Northants - Fineshade, #Grafton Park, Irchester Country Park, Salcey Forest.
Northumberland - Harwood, Kielder, Kyloe.
Notts - Sherwood Pines Forest Park.
Oxon - #Blenheim.
Shropshire - Edge Wood.
Somerset - Bittiscombe, Combe Sydenham, Dunster, Hadborough Plantation, Moor Wood, #Witham Park Woods.
Staffs - Cannock Forest, #Jacksons Bank.
Suffolk - Bradfield Woods, Rendlesham Forest.
Surrey - Alice Holt Forest, #Nower Wood, #Winterfold Forest.
Sussex East - Friston Forest, #Morris's Wood, Wilderness Wood.
Sussex West - #Rabbit Warren, Stansted Forest.
Tyne & Wear - Chopwell Woodland Park.
Warwicks - Claywood.
Wilts - #Clarendon Park, Great Combe, Jacks Castle, Swancombe Wood, The Woodland Park.
Yorkshire North - Clapdale, Dalby Forest, Duncombe Park.
Yorkshire South - #Cawthorne Park.
Yorkshire West - Chevin Forest Park, Harewood.
Wales
Clwyd - #Coed Nant Gain.
Glamorgan Mid - #Llanharan.
Gwent - The Buckholt, #Cwm, Cwmcarn, #Newton Court, Parkwood, Penyclawdd. **Gwynedd** - Coed Llyn y Garnedd, Coed y Brenin, Cwm Mynach, Glasfryn, Gwydyr Forest Park.
Powys - #Ackers Grove, Cefnllysg-wynne, Craigfryn, Held, Trallwm Forest.

Forestry Open Days are being held on the following dates at the woods listed:
10 Mar - Drayton Estate - Northants
3 Apr - Chard Wood - Somerset
1 May - Roundoak Piece - Berks, Kentchurch Deer Park - Hereford & Worcester
3 May - Wray Cleave - Devon
19 May - Drayton Estate - Northants
29 May - Witham Park - Somerset
17 Jun - Holne Woods (2) - Devon
3 Jul - Roundoak Piece - Berks, Nash Wood - Hereford & Worcester, Chard Wood - Somerset, Rabbit Warren - Sussex West.

1 Oct - Broomhill - Glos
2 Oct - Roundoak Piece - Berks,
Chard Wood - Somerset
4 Dec - Roundoak Piece - Berks

Woods listed in the book that have
won or been commended in the
Duke of Cornwalls Award:
Devon - Kiddens Wood, Tavistock
Woodlands, Quicke Estate
Woodlands
Lincs - Stenigot Estate
Sussex East - Wilderness Wood
Wilts - Swancombe Wood
Yorkshire West - Chevin Forest
Park
Wales
Gwent - Parkwood
Powys - Craigfryn, Held

Woods listed in the book that have
won or been runners up in the
Dulverton Flagon:
Glos - Miserden
Lincs - Stenigot Estate
Norfolk - Weasenham
Wales
Gwent - The Buckholt, Coed
Bryntovey
Gwynedd - Coed Llyn y Garnedd

Woods listed in the book that have
won **Forestry Authority Centre of
Excellence Awards:**
Bucks - Burnham Beeches,
Hockeridge & Pancake Woods
Derbyshire - Upper Derwent
Devon - Harcombe, Hembury
Hereford - Bodenham Arboretum
Norfolk - Mannington Wood,
Thetford Forest, Wolterton Wood
Northumberland - Kielder Forest
Somerset - Combe Sydenham
Surrey - Box Hill, Winterfold
Forest
Sussex East - Wilderness Wood

WOODLANDS FOR LEARNING

All the woods in this book offer opportunities for enjoyable learning. Those which make special provision for education and welcome school groups are shown as *Study Woods*. We hope that these will grow in number as the value of studying at first-hand in the forest becomes fully recognised. Many woodland parks and nature reserves are already used for teaching natural history. The Trust, however, is keen to demonstrate the particular excitement of using woods which produce timber and other forest products and are rich in wildlife and landscape. Such woodlands offer an even wider range of study topics which will appeal to children. They show how producing things that people need can - with skill - be integrated with conservation.

Topics immediately suggest themselves.

The variety of trees; how to recognise them; where they come from, both at home and abroad; trees and soil; trees and the weather; leaf shapes and textures; bark studies; how fast trees grow; how long they live; how they spread; how they die; what they provide for us like timber, paper, bark and resin...

Forests - how old are they; the forest in the past; the forest today; kinds of forest; how forests look; enter the forester; forest management; planting trees; caring for trees; felling trees; forest produce in the forest (gates, stiles, hides, bridges, bird boxes...); using wood; making paper...

Wildlife - forest ecology; what plants and animals can we find; where are they living; how are they suited to their habitats; food chains in the forest; birds of prey; forest deer; helping wildlife - unplanted areas, rides, streams, bat boxes, dead trees left...; the wildlife of broadleaved, conifer and mixed woodlands..

Inspiration - woodlands in words; photography in the woods; drawing and painting; music; sculpture; design and craftsmanship in wood...

The relevance of all of these - and many more - to the drier language of the school curriculum is obvious. Science, mathematics, geography, history, technology, economics and art can all be served by the experience of a well-managed multi-puprose forest environment. Many of the individual study topics and attainment targets specified in the national curriculum and public examination syllabuses can be achieved with the help of the forest experience. Where better to undertake environmental education! Or teach field study skills.

The Trust - and many of the woodland owners featured in this book - want to help. At the listed *Study Woods* you will find trees being grown to produce timber and / or small forest produce and evidence of woodland management for conservation. There will be a variety of types and ages of tree and you will be able to see how felled trees are replaced by a new generation in accordance with the principle of sustainability. The owner, whether private or public, (notably Forest Enterprise), is keen to provide some opportunities for teachers to bring pupils to learn about the wood. Usually there will be either a self-guided trail, with explanatory posters provided by the Forestry Trust, or guided visits led by a forester or ranger. To make the visits as profitable as possible, teachers are encouraged to visit and discuss in advance so that the time can be spent as you decide. The forest is seen as an educational resource with learning programmes kept fully flexible to meet curricular needs. Obviously the input that a small private woodland owner can give will be less than organisations like Forest Enterprise and the National Trust where facilities - including study centres and lavatories - as well as educational staff will often be on hand. Look carefully at the individual entry in this book to see what may be available and the arrangements you need to make in advance of the visit.

Educational materials are vital for use both in the forest and in the classroom before and after. The range is increasing and you may well find a pack about the local forest, especially if it is well-known and publicly owned, already available locally. The Trust publishes educational materials itself, details of which are given in this book on page []. Others are available from Forest Enterprise and the organisations listed on page []. Do contact the Trust for further help and information. We are here to assist teachers who are keen to take their pupils to learn from the forest environment.

FOR THE TEACHER

Preparing for a School Visit to a Study Wood

To ensure a successful and enjoyable study visit the secret is to BE PREPARED. The following points will help you with your advance preparation:

1. Contact the Forester and arrange to meet him/her for a preliminary visit, and/or invite him/her to talk to the pupils at the school.

2. Obtain from the Forestry Trust a copy of "YOUR LINK WOOD" and teaching materials appropriate to age and subject - if not held by the forester at your local wood.

3. Discuss the scope and objectives of the visit and obtain a map of the area and a plan of the wood showing all paths, rides, and details of forest plantations. (In the appropriate space in YOUR LINK WOOD note down any additional information about the wood provided by the Forester.)

4. Make a date and time for the

visit and determine the duration and whether it will be a guided or a self-guided visit.

5. If a car/coach park is not available, arrange for a suitable site to park the vehicles adjacent to the wood.

6. Ascertain the proximity of WCs (if any).

7. Make visit preparations including the assembly of the following equipment: camera,compass, secateurs (for collecting specimens - consult Forester first), clipboard, notebook and pencil, metre rule, measuring tape, hand lens, light/temperature meter, quadrat, plastic container or bag for collecting specimens, suitable clothing and footwear.

8. Ascertain from the Forester which materials are suitable for collecting and taking back to the classroom.

9. Ensure that safety considerations have been fully addressed. The pupil to adult ratio should be as low as possible but should at the very least conform to LEA or school regulations. If unescorted, check with the Forester that there are no safety hazards (ie windblow, unsafe trees etc..)where you will be visiting. First aid kit should always be taken, not because the forest is inherently dangerous, but you will frequently be some distance from habitation should anyone require first aid. Finally check your school's liability insurance cover.

Woodland owners should have liability to cover for most eventualities but the onus is on the visitor to take adequate steps to ensure that accidents that might subsequently be construed as the responsibility of the visitor do not carry financial penalties as well.

10. Allow sufficient time for study at the site(s). An overambitious programme will result in a route march to different areas with only superficial knowledge gained from each stop. A few well planned activities will always be preferable to many rushed ones - diversity and interest will come from unexpected discoveries as you walk through the wood.

FORESTRY TRUST EDUCATIONAL MATERIALS

Your Link Wood A *revised* publication for teachers with practical field work and related classroom project work for Primary and Middle Schools. Links the working wood as an outdoor classroom to the National Curriculum. Will cover from Key Stage 1 to Key Stage 3. Publication date and details to be announced later. Provisional price £5. Refunds available to schools who validate material for us.

Key Stage 1 - Trees and Leaves A cross curricular project book for Key Stage 1 of the National Curriculum, produced for us by teachers. It contains ideas for practical and extension activities, plus assessment indicator questions and attainment targets. 21 pages, £2.

Key Stage 3 - Trees in the Forest A cross curricular project book for Key Stage 3 of the National Curriculum. It examines the planting, growing and harvesting of trees for the production of timber and other forest produce, and looks at the different operations which are implied by the term 'Forestry'. The great range of habitats provided by the forest as a whole is also described. Includes attainment target information. 35 pages, £3.

Know Your Trees A small handbook with simple line drawings of 32 common species of tree, ideal for children and beginners as an introductory guide to tree recognition. Short notes accompany each drawing, including details of timber where appropriate. The book is produced by the Royal Forestry Society of England, Wales and Northern Ireland. 50 pence.

Key Stage 4 - Wood Technology A cross curricular teachers pack for Key Stage 4 of the National Curriculum. It describes how trees grow, how timber is produced, the uses of timber, wood quality and defects. It also contains a test pack with ideas for examining the uses and properties of wood. Produced in association with the Timber Research and Devcelopment Association (TRADA). 31 pages, £4.

New Secondary School Pro-gramme Subject to sponsorship this publication *should be available* in the late spring for validation in the summer term. It aims to provide a broad based programme of study for TVEI, CPVQ, A Level, GCSE and Key Stage 4 of the National Curriculum as well as the curricula for Scotland and Northern Ireland. The initial pack will focus on geography and science only - other modules, with mathematics/economics as the next priority will be produced as resources allow. Target price £5.

Forestry with Conservation - Setting the Scene Aimed at adults in general and teachers in particular, it gives short details of forestry and timber worldwide, the historical background and present day situation in Britain, the role of the Trust and how it operates. The main section of the book is a stage by stage description of the various forestry operations and the conservation benefits that are associated with each one. Additionally there is a comprehensive glossary of forestry terms, a short bibliography, and a list of useful addresses. 33 pages, £2.

Tree and Timber Data Sheets A guide to the characteristics of trees and their timber. *Substantially revised*. A single page for each species, covering: site factors, range, tree characteristics, timber and uses, wildlife, other benefits, pests and diseases. Intended to give sufficient background to study the properties of different timber trees and enable project work to be developed. £6.

Forest Management A *new* guide for the general visitor to a working wood. It aims to explain what is being done in a wood managed for timber production and why. It also links this main purpose with other management objectives that must be incorporated in a true multi purpose forest. £1.

Information Leaflet Statistical data on forestry in Britain and the world together with a brief summary of the Trust's role and range of activities. On the reverse is a colour poster illustrating the different stages of forest management, showing how these all contribute to the creation of habitat diversity and the forming of landscapes. 50 pence.

Tree Posters Four separate posters available in either A4 or large format. These are the Tree Charts of Britain and Northern Europe produced by Frederick Warne & Co Ltd. Three broadleaf posters and one conifer poster. Originally available at £12.63 incl VAT for the combined small and large sets, we sell the small set for £1 and the large set at £4. This must represent exceptional value.

Forestry Operation/Wildlife Habitat Posters A *newly available* set of 6 posters illustrating the different stages of forest management and the wildlife benefits associated with them. Unlaminated for indoor use £12, laminated for external interpretive use £30.

Newsletters Back numbers of all copies of Forestry Trust News are available (numbers 1-11). Where originals are no longer in stock photocopies will be provided. £1 each, full set £9.

Tree Labels Some 80 species of tree are covered by the Trust's tree labels. They list scientific name, common name, trade name (where appropriate), and area of origin. The labels are olive green with white lettering, measuring 10.2cm by 6.2cm, fully weatherproofed and have four holes drilled in the corners for mounting on posts or for tying. They are intended for woodland owners who wish to mark species on or near rides and tracks in a clear but discreet manner for the information of visitors. Species stocked include all the main timber trees growing in this country, all native trees and a few of the major exotics. £1.33 each. Send sae for tree label list. Additional species can be ordered for which exact details must be specified (Prices on application - £2 plus).

Information Sheets General fact sheets *newly available* on selected forestry related topics - (1) Causes of tree damage, (2) Forestry and air pollution, (3) The greenhouse effect, (4) Tropical timbers, (5) Soil pH, (6) Dutch elm disease, (7) Tree identification books, (8) Community forests, (9) The sizes trees can reach, (10) Hardwoods and softwoods, (11) Native tree species, (12) Careers in forestry and the countryside, (13) Books about trees, (14) Forestry and woodland organisations. Also

Forestry with Conservation Information sheets (1) Forest management and ground flora, (2) Forestry and water. All sheets are priced at 10 pence each.

Individual Tree Posters Obsolete stock of old Forestry Commission posters reduced to 40 pence each. 75cm by 50cm. To reduce handling costs they are folded for posting. If you would like them unfolded please add £2 to your order value and specify unfolded. Only remaining species are Sitka spruce, Corsican pine, European larch, sycamore and English elm.

There is a minimum order value of £1 including postage. Within the UK please add the following amounts for postage and packing:

Order Value	Add
Under £1	30p
£1 to £4.99	75p
£5 to £9.99	£2
Over £10	£3

Cheques should be made payable to 'The Forestry Trust'

Discounts and sale or return Registered supporters (those who donate £25 or more per calendar year) and retail traders should apply to the Trust for details.

Orders should be sent to:
The Forestry Trust for Conservation and Education
The Old Estate Office
Englefield Road
Theale
READING
Berks RG7 5DZ

EDUCATION MATERIALS FROM OTHER ORGANISATIONS

Teachers will find educational materials relevant to woodland and forestry studies also available from a number of the organisations whose addresses are given on p[]. Forest Enterprise publish educational packs for a number of the major forests in England and Wales. The National Trust is actively developing countryside education programmes and publications for many properties, some of which are woodlands. Likewise, educational materials from the Royal Society for Nature Conservation / Wildlife Trusts partnership and the Royal Society for the Protection of Birds include woodland topics. The Tree Council publish educational material on many aspects of trees and woods especially for the annual National Tree Week in Nov / Dec.

MANAGEMENT

MULTI PURPOSE FOREST MANAGEMENT

Multi-purpose forestry is a frequently used phrase in environmental circles though it may be new to you. What does it mean? Like most catch phrases it will mean different things to different people. The views here are those of the Forestry Trust. You must decide whether you agree with them or not.

In our crowded isle we do not have the space to manage large tracts of forest for a single purpose without regard to many other factors. The days of single purpose forest management are going but that does not mean that forests should be managed so as to mean all things to all people. Rather the forest manager must be aware of the major values of the forest, notably timber, wildlife, landscape and recreation and decide how he is going to reconcile any conflicts between them. Forest Enterprise, for example, follows a multiple purpose management philosophy which integrates recreation, wood production and conservation. The main aim is "to create and maintain attractive and productive wood-lands, to manage them for public benefits and to generate the required return on the assets used". Multi-purpose use is thus an important aspect of present government forestry policy.

Forests are an essential habitat for much wildlife. They can also meet the needs and aspirations of people. The principal human need from the forest is timber and wood products. Most of the other values for ourselves, however cherished, are not essential for our survival. We can survive without a pleasant landscape, without archaeological remains, without recreational facilities. We would be greatly impoverished by their loss but our dependence on them is not as crucial as our dependence on timber and wood products. Everyone accepts the need for timber production. Current arguments focus more on what kind of trees, on avoiding rapid changes of scenery and "getting the balance right". These are all legitimate concerns but can imply that timber production and conservation, in its widest sense, are not compatible. This is the view that the Forestry Trust seeks to dispel, by demonstrating the potential of multiple use.

There are two main methods of achieving multi-purpose forest management.

Firstly by zoning. Zoning for a single purpose is sometimes necessary when preserving archaeological sites and protecting fragile rare habitats such as that required, for instance, for a rare orchid. As part of a complex forest mosaic the overall effect is one of multi-purpose forest management. Such zoning on a large scale, however, contradicts the principle of multi-purpose management. By zoning too extensively the concept of conservation is devalued. The resulting tendency is to manage those areas that are designated for commercial management on a more intensive basis to compensate. The parallel with set-aside is evident.

The second method of multi-purpose forest management, which is not mutually exclusive from the first, is integration. It is this policy which the Forestry Trust advocates for as much of our forest lands as possible. The principal object of management may not always be timber production but all woodlands managed for timber should address conservation measures for wildlife and landscape, and all amenity woodlands should endeavour to harvest the best quality of timber that can be produced without jeopardizing their priority objectives. The first approach is extensive conservation; the second is conservation of resources.

These principles are seldom rejected outright, but there is a tendency to question the emphasis given to one aspect of management rather than another. The relative values of amenity and working woodlands are difficult to compare. They are open to subjective judgements of wildlife, landscape and recreational values. These are accorded lower priority in times of economic hardship - ask any starving peasant in the developing world - but it is fair to say that a nation that imports 86% of its timber, when it is capable of producing far more, is living and importing beyond its means. We have traditionally belittled the importance of producing high quality timber in Britain.

The working wood may not appear such a rich conservation resource as the nature reserve but to understand the true environmental value of a wood one should consider how it is paid for. Despite some funding from Government, now available to many other categories of wood as well, the working forest is a good example of conservation which is self financed and therefore sustainable.

On the pages that follow there are notes on specific aspects of multi-purpose management. Judge for yourself how these have been applied in the wood you are visiting but understand that whatever the individual emphasis, all woods can provide multiple benefits.

However, without careful and sustained management, which costs money, these benefits cannot be maintained. Timber production is not the only method of financing these benefits, indeed recreational and sporting revenue frequently outperform timber as a source of income to woodland owners, but as a sustainable practice for the future, timber production is the key to the multi-purpose forest.

THE FOREST LANDSCAPE

Woodlands, more often than not, are key elements in the structure and appearance of a landscape. It is important, therefore, in considering the management of woodland, to gauge the effect that operations will have upon it and to strike a balance between the demands of forestry and the needs of the landscape. The ultimate objective is an attractive appearance and this can only be achieved by adhering to some of the basic principles of visual design that underlie all matters where appearance is concerned. These are:

1. SHAPE. Shape is determined by edges, and edges are determined by contrasts in height, shadow and colour. The aim is for natural shapes, which are irregular in outline and which reflect the nature and form of the ground where they are situated. It is a useful guide to see shapes as running diagonally to the contour and rising uphill into hollows and downhill on convex slopes. Interlocking shapes are a useful starting point in flat landscapes.

2. SCALE. Scale is determined by size in relation to what is seen of something as part of a whole. It follows that scale will vary from viewpoint to viewpoint. Scale is, therefore, determined by contour and may need to be adjusted from place to place; often larger on top of hills, smaller towards the valley bottom.

3. DIVERSITY. Diversity depends upon the number of different elements of features in a landscape. Uniformity, the opposite of diversity, leads to a dull or monotonous wood and is avoided wherever possible by giving careful attention to varying age structure, by designing satisfactory felling coupes and by creating open space or non planted areas. Water, rocks and contrasting vegetation patterns can all lend variety to a view.

Notional designs in woodland management are first committed to paper - however roughly - and recorded for the sake of later comparison. It is in fact a process of trial and error by elimination, firstly in terms of a perspective sketch, then conveyed to plan form. Sketches, either free hand or traced from photographs, are taken from a number of viewpoints, with salient features described and principles applied so as to create an initial design which can then be refined. Only by analysing each situation in this way is its true potential revealed - and as a result, a better landscape designed.

THE WOODLAND PAST

The woodland and forest areas of Great Britain have a long and fascinating history stretching back thousands of years. Archaeological features representing previous woodland management are often visible in many woods. These include coppice stands protected by earth banks, saw pits, and the platforms where charcoal was made. Some woodlands also contain evidence of earlier land uses such as hillforts, burial mounds, prehistoric house sites and fields. In lowland areas woodland is often the only location where these features have survived the more damaging effects of other changes in land use. From more recent times examples of industrial archaeology can be seen in many areas. These represent the coincidence of metal ores and sustainable fuel source, namely wood.

Today's forest managers are encouraged to conserve important archaeological evidence of all periods. This is possible through the good planning which is necessary to ensure the long term success of woodland. Trees are not planted in such a way as to damage archaeological evidence and care is taken not to cause damage by road construction, harvesting operations or by driving heavy machinery across sites. Vegetation which obscures the detail of features is removed and trees which might damage earlier sites either through root growth or the possibility of windthrow are felled. The open space which is left or created on and around archaeological sites provides a useful variety of habitat as well as conserving the history of the woodland for future generations to appreciate and enjoy.

WOODLAND AND FOREST WILDLIFE

Ancient woodlands, retaining as they do a natural character, are justifiably treasured as habitats rich in plants and animals. There are many fine examples listed in this book which will be a delight for nature lovers to visit. Less well known and publicised is the potential of managed woodlands and forests to provide suitable conditions for wildlife to flourish. Multi-purpose forest management ensures that wildlife conservation is to the fore and you will see evidence of this on visiting both private and publicly owned, notably Forest Enterprise, woodlands. The key to a rich environment for wildlife is variety. A wide range of tree ages and species encourages a variety of plants and animals to adopt the forest. Retaining existing older woodland in places, allowing poorly drained areas to retain their characteristic marshland and bog, leaving some felled areas as open heathland or grassland all help to vary the habitats further. In the modern forest close attention is paid to rides and paths where, at the edges, shrubs are planted or grasses encouraged to suit butterflies and other insects.

It is a characteristic of forests that much more wildlife may be present than is immediately apparent. Patient listening and observation is often rewarded even though it may be just a short snatch of bird song in the tree tops or a quick glimpse of a party of deer crossing a forest ride. For species like birds of prey, especially those which need both refuge and very large territories, the size of our large modern forests is a strong attraction. Deer find refuge in the cover provided by trees in the thicket stage while finding their food in newly planted areas and in rides and clearings. With the expansion of forestry, deer numbers have greatly increased so that damage from browsing and bark-stripping can be a problem. The opportunity is often taken to manage forest herds by careful shooting of weaker individuals by trained staff. This enables numbers to be kept at a level which the forest can support and improves the quality of the herd. Control can be an essential element of conservation.

It is encouraging to discover that some species - unfortunately not all - can adapt their behaviour when their traditional habitats decline and even disappear. Nightjars for example, once characteristic of heathlands in southern England, are breeding successfully in clear-felled areas in the forest. Woodlarks and merlins are other birds to have shown such adaptability. An important goal of today's forester is to provide a forest environment which is suited to as many types of plants and animals as possible. So the focus is on the habitat. However, where essential features, for example, nest sites or safe roosts are lacking special measures to provide them are often taken. As you walk the forest you may see bird boxes affixed to the trees or specially designed boxes with a slit in the base for bats to shelter in. Better still at dusk you may see the bats themselves feeding on the wing. Dead wood is increasingly provided by leaving old and dying trees to decay in situ so that insects and hole nesting birds like woodpeckers may benefit.

We are only just beginning to appreciate what the modern multi-purpose managed forests across the country can contribute to the needs of our wildlife, providing extensive conservation areas relatively free from noise,

disturbance and pollution, where natural sights and sounds can give pleasure to all. Whilst there will always be a need for specialist management for rare species and in such cases advice should be sought from the appropriate authority, the working forest provides unparalled opportunities for this extensive conservation which does not require significant additional resources to achieve it. For any serious study of this subject Wildlife Conservation in Managed Woodlands and Forests by Esmond and Jeanette Harris, available from the Trust, is essential reading.

WOOD PRODUCTION

Growing trees for the production of wood is not incompatible with conservation. Indeed sensitively handled forest management enhances the conservation value of a woodland in several ways. Most importantly, light is periodically increased when thinning or felling takes place and this encourages plants and trees to flower and fruit. The latter encourages birds to feed. Secondly, the removal of rank vegetation, particularly brambles, even to the extent of exposing the soil, for example when timber is extracted, encourages new growth and diversity.

Forest operations are not continuous. The activities are usually years apart and only last for a few weeks or months, so disturbance is not constant.

Thinning is done every five or ten years. Even when there are drastic operations, such as felling and replanting, they do not usually take place over the whole woodland at one time. They do, however, bring the benefit of change, leading to diversity of habitat and thereby increasing the species diversity, before the woodland settles down again for several years without disturbance.

Thus a mature, managed woodland or forest will contain stands of trees at various stages. Areas recently planted will be in the "establishment" stage. When weeding has been completed and the tree branches begin to meet, the "thicket" stage' has been reached. As the trees grow up, their lower branches start to die off, they are in the "pole" stage. Thinning then takes place until the remaining final crop trees are mature. When they are harvested the "regeneration" stage has been reached. Usually some form of clear felling takes place in various sized "clear cuts", scattered through the forest if it is a large one, or in a single clear cut if the woodland is small. These areas are sometimes "naturally regenerated" with seedlings from the mature "mother trees" but more often the felled areas are replanted. These regeneration areas (the clear cuts) are seldom as extensive as the original planting would have been at the start of the first "rotation". Thus a wood becomes more diverse when it is regenerated.

The different wood products, such as fencing posts, garden rustic material, pulp wood for paper production and saw mill logs for constructional purposes, are grown throughout a woodland because the different products depend on the size of the trees. The smaller products come from the young trees but also from the tops of large trees. High quality logs only come from the lower trunk of well grown, mature trees. Hence a diverse range of products come both from the larger trees and from a woodland as a whole.

Britain has become dependent for most of its wood products on imports but top quality timber can be grown here on the right sites and with proper treatment. Conifers (softwoods) are grown producing high quality timber on a wide range of poor soils and upland sites. Three quarters of our total requirement is for them. Hardwoods, from broadleaved trees, require better, more sheltered soils if they are to produce more than merely firewood. They also require more careful tending and for much longer. We cannot, therefore, expect all our woodlands to be broadleaved, and indeed hardwood timber of better quality can be produced if broadleaved trees are grown in mixture with conifers, at least for the first third of the "rotation". This is another way in which wildlife conservation benefits from good forest management because a mixture of evergreen conifers and broadleaved trees provides habitats for a greater abundance and variety of wildlife. The conditions of light and shade vary, the conifers mature and, therefore, seed first, thereby providing food much sooner than would occur in a purely broad-leaved woodland. Hence a wider range of species is provided with suitable habitats.

Thus all properly undertaken forest operations can benefit wildlife, including plants, as well as the trees from which wood products are provided. When the land is first planted young trees are introduced, often including a wider range of species than were there before. For a few years competing vegetation is removed around them, often by the use of chemicals. Properly used these do not harm wildlife and positively encourage a wide range of plants to flourish. When the trees can compete with the vegetation, no work is carried out for some years and woodlands become very dense, providing a habitat for a limited range of species. When the trees start to compete with one another, the poorer specimens are removed and provide small dimension material for rustic work and fencing. If high quality hardwood timber is the ultimate aim, the trees are "high pruned" to remove the lower branches and thus the knots that would otherwise occur in the timber. At intervals for several decades thinnings are carried out to improve the conditions for the better trees by removing the competing poorer ones. Thus by the end of the "rotation" only high quality trees with straight, fat stems, are left to provide large, valuable saw logs (both conifer and hardwood) or in the very best cases, veneer logs.

GOOD FORESTRY PRACTICE

Shelter
Forests provide shelter for the woodland plants and animals which live in them. If well designed they can also protect nearby farmland or houses from wind. A network of shelterbelts can greatly reduce wind speeds on exposed farmland to the benefit of livestock, crops and soil conservation. Shelterbelts with low native shrubs at the edges and taller trees in the centre will be valuable wildlife habitat also and provide good draught-free conditions for pheasants. Within a forest the wildlife which specialises in woodland is dependent upon some shelter being maintained so that moist and still conditions prevail. This includes many species of mosses, ferns and liverworts; lichens which grow on the tree bark as well as other woodland plants like wood sorrel which actually thrives in partial shade. Moisture loving woodland slugs also like the shelter of the forest. Developing some areas where woodland shelter is maintained by felling small glades and avoiding larger "coupes" is helpful for many of these species.

Soils and Erosion
Good forestry practice should seek to avoid excessive soil disturbance and erosion which could affect the future yield of timber and the flora

and fauna of both the land and the water courses within the forest. Cultivation and drainage are used to the minimum extent needed to secure establishment of trees. Scarifying or mounding disturbs less soil than ploughing and is preferable where it is practicable. Continuous plough furrows or drains are avoided on steep slopes to prevent erosion. Drains are cut at very shallow angles, less than 2 degrees. Great care is taken with heavy machinery on fragile soils especially wet heavy soils or steep ground. Where it is necessary to drive over vulnerable soils protective measures such as piles of cut branches are used to reduce the impact, especially close to water courses. Features of scientific or cultural importance such as gravel deposits left by retreating glaciers or archaeological remains are respected and left undisturbed by cultivation and often planted with trees. Fertilisers are used sparingly and targeted at the trees which most need them to avoid overenrichment of soils and water courses.

Water

Good forestry practice safeguards the quality of watercourses from ponds to lakes and from small headwater streams to large rivers. It can increase the diversity of aquatic and wetland wildlife: Careful cultivation and drainage prevents problems from sediments entering streams and lakes. Ditches are stopped well clear of watercourses and the water is allowed to filter through lush bankside vegetation. A balance of grassland or heathland with deciduous woodland is developed on banks of streams and lakes. This provides adequate light and heat from sunshine for plants and animals, including fish, to thrive in the water whilst preventing excessive temperatures in summer. The mixed vegetation of the bankside area is very varied wildlife habitat supporting a wide range of common species as well as specialists which need water and land, like dragonflies and mayflies. Overhanging deciduous trees and shrubs are scattered or clumped along the banks and they provide leaf litter and falling caterpillars which give food and energy to the aquatic wildlife. Heavily shading trees are kept well back from the water's edge to allow bankside plants to flourish and reduce the chances of bank erosion. Special habitats such as flood plains and marshland which are linked to watercourses are treated sensitively, and not densely planted or drained. Damage by harvesting machinery is avoided by timing felling to avoid sensitive periods, and by constructing temporary crossings with branches and timber if machines cannot be routed away from streams.

Leopold de Rothschild Charitable Trust
Lloyds Bank plc
McRobert Trusts
Marks and Spencer plc
Mitsubishi UK
National Westminster Bank plc
Nicholson Nurseries
Norwich Union Life Insurance Group
Plessey Pension Trust Ltd
Provincial Insurance
Prudential
Pye Settlement
Refuge Assurance
Ronaash Ltd
NM Rothschild & Son Ltd
Royal Bank of Scotland
Shotton Paper Company plc
Smallwood
Smith Kline Beecham plc
Tilhill Nurseries
United Newspapers plc
University College of North Wales
Watts Blake, Bearne & Co plc
Whitaker Charitable Trust
WH Smith Ltd
Willis Faber
Woodland Improvements
Yattendon Estates Ltd
Yorkshire Agricultural Society
Yorkshire Electricity

All the above individuals and organisations have made recent significant donations or contributed generously or consistently to the Trust during the last five and a half years. Without their help and the help of many supporters who wish to remain anonymous, who have given lesser donations, and those with whom we have been unable to confirm acknowledgement on this page, this book would not have been possible. To all of them the Trust remains deeply indebted.

Finally these acknowledgements would not be complete without thanking the woodland owners who have agreed to list their woods in this book. In particular those members of the Royal Forestry Society of England, Wales and Northern Ireland and of the Timber Growers Association and other private owners for whom there is no personal benefit in making this offer and often considerable cost. As the years go by we hope that their number will increase significantly, thereby spreading the burden between owners, and the opportunities for visitors to enjoy and appreciate the many values of our woods and forests.

USEFUL ADDRESSES

ARBORICULTURAL ASSOCIATION
Ampfield House, Ampfield, ROMSEY, Hants
SO51 9PA
☎0794 68717

**ARBORICULTURAL ADVISORY AND
INFORMATION SERVICE**
Forest Research Station, Alice Holt Lodge,
Wrecclesham, FARNHAM, Surrey GU10 4LH
☎0420 22022

**ASSOCIATION OF PROFESSIONAL
FORESTERS**
7/9 West Street, BELFORD, Northumberland
NE70 7QA
☎0668 213937

**BRITISH TRUST FOR CONSERVATION
VOLUNTEERS**
36 St Mary's Street, WALLINGFORD, Oxon
OX10 0EU
☎0491 839766

COED CYMRU
23 Frolic Street, NEWTOWN, Powys SY16 1AP
☎0686 628514

**COUNCIL FOR THE PROTECTION OF RURAL
ENGLAND**
25 Buckingham Palace Road, London SW1
☎071 976 6433

**COUNCIL FOR THE PROTECTION OF RURAL
WALES**
Ty Gwyn, 31 High Street, WELSHPOOL, Powys
SY21 7JP
☎0938 552525

COUNTRY LANDOWNERS ASSOCIATION
16 Belgrave Square, LONDON SW1X 8PQ
☎071 235 0511

THE COUNTRY TRUST
Stratford Grange, Stratford St Andrew,
SAXMUNDHAM, Suffolk IP17 1LF
☎0728 604818

COUNTRYSIDE COMMISSION
John Dower House, Crescent Place,
CHELTENHAM, Glos GL50 3RA
☎0242 521381

COUNTRYSIDE COUNCIL FOR WALES
Plas Penrhos, Fford Penrhos, BANGOR,
Gwynedd LL57 2LQ
☎0248 370444

ENGLISH NATURE
Northminster House, Northminster Road,
PETERBOROUGH, Cambs PE1 1UA
☎0733 340345

ENGLISH TOURIST BOARD
Thames Tower, Blacks Road, LONDON W6 9EL
☎081 846 9000

**FORESTRY COMMISSION / FORESTRY
AUTHORITY / FOREST ENTERPRISE**
231 Corstorphine Road, EDINBURGH EH12
7AT
☎031 334 0303

**FORESTRY TRUST FOR CONSERVATION
AND EDUCATION**
The Old Estate Office, Englefield Road, Theale,
READING, Berks RG7 5DZ
☎0734 323523

**FORESTS FOREVER CAMPAIGN / TIMBER
TRADE FEDERATION**
4th Floor, Clareville House, 26/27 Oxendon
Street, LONDON SW1Y 4EL
☎071 839 1891

INSTITUTE OF CHARTERED FORESTERS
7a St Colme Street, EDINBURGH EH3 6AA
☎031 225 2705

INTERNATIONAL TREE FOUNDATION
Sandy Lane, CRAWLEY DOWN, W Sussex
RH10 4HS
☎0342 712536

**JOINT NATURE CONSERVATION
COMMITTEE**
3rd Floor, Monkstone House, City Road,
PETERBOROUGH Cambs PE1 1JY

☎0733 62626

THE NATIONAL FOREST
Stanleigh House, Chapel Street, Donisthorpe,
SWADLINCOTE,Derbyshire DE12 7PS
☎0530 273816

NATIONAL SMALL WOODS ASSOCIATION
Hall Farm House, Preston Capes, Northants
☎0327 36387

NATIONAL TRUST
36 Queen Anne's Gate, LONDON SW1H 9AS
☎071 222 9251

PARNHAM TRUST
Parnham House, BEAMINSTER,Dorset DT8
3NA
☎0308 862204

RAMBLERS' ASSOCIATION
1-5 Wandsworth Road, LONDON SW8 2XX
☎071 582 6878

**ROYAL FORESTRY SOCIETY OF ENGLAND,
WALES AND NORTHERN IRELAND**
102 High Street, TRING, Herts HP23 4AH
☎0442 822028

ROYAL SCOTTISH FORESTRY SOCIETY
62 Queen Street, EDINBURGH EH2 4NA
☎031 225 8142

**ROYAL SOCIETY FOR NATURE
CONSERVATION**
The Green, Waterside South, LINCOLN, Lincs
LN5 7JR
☎0522 544400

**ROYAL SOCIETY FOR THE PROTECTION OF
BIRDS**
The Lodge, SANDY, Beds SG19 2DL
☎0767 680551

TIMBER GROWERS ASSOCIATION
5 Dublin Street Lane South, EDINBURGH EH1
3PX
☎031 557 0944

TREE AID
Room 1B, Temple House, Temple Street,
Keynsham, BRISTOL, Avon BS18 1EJ
☎0272 860662

THE TREE COUNCIL
35 Belgrave Square, LONDON SW1X 8QN
☎071 235 8854

TREE LINK
Ardmore House, 11-15 High Street, MARLOW-
on-THAMES, Bucks
☎0628 890060

WILDLIFE AND COUNTRYSIDE LINK
246 Lavender Hill, LONDON SW11 1LJ
☎071 924 2355

WOODLAND HERITAGE MUSEUM
Brokerswood, WESTBURY,Wilts BA13 4EH
☎0373 823880

WOODLAND TRUST
Autumn Park, Dysart Road, GRANTHAM, Lincs
NG31 6LL
☎0476 74297

WORLDWIDE FUND FOR NATURE
Panda House, Weyside Park, GODALMING,
Surrey GU17 1XR
☎0483 426444

This book was first produced in a pilot version in 1993. It has been extensively revised and added to but we would welcome any suggestions for improvements, whilst bearing in mind that changes are likely to be evolutionary and dependent on the limited budget at the disposal of the Forestry Trust.

In order to cater for a wide range of interests it will not be possible to tailor this book to everyone's liking but we would ask you to give your name, address and specific interest in woodland so we can provide a balance for all interest groups.

Most woodland owners know what is growing and/or breeding in their woods but would welcome specialist information, constructive suggestions and visitors views. We will pass these on. For detailed comments please contact the owners or managers direct.

Your views and knowledge can help us and them to address your concerns, to enhance your visit and to assist owners in balancing the many demands of woodland management.

WOODLANDS TO VISIT IN ENGLAND AND WALES 1994 - READERS AND VISITORS COMMENTS

Comments on the Book:

1. Content

2. Accuracy

3. Style

4. More Information on:

5. Less Information on:

6. Other Comments:

Comments on Woods:
A. Names of Woods (as in book - including County)
1.
2.
3.
4.
B. Comments on Entry (Directions, facilities, description)
1.

2.

3.

4.

C. Other Comments
1.

2.

3.

4.

Your Name and Address (or Tel No) - (BLOCK CAPITALS):

Your Specific Interest in Woodland

Please cut down the line and send your completed form to the Forestry Trust.

The form will fit inside a DL envelope (standard business size - $8^1/_2$" x $4^1/_4$" - 22cm x 11cm) and the address block will line up with the window on a DL window envelope.

Please make sure that you have put your own name and address clearly on the form.

<u>For You Own Record:</u>

Date Sent:

Remarks:

The Forestry Trust for Conservation and Education

The Old Estate Office

Englefield Road, Theale

READING, Berks RG7 5DZ

Planned publication date is March 1995. Pre-publication price is £3.50 plus 50p p&p. Not for general sale outside the UK.

Woodlands to Visit in England and Wales 1995 will contain in excess of 900 woods and will be further revised and up-dated. The 1995 book is offered to readers of the 1994 book using this form only at the guaranteed price of £3.50 plus 50p p&p within the UK. Actual retail price will not be set until 1995 but will be in excess of £4.50 plus p&p where appropriate.

There is no need to send money with this order. Please print you name and address in block letters on the form and send to the Trust at the address overleaf. Acknowledgements will only be sent if accompanied by a s.a.e.

WOODLANDS TO VISIT IN ENGLAND AND WALES 1994 - ADVANCE ORDER FORM FOR 1995

Public support is vital if over the years the Trustees are to build up this service to the level it should reach - that of a really significant recreational and educational benefit to the community.

Anyone giving £10 or more will automatically receive a copy of next year's book.

Any individual donating £25 or more, or company donating £100 or more will additionally be acknowledged as a supporter (unless specifically requesting anonymity - please tick here _____) .

If you would like to support the Trust please tick here _____ and we will send a donation / covenant form together with further information if required.

Please send to the address below _____ copy / copies of Woodlands to Visit in England and Wales 1995 @ £4.00 including postage. I understand that postage is due within 30 days of the book(s) being received.

Name:_____

Address:_____

_____

POSTALTOWN:_____

County:_____

POSTCODE:_____

Trade Terms: Accredited booksellers will be supplied through our distributors. Advance orders on trade terms are available to forestry, wildlife, educational and charitable organisations taking quantities for resale. Please ask for details sending a s.a.e. to the address overleaf.

Please cut down
the line and send
your completed
form to the
Forestry Trust.

The form will fit
inside a DL
envelope
(standard
business size -
$8^1/_2$" x $4^1/_4$" -
22cm x 11cm)
and the address
block will line up
with the window
on a DL window
envelope.

Please make sure
that you have put
your own name
and address
clearly on the
form.

For You Own
Record:

Date Sent:

Remarks:

The Forestry Trust for Conservation and Education

The Old Estate Office

Englefield Road, Theale

READING, Berks RG7 5DZ

Owners

We are seeking to increase the number of woodlands included in the book substantially for 1995. Any woodland that offers some level of access or educational opportunities will be welcome but we place particular emphasis on those which are managed for timber production and wildlife conservation.

Some degree of access, controlled or otherwise, is implicit in inclusion in the book and the more woodland owners who subscribe to the scheme the more readily the load can be shared by all. If you own or manage a wood, preferably in excess of 10 hectares, that subscribes to these principles and share our belief in the wider understanding and enjoyment of our forests being in the nation's interests please send off this form today. The address is on the reverse. We will then send you further details before you commit yourself to going ahead with an entry for 1995.

Advertisers/Sponsors

Please complete the appropriate section on the form if applicable

WOODLANDS TO VISIT IN ENGLAND AND WALES 1994 - NEW ENTRY REQUEST FORM FOR 1995

OWNERS

I would like to offer the availability of

_____ [WOOD(S)]

in the county of

_____ for inclusion

in the 1995 book.

1 Name of Owner_____(as

for entry in book)

2. Size of Wood(s) in hectares_____

3. Level of Access envisaged at this stage (see criteria on

pages 7 to 8)_____

4. Interested in being a Study Wood (where quality timber is a priority object of management, there is a commitment to wildlife and a willingness to run one or more days per year to illustrate the compatibility of these objectives .

(Please initial here_____)

5. Name address and tel no of Contact for the Forestry Trust in dealing with the entry

Name:_____

Position (ie Owner, Agent, Forester)_____

Address_____

_____

PostalTown_____County_____

POSTCODE_____ Tel No_____

ADVERTISERS/SPONSORS

We are seeking advertisers for next year's book together with sponsorship for the book and other Trust projects. The cost of running the scheme is considerable and the book cannot be funded without commercial sponsorship. If you would like details on advertising or sponsorship please complete para 5 and sign here:

STAMP

Please cut down
the line and send
your completed
form to the
Forestry Trust.

The form will fit
inside a DL
envelope
(standard
business size -
$8^1/_2$" x $4^1/_4$" -
22cm x 11cm)
and the address
block will line up
with the window
on a DL window
envelope.

Please make sure
that you have put
your own name
and address
clearly on the
form.

For You Own
Record:

Date Sent:

Remarks:

The Forestry Trust for Conservation and Education

The Old Estate Office

Englefield Road, Theale

READING, Berks RG7 5DZ

Tilhill Economic
F O R E S T R Y

**Skilled staff providing a
Countryside Service nationwide.**

◆ Puzzled over your woodlands?

◆ Have you calculated the impact of lost
Schedule 'D'?

◆ Have you considered your options?

◆ Use the depth and breadth of our practical
experience to fit the pieces together .

Your local manager is your helpline.

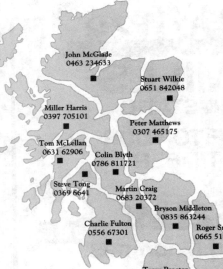

John McGlade
0463 234633

Stuart Wilkie
0651 842048

Miller Harris
0397 705101

Peter Matthews
0307 465175

Tom McLellan
0631 62906

Colin Blyth
0786 811721

Steve Tong
0369 6641

Martin Craig
0683 20372

Bryson Middleton
0835 863244

Charlie Fulton
0556 67301

Roger Smith
0665 510273

Terry Proctor
05242 72249

Tim Liddon
0845 525460

Richard Sochacki
0949 43600

David Owen
06783 206

Andrew Bronwin
0694 781511

Rupert Pearson
0284 728542

Graham Heath
0550 21442

Stephen Smith
0844 279911

Peter Middleton
0892 861305

Roger Lewis
0884 35135

Neil Austin
0252 794771

Head Office 0786 811721

A BOOKER COUNTRYSIDE COMPANY

THE ROYAL FORESTRY SOCIETY
of England, Wales and Northern Ireland

Do you care about trees?

We do!

Joining the Royal Forestry Society is an excellent idea for all who care about trees, their husbandry and their future. For over a century the RFS has spread knowledge about trees, woodlands and forests, and encouraged the multi-purpose, sustainable management of this vital renewable natural resource.

What is the Royal Forestry Society?

It is

- ❖ an independent registered charity founded in 1882;
- ❖ the largest forestry association in Britain with over 4000 members;
- ❖ a broad-based body with open membership bringing together thinking people interested in trees, both **professional and amateur**;
- ❖ a way of learning more about trees and woodlands;
- ❖ a body which believes that tree resources are best conserved and extended through wise management compatible with wildlife, landscape and recreation considerations.

What are the benefits for members?

You can

- ❖ go to local national **field meetings** (over 70 each year) held in a variety of woods, forests and arboreta;
- ❖ meet and exchange news and views with other enthusiasts;
- ❖ attend **RFS symposia** with expert speakers on tree topics;
- ❖ read and understand more about trees, woodland and forests through our **Quarterly Journal of Forestry** (free to members);
- ❖ participate in our annual week-long **study tour** in the UK;
- ❖ join our **visits to other countries** to discover how their woods work;
- ❖ enjoy our famous redwood grove and pinetum at **Leighton** and our demonstration wood at **Hockeridge**;
- ❖ consult our extensive **library**;
- ❖ help influence Britain's policies on wooded environments.

What wider role does the RFS play?

We

 ✧ founded the **Forestry Trust for Conservation and Education**
 ✧ take every opportunity to increase knowledge and appreciation of trees;
 ✧ participate on influential environmental boards, education committees and safety councils, both locally and nationally;
 ✧ conduct arboricultural examinations;
 ✧ conceived and run the **Duke of Cornwall's Award for Forestry and Conservation;**
 ✧ support **Tree Aid** in the Sahel;
 ✧ use our mixed Chiltern woodland at **Hockeridge** for practical demonstration purposes;
 ✧ comment and advise, as a well-informed and impartial NGO, on environmental policies and practices involving trees.

How can I join?

Simply complete the application slip and send it with your cheque to:
*The Director, The Royal Forestry Society, 102 High Street, Tring, Herts.
HP23 4AF.* Why not act now?

1993 subscription rates: **Individuals** - £20 (concessionary rate of £10 available to students and OAP's); **corporate bodies £60; a half year's payment is acceptable after 1st July.**

What happens then?

We will send your membership pack and the address of your local RFS secretary who will keep you informed about events near you.

We look forward to welcoming you.

- -

Membership Application

Name _____

Address _____

_____

Post Code _____ **Membership category** _____

Any special interests _____

I wish to become a member of The Royal Forestry Society and enclose a cheque for £.............

Signature _____ **Date** _____